Abigail Melton and Lilith Cooper are a queer couple who are artists, community organisers and service industry workers. Lili grew up cycling around Cambridge and, when they met, transplanted Abi's desire to walk the world onto two wheels. This is their first book – born out of a series of vegan recipe zines from their first cycle tour. They live in Kirkcaldy, Fife.

Gears for Queers

Abigail Melton and Lilith Cooper

SANDSTONE PRESS

First published in Great Britain by
Sandstone Press Ltd
Willow House
Stoneyfield Business Park
Inverness
IV2 7PA
Scotland

www.sandstonepress.com

Sandstone Press is committed to a sustainable future. This book
is made from Forest Stewardship Council® certified paper.

ISBN: 978-1-912240-96-8
ISBNe: 978-1-912240-97-5

Cover design by Jason Anscomb
Typeset by Biblichor Ltd, Edinburgh
Printed by Hussar Books, Poland

Preface

Our friends and family met the announcement of our planned cycle tour with confusion and alarm. How could two people, routinely unable to leave the house for days on end, manage to cycle from Amsterdam to Spain?

When we left for the Netherlands in 2016, even we didn't know the answer.

Neither of us had ever done anything like this before and we came at the cycle tour with very different experiences – Abi had never cycled more than the 20 minutes to and from work, while Lili had spent more time in psychiatric hospitals than away from their home town. When we boarded the ferry at Harwich, we had no idea how we were going to cope, what this tour would look like, or if we would enjoy it.

Writing this book has been more difficult than either of us imagined. We felt uncomfortable staking claim to the identity of 'cyclists' and struggled to feel our trip was legitimate. We spent hours scrolling Instagram, comparing ourselves to other cycle tourers who had completed their trips in a way we felt we hadn't. We persevered because we didn't want to perpetuate those narrow ideas of what cycle tours and cycle tourers looked like.

Cycling through the Netherlands, Germany, Switzerland and France for three months, we met only two sets of British cyclists, and yet these paths are just a short ferry ride away. As people become more interested in sustainable travel, we want to encourage people to access these amazing cycle routes, and we want cycle-touring culture in the UK to continue to grow. Visibility is only a small part of this. We need city planners, councils, transport bodies and the government to recognise and act on the demand for family-friendly, accessible cycle paths. We also need a cultural shift in attitudes to cyclists.

On the tour, we learnt some harsh lessons about taking up space on the road. We want this book to both take up space and hold space open for other accounts of bike touring or travelling that are too often silenced, minimised and marginalised. Both of us are privileged in ways that allow our voices to rise above many others in our communities. We have tried, in our account of the tour, to articulate the things that made this trip possible for us.

Lili is non-binary and is referred to with the gender-neutral pronouns they/them, which are used throughout the book.

Gears for Queers can be read by anyone, but it is written specifically for the queers, for other fat, disabled, trans, female, femme and non-binary people who are curious about bike touring. To queer something is to trouble boundaries, to question the divisions into binaries: success/failure, commuter/cyclist, mad/sane, travel/migrate, leave/remain. We hope the book does this too.

Take care and happy riding,
Lili and Abi

Gears for Queers

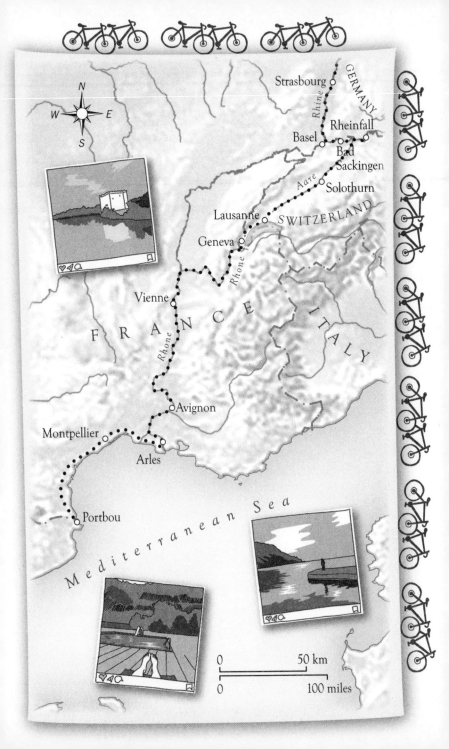

The Netherlands

Lili

Day One, Amsterdam to Durgerdam

Abi and I left the hostel early, hauling our panniers one by one down the steep wooden stairs and depositing them on the damp alley cobblestones outside. I had spent the night lying on the top bunk, listening to drunken shouts and thunder while my mind raced.

Rounding the corner, I was relieved to see our bikes, Patti and Paula, had survived a night in the red-light district. Steel-framed, bought second-hand from Gumtree, they may not have looked like much, but over the months we'd spent fixing them up we'd fallen in love.

We wheeled the bikes over and rested them against the red-brick hostel wall. Slowly, the pile of bags was distributed across the two bikes. I heaved two large black pannier bags onto my rear rack. As I went to clip the two smaller front panniers the bike shuddered against the wall. I held my breath as it ground to a halt midway through falling, leaning dangerously to one side. I gingerly hooked the front bags on and attempted to right it. It was too heavy. Instead, I wrestled a large dry bag with my sleeping bag, a smaller one with our tent, my ukulele and a large hiking rucksack onto the top of the rear rack, securing them with bungee cords. The final flourish was a small fabric bag I attached to my crossbar.

I stood back and examined the result. Abi joined me with a look of trepidation.

'We aren't exactly streamlined,' she commented.

'We'll be fine!' I replied cheerily, silencing my own gnawing worry.

Abi and I emerged from the alley to join the rush of cyclists on the road up towards the train station. I still wasn't used to riding a loaded touring bike; it was slow and bulky. Quick streams of bikes flowed around us on the cycle path. My arms started to ache from the effort of steadying my unwieldy handlebars.

We rode into the gaping mouth of a cycle tunnel beside Amsterdam Centraal Station. Fluorescent orange lights blinked overhead. We surfaced at the back of the station, clambered off our bikes and wheeled them onto the foot ferry. The small boat which crosses the old bay connecting Amsterdam with the sea was busy with morning traffic. I gripped the handlebars of my bike, my nails making crescent-shaped grooves in the grip tape, as the boat ploughed deep furrows into the water.

On the opposite shore, we followed the single road away from the ferry terminal. I patted my pocket containing the folded Google Maps printout of our route.

This was it. After six months of prepping and planning, Abi and I were actually riding our bikes in a whole different country. We weren't cycling to work or the supermarket. We were travelling; we were cycle tourers.

'This is the same bridge. Again.' Abi was barely containing her frustration.

'Eurgh,' I grunted in response.

We'd been cycling in circles for nearly 40 minutes. It didn't seem to matter what configuration of turns and paths we took, we always ended up here, at the same crossroads, looking at the same bridge. It was like a terrible *Choose your own adventure* storybook. The Google map was a useless page of squiggles and words. Maybe if I stared at it hard enough, it would start to make sense and match up with something, anything, around us.

'Are you lost?'

I looked up to see the broad smile of a man, standing astride a heavy Dutch bike.

'A bit,' I conceded.

'Very,' Abi interjected.

I shot her a look; I hadn't wanted to admit defeat.

'Where are you heading?' he asked, laughing.

'Durgerdam.'

Abi's dad had given us several pieces of advice before we left: don't pet stray cats, watch out for bears and don't trust strangers, especially men. I considered this as I rode beside Daan. We'd accepted his offer of a guide without hesitation.

'I don't think it's such a bad thing,' he was saying. 'Maybe the Netherlands should be more independent too.'

We had left the UK in the wake of the EU referendum two months prior, and it seemed inevitable that it would be the first thing people wanted to talk about. What I thought about Brexit and what I felt about Brexit were two very different things. I could understand many of the reasons why people had voted Leave; I knew the EU wasn't an uncomplicatedly 'good' thing; I could see how the referendum had come about. At the same time, I'd listened to my friends who had made Britain their home, temporarily or permanently, express fear, loss, alienation, confusion and worry. Abi and I felt part of a community that had been hurt in a way that was irreparable, and I was furious. I focused on the winding route through a small park.

'I guess I just feel we will lose more than we could possibly gain.' This felt a weak expression of my true sentiments.

'You know where I want to go? Utah.'

This was not the direction I'd expected a conversation on Brexit to take.

'All that wide, open space,' Daan continued, 'the freedom to do as you want.'

We travelled along broad suburban streets, before taking a sharp right down a narrow, cobbled path. We turned into a maze of industrial roads. I glanced behind me to check that Abi was still tailing us, concerned we were about to end up in some kind of Dutch Mormon warehouse complex. At the end of an alley we pulled to a halt at a T-junction, with a large, dark, stone church on the corner. Across the road from us, the tops of masts bobbed in the water. We were on the shore of Lake IJmeer.

'Go straight along there,' Daan gestured left, 'and you will reach Durgerdam. Good luck.'

Fuelled by the fresh air and keen to shake the feeling of being lost, I sped along the shoreside as fast as the weight of my bike would allow. My wheels bounced along the uneven road. I tried to avoid the larger potholes but, distracted by a display of shells in a cottage window, the sails of boats or a glimpse of the sea, I would occasionally hit one, sending my panniers flying up and crashing down. I'd wince at the noise and resolve to pay more attention, until I found myself lost in the moment again.

The sign for the campsite came into view. I sprinted for the finish line, skidded my bike to a stop on the gravel drive and waited for Abi to catch up.

'Have you come far today?' the man at reception asked as he took my passport, assessing my sweaty face, legs splattered with mud, and a grin of achievement.

'From Amsterdam.'

'Oh, so not so bad.'

'It took us two hours.'

He looked up from the paperwork. 'How?'

I walked over to Abi with his laughter still audible. 'We really need a map.'

Abi

Day Four, Amsterdam

After two days' rest in the campsite, I confidently led Lili back along the shore, through the cobbled streets and into the city. Cycling into Amsterdam was simple now we knew the route. We flew through alleys, around tourists already drunk on cheap Dutch beer, and over countless bridges, following the marked cycle lanes which wove alongside every road and lane. Around us, bikes clung to any available railing, locked tight to form a multicoloured wall of metal along each canal. Some were abandoned carcasses, without wheels or seats, broken frames rusted red from time, stuck in their final resting place.

Narrow houses formed a patchwork of different shapes and colours beside the canal. All were a different style or height, the only similarity being the many large windows on each.

We parked our bikes outside a small coffee shop. I pushed through the crowds inside to an empty table nestled in a dark corner. Lili perched on a tiny wooden stool whilst I leant into the wall to avoid elbowing our neighbour.

'Right, who's going to do it?' Lili asked me.

I looked beseechingly at Lili. I was hoping they would take the reins.

Day Four

Lili read my cue. 'Ok. What do we want?'

'I dunno.' I smiled gratefully. 'Something that makes us happy? I don't want to feel ill.'

Lili shuffled over to the busy counter at the back of the coffee shop to buy us a single joint.

I sat back and tried to relax. Smoking weed was not something I'd done often. My brain was taking great pleasure in reminding me of the one unfortunate incident at university when, catastrophically high, I'd eaten a whole family-sized quiche from my friend's fridge then proceeded to vomit it all over the same friend's bathroom suite. Still, when in Amsterdam . . .

Lili returned and placed a rolled joint onto the table. 'It's pure weed. I didn't think tobacco was a good idea. The guy said to take it very, very slowly and only take one or two tokes.'

'Ok, sounds good.' I smiled nervously.

'He also said we should stay here until we feel ok. Shall I get us some drinks?'

I nodded then lit the joint, inhaling deeply. I passed it to Lili who took a toke and then another. I took one more and extinguished it.

We sat for half an hour in the dim light of the coffee shop. I sipped my overpriced orange juice and repeatedly checked the time on the phone.

'I'm not really feeling anything,' Lili announced.

I wanted to get going and visit the Van Gogh museum. 'Shall we have one more toke and then leave?'

The gloom of the coffee shop gave way to the blinding light of a summer's day. I stumbled onto the pavement, unsteady on my feet, and pulled Lili's hand in the direction of the Museumkwartier. The colours of the city were intensifying the more I stared, like someone had turned the contrast up on

9

a TV screen. I looked at Lili who was giggling uncontrollably, and I immediately burst into a fit of laughter.

'Nobody . . . knows . . . we're . . . high,' Lili gasped between breaths.

I nodded, desperately trying to stop laughing. Tears ran down my face. Luckily no one could see me; all their faces had disappeared into a blur.

The pavement fell away from me, and suddenly I was standing in the middle of the road. I rushed Lili to the other side and onto the opposite pavement. I looked around, my eyes would only focus in on the tiniest details, a discarded chewing gum wrapper, the second hand of a clock, the button on a jacket.

'Abi, I'm not ok, I'm really not ok.' Lili looked across to me, face contorted with fear. 'We need sugar, we need sugar.'

I could barely hear them through the invisible bubble that had engulfed me. 'I'm not doing so well either,' I admitted.

Lili's eyes widened. 'No, no. I need you to be ok, Abi. I am so far from ok. Please tell me you're ok.'

'Oh, I'm fine. I'm A-Okay.' My words came out slower than they should. Time was skipping and I was struggling to keep my feet on the floor. I stared at the small scar on Lili's left cheek. How long had I been silent? Seconds, hours? I had to pull it together for them.

I summoned all my resources. 'Let's find some sugar and somewhere to sit.' I was going to look after us, I could do this. All I needed to do was work out where we were. I took Lili's hand and attempted a reassuring smile.

The two of us fell into the nearest supermarket. The packaging was instantly familiar. Thank God, we were back in the UK. Lili held a green and pink packet out to me: Percy Pigs. In the chilled aisle, I picked up two huge bottles of orange juice.

Day Four

The cashier had a strange accent. I couldn't understand her. Where was I? I handed her some odd-looking coins from my purse. They definitely weren't pounds, but this didn't seem to faze her. I gave a mumbled thanks. Walking out of Marks & Spencer and back onto the streets of Amsterdam the bubble broke; we weren't in the UK after all. I suddenly felt very lost.

Lili clung to my hand as I led them confidently along the street. I had no idea where I was going. We just needed somewhere to sit down, anywhere. My brain was working in overdrive as I desperately tried to make out any feature of the city. We crossed a road and then a bridge over a canal. Beside me was a bench. We slumped onto it.

'I can't see anything.' Lili was taking their glasses on and off, staring at the mossy bricks of the canal, partially submerged in luminous green water.

I coaxed some orange juice into them and then took a large gulp. The sugar hit me instantly, throwing the scenery back into perspective. I kept drinking. A group of tourists waved to us from a canal boat.

'We're never going to get back.' Lili had stopped playing with their glasses and now clung to their red pannier bag like a lifebuoy. 'We'll never find our bikes again.'

'Lili, it's fine.' I was beginning to sober up. 'It's only two o'clock, we've got plenty of time for it to wear off.'

Lili nodded their head.

'Stop nodding your head.'

'Sure, sure,' they replied, still nodding but now slower, lolling their head back and forth. They ground to a halt. Suddenly they gripped my arm and came close to my ear.

'I need a wee,' they whispered. 'I really need a wee.'

As they said it, my brain connected with an intense pressure in my bladder. We had each drunk two litres of orange juice.

'I'll get us to a cafe.'

*

11

I walked us steadily along a large road. I had a distinct feeling we were still heading towards the Museumkwartier. Across from us was a monumental red and white chequered brick building. On the ground floor: a cafe. We crossed the road carefully, and I ushered Lili in.

I sank into the high-backed red fabric of a booth which stretched out into infinity. A waiter approached us.

'Do you have a toilet?' The volume of Lili's voice oscillated wildly with each word, ending on a booming 'toilet' that reverberated around the high-ceilinged cafe.

'Yes, just down the stairs there.'

Lili slunk off the sofa and wobbled to the stairs. I smiled maniacally at the waiter who handed me a menu and walked off.

'Your turn.' Lili appeared beside me.

Clinging to anything I could get my hands on: the backs of chairs, the walls, the bannister on the stairs, I made my way into the basement of the building. The toilet cubicle felt safe. Its four walls enclosed me in a tiny space of my own. Maybe I could stay here forever, make it my home, hang tiny curtains along the cubicle wall.

I shook my head cartoonishly. I couldn't let myself get distracted, I had to look after Lili. I gave myself a pep talk: Lili was relying on me, only I could get them back to the campsite safely, I had to do it for them.

Lili was sitting bolt upright in the booth, arms extended rigidly in front of them, eyes staring wildly at the menu in their hands. I slouched in next to them.

'All ok?' I asked quietly.

'Uh-huh.'

It was hardly convincing.

'Let's order something.' I picked up the other menu.

The waiter materialised in front of us. 'What can I get you?' His comforting smile made it obvious that this wasn't the first time he'd had to deal with stupidly stoned tourists.

'Orange juice and lemonade and tea with soy milk and a hummus sandwich, please,' Lili spluttered. 'And no butter in any of it, please, thank you.'

He brought over each item like an attentive nurse.

'Thank you so, so much.' I was intensely grateful for this kind, non-judgemental man. I chewed the food slowly. I poured sugar into my tea for the first time in years. I gradually returned to my body.

'How are you feeling?'

'Better.' Lili smiled at me. 'I think I'll be ok.'

I looked around at the building we'd found ourselves in. Behind us was a grand hall with a high glass ceiling. The floor below me was an elaborate pattern of blue and yellow tiles. A fuchsia sign told me we were in the Cafe de Bazel, part of the city archives, the largest municipal archive in the world.

Lili cuddled into me. I pulled the laptop out of our pannier bag and we watched cartoons. The waiter brought us endless cups of tea. Slowly the colours around me dimmed. I felt the weight of Lili's head on my shoulder and relaxed. Time was returning to normal. It felt like we'd been sitting there for hours. I looked at the clock on the wall. We had been sitting there for hours.

We left a huge tip for our waiter/hero: an apology for doing exactly what tourists shouldn't do in Amsterdam. We emerged blinking from the building.

'We're such idiots.' Lili turned to me and laughed.

'I know, don't . . .' I felt utterly embarrassed to have made such a rookie error. 'Seriously though, are you ok?'

Lili nodded. 'It just felt unpleasantly like being mad, you know.'

*

The Van Gogh museum was a write-off; I couldn't imagine anything worse than being surrounded by a swirling room full of post-impressionist paintings. Instead we headed back to our bikes which, despite Lili's catastrophic predictions, were very easy to find.

I unlocked my bike and wound the chain around the stem of my saddle. Today had been a disaster. Nothing we had done since leaving the UK had convinced me that we could do this cycle tour. In a few days' time we would be leaving the safety of the campsite at Durgerdam. I just hoped we would be ready.

Lili

'Why the FUCK did I bring this FUCKING UKULELE?'

I hurled my rucksack to the ground and stared at it resentfully. This was not how I'd imagined our great departure from Durgerdam. We'd woken up a full hour later than I'd planned. As I'd frantically stuffed clothes into dry bags, Abi had stood bemused. She clearly didn't understand the importance of sticking to our invisible schedule. I hadn't had time to bungee my bag to the back of my bike, or shower, or cook breakfast. I wasn't ready to leave.

I can't do this.

The dam broke and I collapsed into tears. Abi slid off her saddle and, bike still between her legs, shuffled over to me. She put her hand on mine as I exhaled all the tension, anxiety, panic and fear in several loud and messy sobs.

'Ok?' Abi asked.

I looked up at her. She smiled reassuringly.

I nodded, mopping up the tears and snot with the back of my hand.

'Shall we attach this to the back of your bike?' She picked my rucksack off the verge. I'd spent the whole morning refusing her help and snapping at her, trying to regain control over the situation and my spiralling anxiety.

'Thanks. Sorry.'

With it secured onto the top of my rear pannier rack by bungees, we wobbled off along the cycle path.

The two of us were travelling south into the body of the Netherlands. Turning off the lakeside path, we followed the numbered cycle paths, veering right and joining a canal, the water dappled with sunlight. With our route stretching out ahead of us, I began to relax. Even with the weight of the bags, I was comfortable with this sort of cycling. The Fens, which border my home town, share a resemblance with the Netherlands: large agricultural areas, created by draining marsh and wetlands, characterised by dykes, ditches and pumping stations. I grew up riding bikes on unending, straight roads beneath a broad, open sky.

Riding like this breeds its own kind of stamina. I focused my attention on the movement of the pedals, the metal hum of the chain, the idiosyncratic clicks of my bike: the rhythm of riding.

The trees that lined the towpath cast bars of shadow, making the light flicker as we rode. The canal path ended, and we followed the cycle path as it turned onto a road.

Two hundred metres down, we stopped at a roundabout. It wasn't clear which of the three turnings to take. There were no cars, so I took an exploratory pass. At the exit towards Utrecht a bright flash caught my eye: sunlight reflecting water. I knew we were meant to be following a second canal. I didn't want to stop and check a map, keen to cling onto this feeling of momentum. I pointed the way.

We came out onto the broad waterway, double the width of the first. Long industrial barges sheared through the water. The towpath was lined by trees, but with the sun now overhead they offered no respite. Abi was the less experienced cyclist, so I let her set the pace, and on the wider sections of path I pulled up alongside her. For the last year, on every bike ride we'd taken together, I had come up beside her and said, 'Imagine: this, but we're cycling across Europe.' These rides were normally our commute to and from work. It felt strange to have transplanted this familiar activity somewhere completely new. The same action, the same motion, the same push of the pedals was transformed from something everyday to something significant.

'Can we stop and eat something?' Abi's voice broke my reverie.

It was nearly midday and in my panic this morning I'd vetoed breakfast. We'd planned a short ride for our first day, 25km. I didn't think we'd be going for much longer.

'Sure.'

We pulled off the path to a bench that sat looking out over the water and across to the fields dotted with windmills beyond. I pulled a flapjack from my bar bag and broke it in half.

'Not much further now,' I handed Abi her half, 'this'll keep you going.'

'Is this right? This doesn't feel right.'

An hour had passed, and we were still on the canal towpath. It felt like we were cycling the same 100 metres over and over again. The idyllic path of earlier had become a Sisyphean nightmare.

'Let's keep going a little bit further.' I just wanted to keep pedalling.

'We can't just keep pedalling and ignore that we are lost,' Abi called out from behind me.

I didn't reply; I'd spotted a woman walking towards us, carrying her shopping. She was the first person we'd seen in hours.

'Excuse me?'

She looked up, surprised.

'Waar . . . waar . . .' I started. In lieu of Dutch, I pointed at our map.

'U bent van harte verloren?'

I looked at Abi who reflected my expression of total incomprehension.

'Waar . . . ?' I continued.

The Dutch woman began to talk in an animated way, pointing to a place on the map far south of where we were. I pointed to our intended destination and gestured back and forth down the canal. She pointed back the way we had come. Even without understanding what she was saying, her answer was clear: we were lost.

Abi and I discussed our options as the Dutch woman continued away from us along the towpath.

'We need to figure out where we are,' I began.

'Right.' Abi nodded agreement.

'Then we can figure out how to get back on track.'

'The bike route signs don't make any sense, there's no indication of what towns or villages we are near, and this towpath appears to just continue indefinitely . . .'

'So, we need to get off the canal,' I concluded.

We cycled back, towards a junction. The path split and we travelled under a small bridge and onto a road. Agriculture shifted into residential streets, and we were soon cycling through a small village. At a public park I spotted what we were looking for: a wooden board with a map of the area.

'Ok, ok,' I muttered, scanning the board and trying to relate it to the map Abi had open in her hands, 'Mijnden . . . Nieuwersluis . . . Breukelen . . . Oh.'

The canal I had confidently pointed to headed south rather than west. We were nowhere near our intended destination.

Day Seven

I looked over at Abi, trying to read her reaction.

'Why didn't you let me stop and check?' she said. 'You know you can't read maps; you know I have a better sense of direction.'

She paused.

'I can't keep cycling,' she croaked out before her face collapsed.

If I could have gone home then and there, I would have. The whole tour seemed a terrible mistake. We didn't know what we were doing.

I shook my head. I needed to focus on the immediate problem. Whatever we did, it was going to get dark and we needed somewhere to sleep.

'Can I have another look at the map?' I asked Abi. She passed it over without saying anything or looking at me.

'Ok, we're here,' I pointed to the small village, 'and there's two campsites next to each other, here and here.'

I pointed to a road about 10km away. I looked over at Abi, whose eyes were watching my fingers.

She squared her shoulders. 'I'm going to figure out the route.'

She pulled out the Michelin road map from the dry bag on her front pannier rack and silently began comparing it to the map of the bike routes.

'It probably didn't help that this isn't the most topo-graphically accurate map,' she said gently, holding out the bike routes map and offering forgiveness.

The journey to the campsite wasn't more than a thumb's width on the map, but it felt never-ending. We took turns asking the other to stop so we could anxiously check the map. We rode back north through the town of Breukelen along cycle paths, paved in red-brick, that wove past low suburban houses and manicured lawns. In the small village of Mijnden we cycled through narrow streets lined with white brick houses. I stopped at the end of a line of traffic in front of a drawbridge, raised to allow a procession of Dutch holidaymakers cruising in pleasure boats to pass through.

We almost missed the low wooden gate to Fort Spion. It was obscured by overhanging trees and tall grass. Wheeling our bikes back round, we pushed them up the gravel path. We were standing in the shadow of a large grey stone fort.

'Hallo!' A woman striding down the path called out a greeting.

'Er . . . Kamperen?' I ventured.

'Camping, yes?'

'Yes, please.' Were we so obviously English?

'How long?'

'One night.' I paused and looked at Abi. 'Two nights.'

'Of course.' She unlocked the door to a small wooden shed, hidden behind dense bushes, and disappeared inside. We stood outside with our bikes, waiting.

'Are you members?' she shouted out to us.

'Members?' I asked.

She popped her head out the door. 'Fort Spion is a Natural Camping site.' She handed me a small green book. 'To stay you have to be a member, it's 15 euros but it lasts a year and you can stay in any of them.'

I rested my bike against my leg and flicked through the book. The natural campsites or Natuurkampeerterreinen were a scheme of about 150 campsites across the Netherlands. They all catered exclusively for tents, and were designed and managed in a way that was environmentally conscious, and sympathetic to the landscapes they were in.

'I don't think I have enough cash to pay for membership.' I handed Abi the book and scrabbled around in my bumbag.

The woman waved her hand at me. 'You can pay tomorrow.' She looked us up and down. 'You look like you need some rest.'

Abi

Day Eight, Fort Spion

I woke up early to the sun filtering into the tent. I'd slept deeply. Yesterday's exertion had knocked me out as soon as my head touched the dry bag I used as a pillow. Stretching my arms, I unzipped the inner tent, then, turning onto my stomach and shuffling forward to extend my reach further, unzipped the door of the outer tent.

Bright morning light shone in, and Lili began to stir. I lay still on my mat. The doorway acted as a frame for the view outside. The lake glimmered softly, and a warm haze hung in the air. We were beneath the green boughs of an elm tree. This was what I wanted from the tour.

I breathed in the fresh air. I knew being outside was good for me in a way I couldn't pin down. I had escaped the claustrophobic city. I had escaped our tiny bungalow which we couldn't afford the rent on. I'd escaped from the pressures of the everyday and the worries about what I was doing with my life. I felt an overwhelming sense of calm. I was no longer going to be the Abi who ate family-sized bags of Doritos while binge watching season after season of *Peep Show*. Yesterday had been hard, but I had proved that I could do it. I felt excited about the day and all its possibilities.

I stood up and immediately sat back down. 'Oh my God!'

'What's the matter?' Lili asked sleepily.

'Everything,' I mumbled back, rubbing my right calf. 'Everything hurts.'

I allowed my brain to connect with my broken body. My legs were made of lead, I was sure of it. The heavy ache was worse in my thighs but spread all the way to the soles of my feet. Moving my joints sent out agonising shockwaves. Pain radiated from my shoulders down to my wrists. My neck hurt, my back hurt, even my fingers and toes hurt.

'JESUS!' I had just adjusted my pyjama bottoms. I was raw with saddle sore.

It didn't sound like Lili was faring any better as they began to move from their sleeping bag.

'What have we done?' they asked through gritted teeth as they rolled onto their hip and then instantly back again. 'I don't think I can get up.'

I looked at Lili rocking violently from side to side in an attempt to sit up and then at my poor body sprawled on the mat. I couldn't help but laugh.

I was glad we were taking a rest day.

'Here you go.' Lili handed me a pot of oaty mush and apple.

I hate porridge, but I was willing to try and eat it during the tour as it was cheap and light to carry. As I took my first bite, I suddenly realised I'd neglected another part of my body: my stomach. I was ravenous. I shovelled the gelatinous paste into my mouth and then grabbed seconds. Lili did the same.

'I really don't think one flapjack is enough for anyone for lunch.' I side-eyed Lili. I wasn't going to forget their enforced and unrelenting march yesterday in a hurry.

'I know.' They looked up at me guiltily. 'Sorry.'

Day Eight

'It's ok.' I pulled a packet of emergency noodles out of our food bag. 'Second breakfast?'

Lili shook their head and, with stunted movements, prepared a bag for our trip into town. I inhaled my noodles and tried to mentally prepare for the short ride in. I was desperately tired, and the calm of the campsite was hard to resist, but we had jobs to do.

'Ready?' Lili stood over me expectantly.

'I guess so. I'll just pop to the loo first.' I pulled myself off the grass. My body creaked.

An ancient wooden door led to a single toilet surrounded by cobwebs and their eight-legged residents. I sidled in. Sitting down, I let out an involuntary whimper. Weeing was agonising. I waddled back to Lili and my bike.

'I think I'm going to ride standing up,' I proclaimed. I doubted I'd ever be able to sit down again.

Large, white mansions and tall willow trees lined the quiet road as we cycled towards Breukelen. My legs were sore, but I was determined to enjoy the ride. We crossed a canal filled with boats of all shapes and sizes navigating the water, weaving in and out of one another; Dutch tourists on their holidays. The water's edge thronged with people eating breakfast in the sun. On my bike, I felt part of the scene, another holidaymaker enjoying the beautiful day.

I paced the aisles of the supermarket. Lili held up two options.

'What would you prefer, a kilogram of table salt or a small grinder of pink Himalayan salt?'

I sighed. 'I guess the grinder makes more sense?'

'Great.' Lili placed the kilogram bag down. 'I guess we're now officially the most middle-class cycle tourers in the world.'

I laughed and then grimaced. There were hundreds of reasons I didn't feel like a proper cycle tourer and this was just another one. The salt screamed luxury; it screamed glamping. Real cycle tourers probably didn't need salt. They probably ate only mouldy bread and food gleaned from farmers' fields.

Every time I got on my bike, I felt like I was being sized up. At 18 stone, I didn't look like a cyclist. I didn't feel like one either.

It hadn't always been this way. As a teenager I'd loved cycling on my simple mountain bike. Its purple frame had been a perfect fit, every turn of the pedal a natural extension of my legs. I'd ridden it as quickly as I could around the neighbourhood, watching the numbers tick higher on the speedometer my parents had installed.

It didn't take much to break my love affair with my bike. A throwaway comment by an older boy who looked at the large, comfortable gel saddle cover I used and remarked, 'Guess you need that for your fat arse.' I immediately removed the cover.

I stopped cycling. My oversized body had become an object which people felt compelled to discuss, to criticise. I couldn't verbalise the shame I felt, but I knew that if I stopped cycling, stopped exhibiting my body in motion, I might become invisible again.

When I got back on my bike as an adult for my commute to work, it was hard not to feel that same shame. I felt exposed. I knew that the surprise which registered on people's faces when we told them about the cycle tour had nothing to do with Lili. They were looking at my fat body and deciding what it was capable of.

We wandered out of the supermarket into the sunlight and sat on a bench in the small town square. The shops around us were mostly closed or were bargain shops, a stark contrast to the gentrified streets along the canal.

Day Eight

'How are you feeling?' I asked Lili.

'Tired, dazed. You?'

'Tired.'

It was not yet midday but yesterday had completely exhausted us.

'Let's go back to the campsite.'

The afternoon at Fort Spion passed quietly. My feelings about the tour oscillated between excitement and anxiety. Travelling was all I had thought about since leaving university three years ago, but I'd never found a way to do it which was affordable, or which fitted with my values. When Lili first mentioned cycle touring, on our first or second date, it made perfect sense. I wouldn't be pumping carbon dioxide into the atmosphere just so I could take a few nice Instagram pictures and enjoy the sun. I wasn't going to be just jumping into another culture, spending money in the tourist areas and then jumping back out again. I'd have the opportunity to experience each tiny place, to see much more of a country than was possible by train or plane. All it would take on my part is getting on my bike.

I settled next to Lili on a bench overlooking the lake. So much of my life was spent inside; working, eating, sleeping, and now I was planning to live predominantly outside for the next year. It felt like a necessary change. My head was beginning to feel clearer.

I watched the sparrows flitting between the bushes beside the lake. A Red Admiral butterfly floated onto the arm of the bench. A large black fly swooped down onto my leg.

'OUCH!' I yelled.

Lili jumped in alarm. 'What?'

I pointed to the fly on my leg. 'It's biting me! What the fuck is it?'

Lili looked in horror at my leg. 'Well, wipe it off!'

The fly continued to devour me.

'Can I do that? Are you sure?'

'YES!'

I prepared myself for the fight of my life. Lifting my hand, I softly brushed it off. The sated fly buzzed away happily.

'What the hell was that?' I asked Lili, wide-eyed in panic. 'It just wouldn't stop biting!' The bite was bleeding and radiating pain up my leg. 'And it really hurts!'

'I have no idea.' Lili had jumped up and was scanning the sky.

I looked over at the tent. 'Maybe we should head inside.'

Abi

Day Nine, Fort Spion to Paalkampeerterreinen

'Jesus Christ.' I was trying to lower myself onto the saddle. 'Do you think we'll ever adjust?'

Lili was a much more experienced cyclist and my only reliable reference for what lay ahead.

'We should do.' They let out a moan as they sat down.

We set off along a road which floated between two wide lakes. The flatness of the landscape left me feeling like we were cycling across the water. Midges hung in dark clouds along the side of the road, and occasionally Lili or I would swerve wildly to avoid them but would usually end up with a face full of bugs.

Our destination was our first wild camping spot, nestled in Hoge Veluwe National Park. 'Wild Camping' is any camping outside of designated campsites, and it's illegal in most European countries. However, the Netherlands offered a system of Pole Camping sites or *Paalkampeerterreinen*: areas in forests and woodlands where people could legally wild camp, marked by a wooden pole which the campers must stay near.

We needed our money to stretch as far as possible, so wild camping was an inevitable part of the tour. I found the idea terrifying. As we cycled along the quiet lanes, I worried about all the risks we were taking. There would be no gates or fences to protect us tonight. The tent was just a flimsy piece of fabric. We would be completely vulnerable.

I'd read a lot about people's experiences of wild camping and the joy and excitement they felt. None of the cycle tourers we followed on Instagram seemed as scared as I was. I didn't know if I would be able to push down my fear to enjoy the experience. I wasn't even sure which fears were worth taking notice of and which were over exaggerated by a society fixated on the harm strangers could do to you.

The long road ended, and we rolled onto a white sandy path surrounded by dry open heath. The path dipped and dived like a pump track. My legs, which had had time to loosen on the flat roads, started to seize again, my muscles screaming out at every uphill.

'I thought the Netherlands was supposed to be flat?' I shouted ahead to Lili as we laboured up a steep incline. My breathing was coming in ragged gasps. What had made me think I could do this?

'I'm sure it'll even out,' Lili shouted back. They continued cycling forward, lost in a race that only they were competing in.

The morning cool had given way to a fierce heat. I could feel beads of sweat dripping down my back as the temperature crept into the thirties. We darted in and out of woodlands of looming pine and gnarled birch, their shade a welcome relief on a hot day.

'I need to stop for water!' I looked at my watch. We'd been cycling constantly for three hours.

Lili let out a huge bodily sigh and cycled back to me. I took a large glug of warm water from my bottle. Salt from my sweat had crusted onto my face, I could taste it in the corners of my mouth.

'Ready?' they asked, keen to get going.

Day Nine

I looked at Lili in disbelief. I felt ready to collapse. How did they not realise I was struggling? The difference in mine and Lili's fitness levels was becoming more and more apparent. They were used to long-distance running, ignoring their body's needs in order to achieve their goal. This was already the second-longest cycle ride I had ever done, the longest being our first day on the tour. I was pushing myself to my limit.

'Abs?' Lili asked.

'Yeah, I'm ready.' I wanted to do this tour. I was determined not to let Lili down.

We pushed on. The meadows of heather in pinks and purples, blues and greens, took on an almost luminescent quality as the temperature rose and rose. I started stopping often to drink water, pulling to the side of the narrow path to allow leisure cyclists and walkers to pass by. I needed to listen to my body. I'd fainted in the past from heat, I wasn't willing to do it again in the middle of nowhere. Lili stopped with me. I could read their frustration in the curtness of their voice and the restless tapping of their hands and feet.

The heath gave way to woodland, but here the hills became longer and larger. The dry dirt track kicked up dust onto my panniers and legs. Lili's pace didn't give us time to stop and enjoy the scenery, we were getting to the campsite as quickly as possible, even if it killed me.

I reached the top of a huge hill, my legs burning, my body hungry and tired. Lili was waiting for me, one foot on their pedal, ready to begin again as soon as I caught up. Ahead of me, another hill rose high into the forest. I felt something snap inside of me.

'I can't fucking do it!' I choked out. I pulled my bike to the side of the path and let it fall into the shrubbery. 'I thought I would be ok, but I'm not. It's too much.'

This was my limit. I had failed. I felt a huge swell of frustration and shame form within me. I burst into tears and sat disconsolate on the twig-strewn floor.

Lili walked over to me. Their face had softened. They put their arms around me and waited until my big gulping sobs subsided.

'It's ok. You can do this. You're doing so well.' They pulled something out of their bumbag. 'Open up.'

I opened my mouth and Lili popped in a glucose tablet. I knew Lili neither deserved nor wanted to be stuck on this tour with a big, fat, sweaty mess of a person. I knew I was only going to keep disappointing them.

The orange tablet dissolved quickly on my tongue. I opened my mouth for another sweet.

'Maybe I *can* do this,' I whispered. The wave of emotion was retreating.

I ate a few more sweets. I didn't want to admit to Lili that they were helping, that I'd just needed sugar. Their transformative effect on me was a stark lesson in the ways I needed to maintain my body during these long workouts. I couldn't cycle to Spain on willpower alone.

'You can do this.' Lili smiled and gave me a kiss. They pointed to the map. 'Look, we're so close. I promise we can stop as much as you need to.'

I felt better getting explicit permission to stop regularly. It wasn't something I could give myself.

We walked up the last hill and then cycled a short distance deeper into the forest. The Paalkampeerterreinen was around this area somewhere and we began to pedal up and down the winding tracks to find it. We only had a thick pencil mark on our map to guess by. We'd translated this mark from Google Maps, and right now it seemed that the crucial details had been lost. Who would have thought it would be so hard to find a wooden pole in the middle of a forest?

Day Nine

'There!' I'd spotted the dark green of a tent canopy in the undergrowth.

We pushed our heavy bikes into a small clearing where two other tents were already set up. I was relieved to have company for the night. At least now if a fortuitous murderer stumbled upon our tents there was only a one in three chance we'd get killed first.

I took a look around; four logs formed a square around the ashen remains of a fire, a dense area of forest to the side of the clearing looked perfect for a makeshift toilet. An old-fashioned water pump stood next to the two-metre wooden pole we'd been looking for.

'There's a big notice on the pump which says "Niet Drink-baar", so I'm guessing we're going to have to find water elsewhere,' Lili announced.

I was way too tired to move. I looked up at Lili in dismay. The last thing I wanted to do was get back on my bike.

'I can go get water?' they suggested.

I nodded gratefully. 'Do you mind? I'll put up the tent.'

'Nah, it's not too far to the nearest town. I'll be about an hour. Come find me if I'm not back by then.'

Lili set off and I pitched the tent. We only had one work-ing mobile phone between us; the other was a dumb phone, uncharged and with a SIM card which hadn't been set up, lying in the bottom of an unknown pannier bag. The know-ledge of this began to sink in as the time ticked by. How would Lili contact me if something went wrong?

I sat on the log near the fire pit. We'd made an active decision to leave technology behind. I hated how much time I wasted on social media and the internet. I hated the pres-sure which came from people being able to constantly contact me. I accepted that it was important for us to have a phone for emergencies, or when we wanted to chat with family, but surely we only needed one. Or at least, that's what we'd decided pre-tour. Sitting alone in an unfamiliar country in the woods, I began to wonder if we'd made a mistake. I considered finding the other phone but, without internet, there was no way I could set it up. Images of lorry collisions filled my mind. I wouldn't know if anything happened to Lili. I would be stuck alone, in the middle of a forest, whilst they lay dying in some hospital bed.

Thirty minutes passed. Then 50. Still no Lili. At 60 minutes I began to prepare my bike. I was going to have to go and find them.

I put on my helmet. From out of the bushes a familiar face appeared.

'I thought you were dead!' I shouted, throwing myself into Lili's arms.

'I'm ok.' Lili was breathing hard. 'The town was much further than I thought, I had to race back.'

They produced a pannier bag full of water and food. I felt suddenly very thirsty.

'We need to set up our second phone as soon as possible.'

'Agreed,' I said, in between gulps of cold water.

Lili

Day Ten (1am), Paalkampeerterreinen

I opened my eyes to darkness. Sleeping in the tent, I'd gotten used to waking up a few times in the night, but this was different. Something was digging between my shoulder blades. I shifted onto my side and shot up with a yelp. Something hard had hit the bone at the top of my arm. I was suddenly aware that I could feel the ground underneath me in all its complexity: hard earth littered with twigs and stones. The airbed we'd purchased from a company in the States was now just two sheets of thin and very expensive plastic. My body ached with a heavy, almost unbearable desire for sleep. Could I lie back down and deal with this tomorrow? I shifted and winced as a pinecone dug into my thigh.

'Abi.' I prodded at the lump of sleeping bag I could make out next to me. 'Abi.'

'Mmmm.' Abi rolled to face me.

'My airbed has a puncture.'

A solitary hand emerged from the sleeping bag and felt around me to test my statement.

'Oh, ok.' She sat up. 'Where's the repair kit?'

*

Experienced hikers would probably think nothing of mending a punctured airbed, but I was quietly pleased that, in the pitch black of the forest, we'd managed it. I rolled out of the tent, pulled on my shoes and stepped into the clearing. The night before I'd felt on high alert; my brain interpreting everything unknown as a threat. I'd even convinced Abi we were safest cocooned in the inner tent, eating spicy Doritos and chocolate soy milk for dinner, rather than cooking in the wilds of the forest. The stillness of the morning was matched by my own sense of calm. We'd spent the night here, casting a spell that had made the space our own.

The rules of wild camping are clear: when using the toilet, keep 50 metres away from water and dig a six-inch hole minimum, covering this over with earth when you've finished. In England, Abi had attempted to buy a small trowel for this purpose online. What arrived in the post was a large collapsible shovel with a serrated blade on one edge. It was better suited to burying a body, and we did not pack it.

'What do you think?' Abi had emerged from the tent and was pacing back and forth. 'It doesn't feel like it's good manners . . .'

Last night, we'd headed into a dense band of trees across a dirt track. Squatting to wee, I'd spotted several deep holes that we assumed had been pre-dug by our companions in the pole campsite. With no trowel of our own, our discussion of toilet etiquette was becoming increasingly urgent.

'Fuck, I can't hold it.'

Abi returned looking sheepish.

We followed dry mud trails through dense forest. The light was low and soft, filtered through the trees. Occasionally, the bright sun burst through gaps in the canopy in a flash of light. The Dutch system of cycle paths was starting to make sense; the numbers indicated the numbered intersection we were heading towards rather than the route itself. We made steady progress. The path gently rose and fell through the undergrowth. We paused only to give way to walkers or other cyclists on narrower sections. I felt increasingly comfortable steering my juggernaut of a bike, but I was not confident enough to feel I could avoid a collision.

We cycled back and forth along the track; the pole campsite where we had planned to stop for lunch, and potentially for the night, should have been here. I strained my eyes to try and discern the tall pole amongst the trees without success.

We settled on a bench to make lunch. I pulled our gas stove and pans out of the panniers, watched over by four curious horses in the field opposite. As the pasta boiled, they stood and sniffed the air, occasionally sprinting to the far side of the paddock and then back again, reacting to things we couldn't see. I kept a watchful eye on them.

'What if they jump over the fence?' I asked Abi.

She looked at me. Realising I was serious, her face softened from mocking to reassurance.

'They won't, don't worry.'

Not worrying is easier said than done. I didn't know how not to be afraid of everything. The four horses triggered a rising panic that settled on the front legs of the largest horse. My brain conjured up images of the devastation a single kick could cause to the softest parts of us. I remembered how last night's anxiety had dissipated just by staying in the space. I sat it out, and the longer I sat there the calmer I felt. By the time we were eating, I had relaxed into their company.

'I don't think we're going to find the pole campsite,' Abi said as she scraped her bowl.

'Let's keep going then.'

*

I heard Abi whoop behind me and looked up to find the source of her excitement: a blue 15 encircled by stars in the corner of a sign. We had joined the EuroVelo 15.

EuroVelo is a network of long-distance cycle routes in various stages of completion. They add up to more than 45,000km and stretch from the Nordkapp in Norway to the southernmost tip of Italy, from the west coast of Portugal east to Moscow. Number 15, the Rhein route, or Rijnfietsroute in Dutch, was the first to have consistent signs the whole length – from the sea at the Hoek van Holland up to the source of the Rhein at Lake Toma. This was the route we planned to follow from the Netherlands, the length of Germany and into Switzerland.

We left behind the national park and rode out from the shade of the forest onto quiet farm roads. A patchwork of green pastures used for dairy farming stretched as far as I could see. We'd been chatting the whole way through the forest, on the road we travelled single file. I sang to myself.

'Lili! It's right back there.'

Fully absorbed in a tune, I'd been cycling on autopilot and missed the turning to Leersum.

The campsite was round the back of an old farmhouse. After wild camping, the simple facilities felt suburban. We put up the tent in a small circular pitch cut into the meadow.

At 10pm, the sky burst into fireworks.

'Maybe they are marking our first day without incident,' Abi said, laughing.

Abi

Day Eleven, Leersum

'Ah, crap . . .' Lili let out a deep sigh. Their airbed had deflated again.

We both crawled out of the tent and sprinted through pelting rain to the campsite kitchen. The miserable weather was mirroring my mood perfectly. The cycle tour was harder than I'd anticipated; the physical and mental exertion greater. We'd got lost, been attacked by mystery insects and now we were dealing with a temperamental airbed. It felt like the universe was intent on making this trip as difficult as possible.

In the kitchen, we filled up a washing-up bowl and, section by section, immersed Lili's airbed in water. I tried to will myself to stay positive; if we could find the hole in the dark, in the middle of the night, we could find the hole this morning.

After around an hour it became clear that there was no hole. I felt as deflated as the mattress. Were we really this useless?

Lili exhaled through their teeth. They had picked up the iPod and were scouring the internet for answers to our problem.

'What?' I asked as Lili's features dropped.

'Chemicals in insect repellents, such as DEET, can cause wear to airbeds. This can result in invisible leaks which cannot be fixed by conventional patches,' Lili read aloud.

'Oh, for fuck's sake,' I moaned.

We'd been smothering ourselves in insect repellent since the incident in Fort Spion. Now the damage was done. Lili was going to need a new airbed.

'We'll just have to buy a new one when we next pass a camping shop.'

'If it's not too much money,' Lili added.

I walked over to sit at a picnic bench near our tent whilst Lili organised a replacement mat to be sent back to the UK under the warranty. I felt the overbearing presence of perfect-cycle-tourer-Abi. The Abi who didn't make simple mistakes, the Abi who knew what she was doing. I was being haunted by the idea that I simply wasn't good enough to do this. That the mistakes we kept making would be remedied if only I was a better person.

I felt Lili's arms wrap around me.

'Come on, let's go out.'

Lili guided me into the town centre, past identikit houses, children's play parks and a field of pygmy goats. We arrived in the square of a park where a brass band in traditional dress played oompah versions of classic pop tunes from a white pagoda. Food vans lined the side. One selling poffertjes (small, round Dutch pancakes) sent puffs of icing sugar up into the air. The sweet sugar mingled with the smell of smoked rookwurst sausage which wafted from another tiny wooden stall.

As much as veganism was growing in popularity, it was unlikely we would find anything to eat at a small-town market. I knew what I was missing. As a child, I had stayed at a campsite/theme park in the Netherlands on a kind of souped-up Butlin's holiday. There, my brothers and I had

Day Eleven

eaten as many poffertjes as we could. It felt like I was missing out on an essential part of travelling: sampling the traditional food culture. I looked wistfully back at the pancakes, my stomach growling.

'How cool are these?' Lili directed my attention to a line of brightly coloured canvases.

They were each between one and three metres square and depicted everything from Dutch pastoral scenes to cult movie icons. All were crafted from thousands of freshly cut flowers.

I walked up and down, amazed by the skill that had gone into each intricate design. My idea of a flower festival was something akin to the Sandringham Flower Show: a strange mix of village fair, gardening stalls and obsessive fans of the Royal Family. Most West Norfolk schoolchildren got coerced into visiting at least once, and I had expected something similar here. What we were seeing was closer to an outdoor art gallery.

'I think these are only the kids' ones . . .' Lili was looking over the top of the moving crowd, spying something I was too short to see.

They pulled me forwards, past the edge of the park and around the corner onto a long road. All I could see was the heads of people in the crowd and, in the distance, white smoke billowing into the sky. The crowd ebbed and flowed, and I caught glimpses of a large vehicle ahead. The smoke was coming from the exhaust pipes of an articulated lorry, lights flashed loud while heroic music played. Slowly it transformed into the robot Optimus Prime.

'Oh my God!' The robot was made of thousands of flowers, painstakingly attached to its framework. I looked behind the lorry and saw more flower sculptures stretching into the distance, a myriad of colours set against the grey day.

*

'Which was your favourite?' Lili asked as we left the festival.

'Hmm, it's a hard one. Maybe the giant pandas? Or the meerkats playing bongos?'

'I liked the floral tribute to Pink Floyd's *The Wall*.'

'I thought as much!' I laughed.

I took Lili's hand and we ambled back to the campsite. It didn't matter that we were making mistakes. Getting lost on our first day had led to the discovery of the Natuurkampeer-terreinen without which we would never have seen the festival. Maybe the universe had some treats in store too.

Abi

Day Twelve, Leersum

'Porridge is ready!'

Lili had been up for a while, enthusiastically cooking and packing for our day's ride. I was stationary in my sleeping bag, staring at the orange ceiling, exhausted. Raindrops on the outer tent cast moving patterns of light across the fabric. I really didn't want to cycle today.

'Are you all right?' Lili popped their head in.

'Uh-huh,' I muttered in a noncommittal way. I couldn't look Lili in the eye. I didn't want them to see that I was struggling.

'Are you sure?' Lili probed.

'I'm fine! Just, I dunno . . . leave me alone for a bit.' I turned over, hiding my head in my sleeping bag.

I heard Lili zip up the tent and walk away. I just needed to sleep, or cry, or cry and sleep, anything to stop the deep sense of wrongness that was creeping through my body.

The tent unzipped again.

'I've made a decision,' Lili announced.

'Yeah?'

'I think we should stay here one more day.'

'Why?' I stuttered.

41

'You obviously need to,' Lili began, and my relief was instantly overshadowed by a nagging shame. I was convinced I was, and could only ever be, a burden to Lili and that this tour was proving it, until, 'and to be honest, I'd like to stay too. What's the point of this trip if we aren't enjoying it?'

I finally let go of the tears that had been building up. Lili crawled in and held me tight. I tentatively allowed myself to be comforted. My eyelids began to droop. Exhausted, I fell back asleep to the patter of rain on our tent.

I awoke to bright sunlight shining in, bathing me in an orange glow. Disorientated from sleep, I allowed my brain some time to figure out where I was. The tent was unpleasantly hot.

I stumbled out, tripping over a guy rope. Lili was outside at the picnic bench, typing on the netbook, maps sprawled on the table.

'What are you up to?' I croaked. In the cool air, my head was beginning to clear.

'I'm just getting in touch with Max to say we'll be a day later than planned. How are you feeling?'

'Better, I think.' I joined Lili at the bench.

Max was one half of a Dutch couple who lived about 30km down the Rhein in Wageningen. We'd contacted them on Warmshowers to see if they could host us for a night.

Warmshowers is the bike tourer's equivalent to Couchsurfing. It's a website designed for cyclists looking to stay for free with other cyclists around the world. Aside from free accommodation, you get a wealth of local cycling knowledge, advice and maps. We planned to use it to save money on campsites, especially in countries where we couldn't wild camp. We had a few criteria for people we contacted: we would only choose hosts who had lots of pictures, who had hosted or been hosted before, or who had been on a tour before. Our only absolute rule was we wouldn't stay with single men.

Couchsurfing is hard to navigate as a woman. I was used to being told not to make myself vulnerable yet felt silenced by #notallmen when I tried to discuss the endless calculations and judgements I was making about risk. It was hard to balance my desire to remain open to new people and experiences with my practical concerns for our safety. Single female hosts were hard to come by, presumably for a similar set of reasons, so we'd settled for couples. However, Max's partner was away in Thailand.

'What do you think?' Lili asked.

I was grateful to be travelling with Lili as I didn't have to explain or justify my fear. Out of touch with the rest of our community, seeing life often through the lens of the cycle tourers we followed on social media, I felt lucky we had each other to reflect with, to validate how we were feeling, to probe things. We may not have had the perceived safety of a man travelling with us, but I was never worried my fears or discussions of safety would be minimised or silenced.

'We could give it a go? He lives in student accommodation, so I'm sure there'll be other people about.'

Lili nodded. 'We can always leave if we get bad vibes.'

We knew it was important to respect our gut feelings above all else. As a queer couple, we'd gotten used to making constant quick risk assessments of people and places. Should we hold hands here? Do we feel comfortable about kissing here? Shall we tell this person we're together, or are we just friends today? I knew that if I ever felt unsafe then Lili would respect that, and vice versa. I was happy to give Max's house a shot.

The evening's supermarket shop gave us a clue why I'd

been feeling so miserable that morning. I looked down at the basket loaded with junk food and turned to Lili.

'What's the date today?'

Lili checked the phone. 'Oh. Ovulation.'

'Ovu-fucking-lation.'

Lili

Day Thirteen, Leersum to Wageningen

We had settled into a morning routine. I would shuffle out of my sleeping bag and sit in the porch, boiling the water for a cup of instant coffee. While I drank this, I would make porridge – throwing oats, water and whatever combination of nuts and dried fruits we had into a pan. I would top Abi's portion with a thick crust of sugar. We would then go through the pantomime: I hand Abi the porridge through the tent door; she takes a spoonful and spits it out like a petulant child. I zip her into the inner tent.

I sat, watching the water boil. Legs straight, I reached for my toes and felt a sharp pull behind my knees. Although I would always want to keep going, I was glad we had taken an additional rest day.

'Gas canister?'

'C.'

'Swimming goggles?'

'Why did we unpack those?'

Abi shrugged.

I looked down at the page of my small notebook. 'Two.'

Before we left, I had used duct tape to label the larger rear panniers A–D and the smaller front ones 1–4. In my notebook I'd recorded what we packed into each one. In theory, everything we needed for an overnight stay was in panniers 1, 3, A and C. In the three days we'd spent at Leersum we'd managed to spill everything out into the front porch. It took nearly an hour to pack up again.

As Abi dismantled the tent, I walked over to our bikes. I put my thumb and forefinger around Abi's rear tyre and squeezed. The rubber gave slightly. With the additional weight of our pannier bags our tyres were deflating faster than usual. Wanting to avoid a flat, I retrieved the handpump. I unscrewed the small plastic nubbin on the tyre valve and immediately encountered a problem. There wasn't enough of the metal valve sticking out for the tyre pump to grip onto.

'Fuck.' I threw the snapped tyre lever onto the grass. Abi's rear wheel had racing tyres and inexplicably deep and narrow rims. I could feel the sweat dripping down the small of my back, my fingers pulsed with the effort of levering the stiff rubber off. Abi's wheels were the only new part on either of our bikes. They were the only part of our set-up that neither of us was totally comfortable working with. Predictably, they were now the part causing trouble.

I made another attempt. I wiggled the first tyre lever in, using its curved edge to pop the rubber over the rim, and secured it in place by hooking its bottom around a spoke. I wrestled a second in, an inch along.

Pop. Hook.

I fought to get a third lever in, using all the strength in my fingers to push it between the rim and the tyre wall – now taut with the tension of the other two levers.

'Gahhhh.' I held up the inner tube triumphant.

'I'm going to see if he has a nut or something I can use,' I called to Abi, gesturing at the man working in the garden beside the farmhouse.

Day Thirteen

In his shed, the man pulled down old cigarette tins and small cardboard boxes filled with nuts, screws and washers of every size until we found one that fit on the inner tube valve. It was an imperfect solution, but it allowed me to re-inflate the rear tyre.

We left Leersum in the heat of midday, stopping at the caravan shop in town where I bought a thin foam mat to sleep on. I attached it to the growing pile of stuff bungeed on top of my rear pannier rack.

We followed the EuroVelo signs, meandering downhill until it felt like the road fell out from under us and we were on the banks of a large bright river. I don't know what I'd expected of a river so close to the sea. I was struck by the sheer width – the vast body of water that lay between us and the opposite bank. The large flat bottom boats that transported shipping containers looked like toy boats on a pleasure lake. The river here is tamed, managed by dams. The lack of visible current made the water a single sheet of light, more like a plateau than the muddy winding rivers I knew. We would be following the Rhein until Basel, 700km away. It was 20km along the river to the turning off to Wageningen, and we were silent, lost in thought.

In *A Time of Gifts*, Patrick Leigh Fermor recounts his 1933 journey on foot from the Hoek van Holland to Constantinople, including a period along the Rhein. I'd read it as a teenager and it was the starting of an idea, a single point on a continuous line that led to this moment – my first sight of the Rhein. When I'd left hospital in 2014, I had the crane from the title page tattooed on my wrist. I was setting an intention: one day my world would be bigger than a hospital ward.

*

I'd assumed a route along rivers would be relatively flat. I stared up at the sheer road we needed to take towards Wageningen. The town sprawled up and away from the river's banks, and the road into the centre was a steep climb. My arms strained as I pushed my bike up the pavement.

When the road levelled out to an acceptable incline, we agreed to start cycling again. Without thinking I swung my leg over the back of my bike. It collided into my sleeping bag, rucksack, ukulele and newly acquired camping mat. Off balance, I couldn't stabilise my bike and it crashed to the ground.

'Shit!'

'You ok?' Abi asked.

I was flushed with the irrational annoyance born of embarrassment. I put my foot against the front wheel, grappled the handlebars and levered my bike upright. Tucking my leg over the crossbar, we set off.

We cycled along regimented suburban streets, and up the high street through the town centre. Breathless, we reached the campus of the agricultural college that dominated Wageningen. The large central thoroughfare ran parallel to the river and we cycled from one end of it to the other trying to locate Max's student accommodation. In the baking August sun our tempers were fraying. On the third lap, we stood in the shade and I dug out our phone: an old, mostly unusable, Samsung.

'Can we not buy some data?'

'I don't know.'

'Give it here.' Abi took the phone and worked on it for a minute. 'There, we can use data for 24 hours, but it costs, we can't keep doing this.'

I wasn't sure if she meant buying data or getting lost. She pulled up Google Maps. Max's accommodation was at the opposite end of the campus. She raised an eyebrow but didn't say anything more.

'Is this right?' Abi asked, wheeling slowly up the driveway.

'Looks right.' I pointed down to the tarmac where 'Sex, Drugs and Droevendaal' was scrawled in large chalk letters. Droevendaal was a small, self-governing village of single-storey houses. These were connected by a blocked framework of concrete slab pavements and hundreds of winding short-cuts worn down in the long grass and through overgrown hedges. A wooden noticeboard had a paper map with the numbered grid of houses pinned to it, and an announcement they were seeking nominations for a new mayor.

We leant our bikes against the wall of Max's house and rang the bell.

'Hallo?' The door was answered by a lad of our age.

'Hi . . . we are friends of Max's . . .'

'The cyclists!'

We came through to the cool, white interior of the kitchen.

'I am just studying but help yourself to tea.'

He fell back into a nest of books and papers on one of the two futons. Abi settled on the other while I stepped out and pulled our books from the pannier bags.

An endless stream of people passed through the kitchen – coming and going, looking for someone that lived there, or someone that used to. No one seemed surprised to find two strangers sitting reading. We were joined by a tall boy, who sat tapping his fingers on the fish tank between the sofas, causing the small fish to scatter in shock waves. He was staying in a tent in the front garden while trying to sort out somewhere to live.

'Is it good?' A young man with a tousle of blonde curls was standing at the doorway. He gestured to my book.

'I'm enjoying it – nearly finished though.' I held up the remaining sliver of pages. He pulled an identical copy of *The God of Small Things* from his rucksack.

'I've only just started.'

I laughed.

'Lili and Abi, right?'

'Yes!'

'I'm Max.' He stretched out his hand. 'Shall we get your stuff inside? I thought we could maybe ride down to the river for a swim? Don't feel you have to – I know you must be tired . . .'

I looked at Abi. She nodded.

'Sounds good to us!'

'We'll pick up my brother Bart on the way,' Max explained as we climbed onto our bikes.

We were joined by his friend Justin as we rode down from the campus through Wageningen. The pavements were busy with students. We waited at a street corner for Bart, who pulled up on a postbox-red racing bike, a gleeful smile under a shock of bright blonde hair. The five of us flocked down the high street.

I love riding bikes as part of a group: not in a peloton or a cycling club, (which I've never done, although I'm sure it is fun), but as part of a gang: riding to school, around the suburbs on long summer afternoons, from work to the pub. Whilst normally as a cyclist I am cautious, trying to make myself smaller, in a group I feel part of something bigger than me, a fluid whole which expands to fill or claim space. Racing the boys, swerving around cars or pedestrians, conversation shouted amongst us, I felt part of an undeniable, joyful, presence on the road. I stopped worrying about whether a car had seen me, or if I was an inconvenience. I knew they could see us, and they could just damn well wait.

Day Thirteen

We wheeled down to a sandy path, locked our bikes and followed the boys on foot through a wooden gate. The sky was an electric blue, and we cut a line through the tall grass, following hidden paths, winding under the concrete bases of electricity pylons, scrawled with graffiti. Static crackled in the air. It felt like the drumming heat came not just from the sun, but the soil, which had been baked over the day and hummed beneath our feet. At an empty beach, the boys stripped to their shorts, yelling as they ran into the water and bringing big handfuls up to their shoulders to prepare their bodies for the cold before they dived in. They began swimming across the wide river, dodging ferries and barges. With tired legs, Abi and I sat reading. Two huge dark brown cows slumbered just along from us, sharing the shaded bank.

Abi

Day Fourteen, Wageningen to Arnhem

Max was sipping coffee at the large wooden table when Lili and I wandered sleepily through to the communal kitchen.

'Help yourself to anything,' he said, gesturing to an array of breakfast foods, teas and coffee.

'Thanks. We're going to make porridge, would you like some?' Lili asked.

Max nodded enthusiastically.

As more people emerged bleary-eyed from their bedrooms, more oats were added to the pan. It was beyond me how so many people could be so excited about porridge, but I accepted my breakfast graciously. Max produced some foraged black-berries and pears, and others donated nuts, syrups and spices for the meal. It felt very wholesome sitting around the table with this large group of people. It was a feeling I missed from university. It had been a while since I'd felt a part of a strong community like this. We chatted a lot about our cycling plans and then about school systems around the world. It was Max's first day as a teacher, and he was feeling nervous.

'I just hope I can make a difference,' he mused as he idly played with his spoon.

'I'm sure you will,' Lili replied.

Day Fourteen

I smiled but wasn't convinced. I'd left a teacher training course a year ago after a poor period of mental health. It had been precipitated by an overwhelming workload and the realisation that teaching was radically different from what I expected or remembered. The government had turned schooling into a business, squeezing out joy and creativity and ending any chance of social mobility. I was not prepared to hold up hoops for children to jump through.

I hoped for Max's sake that it was different in the Netherlands.

'Let's take a look at your bike,' Max suggested after breakfast.

My tyre had developed an egg-shaped bulge in it after Lili had removed it in Leersum. Max had noticed it on our river ride last night and had recommended we replace the inner tube before it blew. He was a semi-qualified bike mechanic and we were grateful for any help we could get.

'You're going to need to use an inner tube with a longer valve,' he said, examining the problem. 'Let's take it off and I'll lend you one.'

Bright, hot sunlight peeked from above the tall trees as we began our fight with the tyre. It was frustrating work; we would get a lever in between the rim and the tyre only to have it snap in two or stubbornly wedge tight. Max watched our developing struggle and confidently stepped in. Whether he thought it was our inexperience or our weak female hands which made us incapable of tackling this basic task, his confidence was soon put to the test.

'How did you manage to get these off at all?' he asked Lili, panting with effort.

Combining our strength, we began again. One lever in. Another. A third. Pulling and pushing, the levers awkwardly jolted, threatening to snap or fall out during even the smallest lapse in concentration. Finally, we slid the tyre off. We were red-faced and sweaty but pleased with our small victory. Max handed us a tube from a pile in the garden.

'Oh crap!' he exclaimed, looking at his watch. 'I'm going to be late. Can you manage?'

'Sure,' I said with false confidence.

'Good luck,' he called.

'Good luck to you!' Lili replied as Max cycled off.

We looked at the wheel lying on the grass.

'Right. Let's get this tyre back on.'

As we pumped up the tyre, we heard a pop and hiss of air. Lili and I looked at the deflating tyre in disbelief. Frustrated and exhausted by the hard work, I searched for bike mechanics in town.

'It will be around an hour,' the mechanic announced.

I sighed and handed over the bike. 'Dank je.'

It had taken us 40 minutes to walk the bike in and now we were stuck for another hour. I wasn't sure if we were ever going to leave today.

'What do you want to do?' Lili asked, looking completely dispirited.

A cafe called *Bagels and Beans* was advertising vegan food. The two of us sat inside, next to a large glass window which overlooked a market square littered with bikes.

A waitress in an orange uniform brought over two seaweed bagels and some tea. The warm comfort of hot drinks and carbohydrates washed over me. I felt instantly better. We may have been delayed, but at least we had problem-solved effectively. Lili smiled happily. We could do this.

'Oh my God!' I hung my head over the handlebars of my newly fixed bike. Sweat was dripping down my forehead. My good mood had wilted as soon as we had left the air-conditioned cafe.

Day Fourteen

'What?' Lili asked, alarmed.

'We're so stupid.'

'Why?'

'If we'd wheeled your bike in, we could have cycled back together. It would have only taken ten minutes.' It was already midday and we still hadn't started out. 'Do you really think it's a good idea to go today? It's so hot already.'

I was close to panic. I wanted to leave but after this huge delay, I didn't know if we had time to reach our destination.

'I think we should get going.' Lili's voice was sure and steady. They gave me a big hug.

I buried my face in their shoulder and began to calm down. If I stayed for another day, I would lose the rhythm we'd been building; the steady passing of kilometres, the comfort of our camping routine. It might be hot, but it would feel cooler once we were moving. I took a long steady breath.

'Ok, let's keep going.'

Back on the route, Lili rode ahead of me and I began to relax. The path ran along the river and a cool breeze eased the heat of the beating sun. After the constant stops and starts of the day it felt freeing to get back on my bike. My legs relaxed into the slow motion of the pedals.

Then Lili took a magnificent wrong turn back down the steep hill from yesterday.

'Oh, fucking hell! LILI, STOP!'

Lili sped away, not hearing me.

I looked wistfully at the flat path to my left – the correct route – and headed down to catch them.

'We've gone the wrong way.' I broke the news at the bottom of the hill.

'I don't think so.'

'Lili—'

'I'm 100 per cent certain it's this way.' They placed one foot against their pedal, as if ready to cycle off.

'Look, let's just look at the map and see.'

Lili frowned.

'Please? We don't want another detour.' I played on their guilt from our first day's drastic route change, anything to make them see sense.

Reluctantly, Lili looked at the map and let out a quiet, 'Oh.'

'It's ok.' I gave them a hug. When was this day going to give us a break?

We'd made a horrible mistake: cycling in the middle of the day was excruciating. It was easily 30 degrees and there was no shade on the path. I could feel the heat clinging to me. I felt suffocated by it.

I switched positions on my handlebars again, trying to minimise the pain which radiated through my hands, along my forearms and down my shoulders and back. All I could think about was how unfit I was; how I just wasn't made for this; how I shouldn't have bothered to do this; how everyone who looked at my fat body and decided my limits had been right.

Lili was faring no better. We cycled in grim silence, determined to reach our destination.

We stopped to pop glucose sweets into our dry mouths and to take large swigs of our dwindling supply of lukewarm water. The cool waters of the still Rhein mocked me. We didn't have time for swimming. I kept going.

At the village of Renkum, we turned onto a path which ran beside a motorway. Fumes from the lorries filled my lungs. I pushed on, waiting for the turning back onto the small roads and paths we were used to.

Finally, we barrelled down the steep path onto a quiet road. My relief was instant. The roar of the motorway died to a distant hum. It was the first shade all day and the sudden drop in temperature felt as refreshing as an ice-cold drink.

A group of bikers in full leathers stood beside a map board, cooling themselves with makeshift fans under the shade of the trees. Even with our new-found confidence navigating the Dutch cycle paths, it made sense for us to use the infrastructure around us to check our position. We nervously sidled over to the board.

'Wil je er een?' A female biker approached us, holding out a plastic bag.

'Um.' I looked into the bag. It was full of hard-boiled sweets.

She smiled and pushed the bag towards us.

'Dank je,' I said, taking two and handing Lili one.

The sweet was sticky in its wrapper. I popped it in my mouth. We started to cycle along a small road, beneath tall elm and oak trees. The sourness flooded my mouth with much-needed saliva. I savoured it. The sensation took my mind off the pain and heat.

'This sweet is amazing,' Lili said. 'We should definitely get some for the rest of the tour.'

I nodded enthusiastically.

Our last obstacle was, once again, the steep banks which lined the river route. Lili pointed up a very large hill.

'There is campsite up that hill within 2km. Or, we can continue to the campsite we had originally planned to stay at, but it's another 10km.'

I looked up the hill, my legs in agony and my body aching. I clung to a vague hope that the next campsite would be along the flat path. 'Let's try the next one.'

After a day like today, surely I couldn't possibly make another bad decision.

We continued for another 4km through dense forest. The sunlight filtered green through the leaves. The shade provided respite from the heat. I was sore, but the pain was temporary.

Then I saw it. Towering above me. It was the hill to end all hills. A rough dirt track between spectacular pine trees, weaving towards a distant peak. Our Dutch Everest, and the only way to the campsite. I let out a low moan.

I stood at the bottom of it, willing myself to move. An elderly female couple on Dutch bikes pedalled past us. They began slowly but surely ascending. I watched in despair. How was I so, so unfit?

I looked at Lili and they looked at me. Determination shone on their features, we nodded to each other and then swung our legs off our bikes. We began to push. I stopped at intervals to catch my breath. Finally, we reached the summit.

'That better be the last one.' I turned to Lili who was scouring the map.

'I think so.' They smiled.

We cycled the last 5km towards the campsite where I collapsed.

Through all the pain and the heat of the day I had felt utterly miserable. At no point had this cycle ride felt possible yet I had kept going; my body had kept moving. I couldn't help but feel proud of myself.

Lili

Day Fifteen, Arnhem

I was lying on top of my sleeping bag, my sweat sticking the silky fabric to my bare skin. I stretched my arms above my head, grateful we had invested in a larger three-person tent. I didn't want to get up. Every time I tensed to sit up my muscles let out a symphony of complaints. The heat wasn't helping the intense feeling of tiredness. I could just lie here forever, unmoving.

The temperature rose a degree. I couldn't stay another minute in this tent.

I hauled myself out and into the cooler air outside. Beside the tent, in the shade of a large oak tree, I laid out our tarp. I weighed it down in each corner with boots and water bottles grabbed at random from the tent porch. I sprawled across it, lifting my legs at intervals to peel my skin from the tacky surface. Even in the shade, it was too hot.

A T-shirt landed beside me. Abi was awake and throwing clothes out of the inner tent.

'I spotted a washing machine last night,' she explained.

Although we'd packed several variations of clothing layers, in the unrelenting heat of the last two weeks we'd been wearing the same clothes over and over. Pulling on my cycle shorts after a week of continuous wear was unpleasant. I'd come to dread undressing after a long ride, and the whole inner tent smelt increasingly musty.

We hung a washing line from the oak tree to Abi's upturned bike, stabilised by its pedals. The wet clothes flapped in the breeze. I mimicked them, moving restlessly around on the tarp. My body needed rest, but I was struggling to tolerate an empty day, void of structure, stretching out before me.

'I'm going to the supermarket, do you want anything?'

Every time I'd been in hospital, the big Tesco in Fulbourn had been the first place I was allowed to go on leave. I would prepare a detailed list, but even though I knew exactly what I wanted to buy, I would still drag the nurse or HCA accompanying me up and down the aisles. After weeks starved of stimulation, I wanted to drink in and gorge on everything the supermarket had to offer – colours, sounds, smells, unfamiliar faces. In a time where I had no choice about where I slept, what I ate, or what medications I took, I was making the most of being able to exercise consumer choice. Once I was in 'recovery' and out of hospital I still found pleasure and comfort in wandering up and down supermarket aisles.

Stepping through the automatic doors, I set myself a task. It already felt impossible to eat enough on the tour. I walked up and down the aisle of the supermarket, enjoying the chill of the coolers that sent goosebumps shivering up my legs. After years of eating disordered behaviour, I had reached something of a balance – food or what I weighed weren't the most important things in my life. I idly picked up boxes of crackers, read the ingredients, returned them. Nine days into the tour, long days of cycling and the limitations of camp stove cooking meant my clothes were already feeling loose.

Day Fifteen

Abi had asked for chocolate soy milk. I turned down the aisle. Next to the usual soy milks was a soy macchiato drink. I threw it into the basket. I may have struggled to eat more but I had an infinite capacity for consuming coffee.

Returning to the campsite, there was no sign of Abi. I heard a rustle.

'Abs, you all right?'

'No,' a voice said from the tent. 'I feel all wrong.'

'Is it not really hot in there?' I walked over. 'Why don't you come out?'

'No.' Abi unzipped the small window at the top of the tent door. I peered in to see her face, pixelated and angry through the mesh. 'I'm a tent goblin.'

I unzipped the tent door and clambered in beside her.

'We should have kept riding today; we should have just kept riding,' she repeated, lying on her side with her face turned away from me. I stroked her hair.

At home we'd coined the word 'crashing' for a physical and emotional comedown from a high intensity period. It was a feeling that saw me invent endless tasks around the house so I didn't have to face it, or saw Abi obsessively playing *The Sims* for 72 hours after a week of work or a big event. I hadn't imagined carrying it with us on the cycle tour. Surely away from the everyday pressures of life, surrounded by nature, we should be saturated with wellness.

I sat up and opened the laptop. I clicked through website after website until I found it. The familiar twee music played. The camera swept over green grass to the white tent. The reassuring face of Sue Perkins appeared on screen. Abi sat up and sniffed, drawing the laptop towards her.

'Is it the new season?'

Lili

Day Sixteen, Arnhem to Aerdt

In the cold light of the morning, 6.30am seemed unreasonably early to start. I switched the alarm off and started willing myself upright, bargaining with myself for an additional few minutes lying down before the inevitable.

Both of us moved sluggishly through the morning routine, and we left the campsite about 8.45. The rush of air on the sweeping downhill route blew the sleep from my eyes. We sped out of Arnhem following the blue EuroVelo signs.

I was riding a few metres ahead of Abi. Turning around a corner, I started, tensing my fingers ready to pull sharply on my brakes. A huge dark shape loomed towards the path. My brain worked frantically to figure out what it was. I disentangled feet . . . ears . . . tusks . . . trunk? A yelp from Abi confirmed she'd seen it too, and I stopped for her to catch up.

'Ermm . . . why is there a mammoth here?'

'I have literally no clue.'

I'd been desperately trying to make sense of something nonsensical: a life-sized stone model of a mammoth.

We continued cycling through the delta: a broad flood-plain where the water had been pumped and drained to create fields. It was only ten o'clock, but already the sun was beating down on the flat and exposed farm roads. In the small village of Pannerden, about five minutes from our intended campsite at Aerdt, we stopped at a cafe. Tables and chairs spilled out onto the pavement. We propped our bikes up and sat. I drank a coffee while we looked over the map; we'd expected to be riding for much longer.

'Should we keep going?' Abi asked.

'I think let's just take today as a semi-rest day and leave early tomorrow for Germany.'

We followed the road past the church and village hall where children in medieval costume ran in and out of some event. The houses turned into fields, and we swerved around tractors, which trundled along the narrow roads to the campsite.

'Ah.'

Abi was searching her bike for the source of a strange squeaking noise that had been following her the last two days. Beside our tent, in the shade of two old fruit trees, I watched from a bench as she slowly eliminated suspects from her line of enquiry. Finally, she removed her rear pannier rack, beneath it her tyre had worn a sizeable hole in her plastic mudguard.

'Oh, shit.' She set about removing the mudguard.

I was not the only person observing her labour. Earlier in the day we had attracted the attention of the campsite owner's granddaughter. She had walked us around the campsite reception, a glass conservatory busy with strange paintings, clocks and ceramics, and babbled in German whilst we nodded along (she lived over the border). I had tried to avoid staring at the crucifixes which crowded the walls. Now she was cycling laps of the car park, and every few minutes her small face would appear, still struck with curiosity about the visitors who were not an elderly Dutch couple.

'RIP,' Abi said solemnly as she threw the mudguard on the ground.

The first casualty of the tour.

LILI'S POOR IMITATION OF A LENTIL DAL

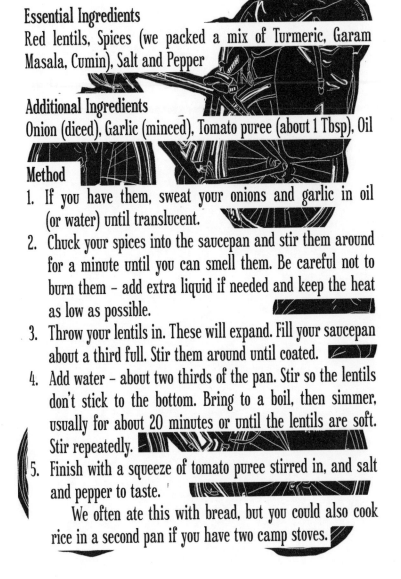

Essential Ingredients
Red lentils, Spices (we packed a mix of Turmeric, Garam Masala, Cumin), Salt and Pepper

Additional Ingredients
Onion (diced), Garlic (minced), Tomato puree (about 1 Tbsp), Oil

Method
1. If you have them, sweat your onions and garlic in oil (or water) until translucent.
2. Chuck your spices into the saucepan and stir them around for a minute until you can smell them. Be careful not to burn them – add extra liquid if needed and keep the heat as low as possible.
3. Throw your lentils in. These will expand. Fill your saucepan about a third full. Stir them around until coated.
4. Add water – about two thirds of the pan. Stir so the lentils don't stick to the bottom. Bring to a boil, then simmer, usually for about 20 minutes or until the lentils are soft. Stir repeatedly.
5. Finish with a squeeze of tomato puree stirred in, and salt and pepper to taste.

   We often ate this with bread, but you could also cook rice in a second pan if you have two camp stoves.

Germany

Lili

Day Seventeen, Aerdt to Wesel

In the darkness I moaned and groaned and packed my sleeping stuff up around me. We had a long day ahead.

Abi and I set off at 7.30am, with the aim to get some miles in before breakfast. It was a cool morning and I wore my thermal layer underneath Abi's vest top. The sky was milky, casting a pallid light across the low fields. We rode through the still air, and I noticed the profound silence – aside from the lack of cars or people, there was none of the constant hum of insects, who had not yet taken flight. I may have been struggling with the early starts, but times like this felt worth it.

After a few wrong turns through the fields, tracks and agricultural roads that surrounded the campsite, we bounced down an unmarked and unpaved path. This bisected a bike path running on top of a long dyke. Here the Rhein route split, with options on both sides of the river. We chose to stay on the side we were on and turned left. This, like many of the decisions we'd made, was an arbitrary one.

'Are we in Germany yet?' Abi asked.

I shrugged. 'That's German, right?' I said, pointing at a sign on a crossroads. It was an unfamiliar shape, red instead of green. We'd crossed over an invisible line, the border between the two countries, somewhere back along the path. The Netherlands was behind us.

'Oh, that was anticlimactic. I expected . . . something.'

We stopped at the next bench and while Abi ambled off to pee inside an abandoned building, I started constructing our celebratory breakfast. Stuffing the sandwiches into our mouths, I marvelled at the perfect combination: peanut butter, chocolate spread and banana. Sweet, salty, soft, cool, claggy. I shot Abi a stupid grin, my mouth full. I was quietly thrilled we were in a whole different country.

We climbed gingerly back onto our bikes and pushed off. Though we were in a new country, the scenery was indistinguishable from the start of our ride. We carried along the same straight path, over the uneven light grey paving stones, along a tall dyke. The light gauze of the early morning was lifting, and I could see across the low wetlands to the river. Looking the other way, across meadows and fields and the irregular boundaries of trees, I could make out the stark spires of churches, jutting out of clusters of houses in the near distance.

Arriving into Emmerich am Rhein, the path split. I looked around for a route sign but couldn't see one. I stood at the junction, staring up at the main road which crossed over the path ahead of us. Looking at the map, it was clear we needed to get up there, somehow. We wheeled our bikes off the path, across the grass and straight up the steep bank to the road, hauling them over a barrier onto the pavement. As I grappled the handlebars over, I considered how much stronger I'd gotten in just a few weeks.

I rode under Emmerich's town sign. *Partnerstädt King's Lynn*. Wheeling back, I took a photo of Abi pointing enthusiastically at this link with her home town. It seemed a good omen.

Day Seventeen

In the Netherlands I had felt increasingly comfortable navigating the Dutch cycle network, fluent in both the language of the signs and where they were placed on the path. I thought the way Dutch street planners imagined a cyclist would think.

As we cycled into the centre of Emmerich it became apparent that the German town planners imagined cyclists thinking very differently. It felt as if I'd switched to a different user interface, and nothing was where I thought it was. I quickly lost sight of the Rhein route.

We wheeled into the town square, where I found a board displaying a tourist map. As we stared at it, a man approached us.

'Hallo, sucht ihr etwas?' He seemed to be offering help.

'Hallo, ja. Wo ist die EuroVelo?' Abi ventured. He looked at us quizzically.

'Er . . . der Rhein?' I tried.

He laughed and pointed through the archway of a building to our right, where I could see the glint of water.

'Danke, danke!' I called as we cycled off.

We continued from Emmerich as the sun rose steadily higher. The route followed the main road away from the river, through suburban streets that blurred into each other. The Rhein Radweg signs pointed us off into the village of Bienen. We swung round the tall spire of the church at its centre.

'I feel like we're going in a big circle,' Abi shouted behind me.

I shrugged my shoulders in response; without a decent map or GPS we didn't have much choice but to follow the route signs. We emerged again about 100 metres down the road we had left. I could see Abi was frustrated at this scenic and unnecessary detour.

'I guess it's just trying to keep us off the main road as much as possible,' I reasoned.

She didn't look convinced.

A little before midday, we arrived at Rees, the oldest town in the lower Rhein area. We cycled through streets paved with irregular red bricks and lined with tall houses. I was getting hungry. Spotting the green of a park, we rested our bikes against an old stone wall and sat on the grass beside the figures of three oversized inanimate ladies in bathing suits, made of painted metal. They were watching a single metal figure in a blue bathing cap suspended in the middle of the pond on a red and white ring. This was just one of the sets of sculptures populating the park. After eating our sandwiches, we took a turn around the water, past tall, rust-coloured, sheet metal figures, to the Frog King, a huge reclining bronze frog wearing a jauntily angled crown.

Back on our bikes, we immediately took a wrong turn, still struggling to spot the signs, and came onto a promenade, lined with restaurants and busy with trade. Retracing our steps, we re-joined the route and continued through the town. We cycled past large plastic ice cream cones advertising the wares of the shops they were chained to. The wooden signs of bakeries and the green neon crosses of pharmacies jutted above us. We turned off the street up a smooth, steep cycle path marked by brightly coloured, geometric shapes of metal, and came onto the epicentre of Rees; the Sculpture Park was opened in 2003 and is home to work by Dutch and German artists which spill out onto its streets, blending with the everyday objects of a popular tourist town.

My heart dropped a beat as I saw it was another 27km to Wesel, where we had at some point hastily marked a campsite on our Michelin road maps. The steam ran out of my legs, but continuing felt far less effort than changing plans. Wikipedia now tells me that there are three campsites in Rees, but we didn't know that at the time. After the disaster

Day Seventeen

of our first day in the Netherlands, I was committed to sticking to 'the plan'. Leaving Rees behind we joined a bright exposed path along a dyke, peopled with walkers, cyclists and families.

An hour later and our water bottles were empty. Despite our early start I was struggling in the heat. A left-hand turn off the path brought us into thick shade and the steps of a church, the end of the main road of a small village. In the late afternoon everything was quiet, the wooden shutters were closed on the only shop. We returned to the glade and sat on the cool stone steps opposite a large family who were also enjoying a break from the relentless sun.

'We have to find some water soon.' Abi squeezed the last lukewarm drop from her bottle.

Everything in me wanted to just keep going, but Abi was right, we needed water.

The route wound along the river, away from cars, towns and shops. Thirst drove us off the path and away from the security of the EuroVelo signs. We rode into the town of Bislich and headed towards the church spire. I spotted a man in the driveway of a house, getting out of a car with his son. We pulled onto the pavement, and he looked up at us.

'Hallo,' I began. 'Spreckenzie . . . English?'

He looked hesitant. 'Ja, a little.'

'Are there any shops near?' I gestured to my empty water bottle. 'Ein Supermarkt?'

He looked at his watch and shook his head. They would be closed by now. He gestured for my water bottle.

'I can . . . in my house.' He pointed inside.

'Oh my God, that would be amazing.'

He took my bottles in his hands, and his son took Abi's from her. They came out five minutes later, bottles full of ice-cold water. We put them against our cheeks and the back of our necks and let the condensation trickle down. Oh, to be cold again!

'Danke! Danke!' I called out as we cycled off. Stopping back on the route, I took a mouthful. It was beautiful, ice cold, and . . .

'Oh no!'

'What?' Abi was poised to take a sip.

'Don't drink it, it's fizzy.'

Abi thrust the bottle at me. Her childhood migraines meant she had had to take a lot of dissolvable painkillers, and as an adult fizzy water makes her gag. Stopping at a bench, we sat while I stirred the handle of a metal fork into the water to flatten it enough so that a sip didn't send her off retching.

In the distance, I could make out glinting, white forms which, as we pedalled closer, didn't disappear like a mirage but materialised into a huge field of baked earth, populated with hundreds of boxy white caravans and mobile homes. Children ran gleefully between them, to and from the beach at the bank of the Rhein. We pedalled up to reception along-side a long line of cars. Abi balanced my bike while I went in and booked a pitch for the night (already half the price of camping in the Netherlands). Waving a hand towards the huge field, the receptionist said we could pitch anywhere we could find.

Amongst the countless caravans there weren't many tents, and we were too tired to look for an elusive good pitch. Abi spotted a clear area and I shrugged agreement. The earth was baked. There was no shade to speak of, and in the oppressive heat of the sun we attempted to get the pegs into the rock-hard earth. Not even the full weight of my hiking boots would do it. As Abi continued to struggle, I ventured to the caravan next to us, where several shirtless lads were drinking and chatting.

'Hallo! Hast du ein . . . Hammer?' I said, gesturing a banging motion and pointing to Abi struggling with the tent pegs.

'Ja ja!' A man disappeared into his caravan and emerged with a mallet. I turned back to Abi, to the sight of three other men heading over to her, gleefully wielding mallets and very keen to assist. We got the tent up quickly and returned the mallets to their various owners. One was confused why we hadn't brought one with us. Clearly, we didn't need to as it only took a few minutes' struggling with a tent peg to summon three.

Light-headed, and both walking like John Wayne, we located the onsite supermarket. At the rear there was a walk-in fridge for drinks. I stood in the cool like a zombie, swaying gently amongst the brightly coloured bottles of unbranded pop. I could feel every kilometre of the ride in my aching limbs. We bought ice lollies, four rolls, pale vegan sandwich slices, sauerkraut and some lemonade. With a lolly hanging ungainly from my mouth, I proceeded to construct messy sandwiches on a wooden bench. We ate hungrily and watched two groups of teenagers playing out familiar summer holiday dramas.

I was woken by the crashing sound of thunder and flashes of light. Opening the tent, I could see huge clouds in the distance. Suddenly, a bright fork of lightning burst out from underneath them, zigzagging rapidly down to the ground a few miles away.

'Wow! Have you ever seen anything like it!' Abi exclaimed, excitedly peering at the clouds as they came closer and closer.

I refused to move from my mat. 'Abi, please lie down.'

I mentally listed all the things that were a) taller than us and b) more conductive.

'Statistically, it's very unlikely to be struck by lightning,' Abi said.

I wasn't reassured. After an hour of waiting, listening and praying, the storm eased off into heavy rain and I began to drift into sleep.

Abi sat up in her sleeping bag.

'Where are you going?' I asked, wide awake and struck by panic.

'I need the loo.'

'But it's not safe, the thunder might start again.'

Abi sighed. Concealed by the sound of the rain, she squatted in the porch and peed into a saucepan. I listened as she unzipped the tent door and upended the pan onto the grass outside. The sound of her peeing inevitably meant I needed to go. Swapping places, I grabbed the saucepan and held it between my legs. The rain stopped suddenly, and after a moment's silence was replaced by the sound of a confident stream of liquid hitting a tin pot. Abi started laughing.

I was suddenly aware of other tents around us. In an effort to make it seem less obviously like someone was weeing in a pot, I practised my pelvic floor exercises and stopped and started the flow. I emptied out the pot and left it to sit in the rain outside: the tell-tale pot. As I lay down next to Abi, she was shaking with laughter. Apparently, my attempts to disguise the noise had only made it more obvious.

She cackled. 'We'll just have to call you Piss Pot Lil from now on.'

Abi

Day Eighteen, Wesel to Gotterswickersham

Yesterday had been our longest day; I woke up starving.

'We're all out of porridge,' Lili announced.

I silently rejoiced. Lili trundled to the onsite supermarket to choose some breakfast rolls while I reluctantly dismantled the tent.

'Are you sure you want to leave?' I pleaded. Lili had returned and was side-eyeing my half-arsed efforts to pack up.

'I just don't want to stay in this huge park where we're so exposed.' Lili glanced up at the temporarily cloudless sky. 'Besides, I have a good feeling about the next campsite.'

I grimaced. My legs were barely functioning and even though the next campsite was only 25km away, it felt like an insurmountable task. I really wasn't sure I could take another day of pain.

'Look, I promise if you cycle with me today, we can have a rest day, or two, and I won't even complain,' Lili beseeched.

'Ok,' I relented. Anything to have two rest days.

Lili pulled out a bag of four rolls, each a different shape and size.

'I didn't know what to choose, so it's a lucky dip,' they said, taking a round roll and scoffing it in two monstrous bites.

I grabbed a triangular roll covered in sesame and took a bite. I knew immediately something wasn't quite right.

'This is a pastry.'

'Oh shit.'

'It's probably got butter in it.' I frowned.

'I don't have any money to get more.' Lili was already half-way through their second roll.

We looked at each other. My stomach was empty, and I'd learnt the consequences of not fuelling properly before a ride. I took a deep breath and ate the probably-not-vegan pastry.

We cycled along the river. A barrier covered in padlocks, mementos from holiday romances, separated us from the water. In the distance stood the impressive Rheinbrücke, its deep red suspension cables creating a triangular point 130 metres above the centre of the Rhein. After Wesel, the route signage took us inland, over and around canals and rivulets which criss-crossed the flat landscape. We cycled in silence; I was still feeling guilty about the pastry.

'Do you think it was wrong to eat it?' I asked.

'No,' Lili replied. 'We don't know for sure it wasn't vegan,' they continued. 'And even if it wasn't, what's the big deal? It was a mistake. It wasn't like you just bit a huge chunk of ham.'

I wasn't convinced.

Since going vegan three years ago I'd gotten used to being asked hypothetical questions designed to catch me out or somehow prove I wasn't a 'real' vegan. Questions like: 'If you were stranded on a desert island, and the only food source was animals, would you eat them?' or 'If you were attacked by a bear and you had a gun, would you kill it?' Or my new favourite: 'If you were in a building and the building collapsed and you were pinned under rocks and couldn't move your arms and legs and next to you is a baby and the baby is being slowly smothered by a pile of bacon and the only way to save the baby's life is to the eat the bacon . . . would you do it?'

I wasn't interested in defending my veganism to anyone, but this tiny pastry was weighing on my mind. I felt like I'd failed the vegan test; it wasn't exactly a survival situation.

'Cut yourself some slack,' Lili said. 'We do our best. It doesn't mean you're not a *real* vegan because you may or may not have eaten something containing butter.'

'I guess so.' We pedalled on. 'I hate feeling guilty about food. And what about my vegan superpowers?'

Lili laughed. 'It's a three-strike system.'

As we wound along the river, the feeling began to wane.

Although we had no idea what the vegan scene was like in different countries, we were both confident that wherever we went, we would be able to get the basics and cook for ourselves. I stopped worrying. We now knew to be more careful when picking rolls in Germany. It was all part of a steep learning curve.

The path continued lazily onwards, sometimes next to the water, sometimes through farmland where sheep grazed contentedly. Small villages passed one by one, providing snapshots of life along the river. We entered the Momm-Niederung nature reserve just outside of Voerde where we listened to the calls of unknown waterfowl, hidden from sight by thick marshy knolls.

In Gotterswickersham, a rural suburb of Voerde, I spotted a sign between two houses: peeling lettering across the faded background of a sun.

'Lili! Stop!'

Lili turned and wheeled up beside me.

'Do you think this is the campsite?' I asked.

We were in the right town, but the sign looked ancient and the campsite seemed empty.

'*Göwi Camping* – it certainly seems right . . .'

'I guess we should have a look.'

We walked up a gravel path to find a derelict campsite perched on the banks of the Rhein. There were two static caravans and several overgrown, empty pitches. On the door of a house by the entrance hung a notice and a phone number. As we were working up the courage to call the number, a man and a woman appeared from the nearest caravan.

'Hallo, wollt ihr heute Nacht hier campen?'

Lili and I looked at one another, we'd picked up the word 'camping'. Struggling to come up with an immediate reply, we were relieved when the man asked: 'English?'

'Ja, ja!' we exclaimed. 'We want to camp here tonight.'

'Ah, the man is away now. You could telephone?' he replied, throwing our lack of language skills into sharp relief once again.

'Ah, thanks,' Lili replied and, in a moment of hubris, dialled the number.

We all stood watching. I couldn't help but feel relieved that it was Lili attempting the phone call. In France, I was to be the main conversationalist for situations like this; in Spain it would be back to Lili. In the Netherlands and Germany, working out who would lead the conversation was mostly decided by who could pull the most pathetic, terrified face. I usually won and Lili usually ended up with the hard job of speaking in a language neither of us knew.

Lili's garbled German became more and more strained as they spoke on the phone. It seemed that neither party could understand the other. Hearing Lili's frantic tone and watching them obviously struggle, our helpful German caravan man came to the rescue.

'Please, I will.' He gestured for the phone.

Lili practically threw it at him.

Day Eighteen

Our multilingual saviour relayed some questions and answers back and forth: how many nights, how many people, how much money?

'He said you can put your tent here. He will be here soon for money. I will show you where to go.' Our new neighbour smiled at us.

Showing us the large pitch next to their caravan, he asked the usual questions – where are you heading, where are you from – and then turned back, assuring us that if there was anything we needed we could simply ask.

We pitched our tent and looked around the site. Other than the couple in the caravan we were completely alone. Pink plastic flamingos, missing their legs, lay discarded on an old pitch. A wooden swing hung uselessly from a single rope. In the bathroom faded pictures told a story of a small hippy camping community in the seventies: the campsite brand new and the pitches full of caravans. It looked like an idyllic place. Now, 40 years on, the campsite felt lost in time. It was hard not to feel like we'd stumbled on something that should no longer exist, that had managed to resist the march of neo-liberal capitalism but was now reaching the end of its life. I was filled with utter sadness for this melancholic place filled with old memories.

We left for a walk around the small village. A white church stood across from the campsite, its bell tolling every quarter hour. Along the river and into the distance stretched a park filled with young families and elderly couples.

'Shall we keep walking?' Lili asked.

'Um . . . maybe not.' My legs had not recovered from the long cycle ride the day before. Instead we gravitated back to the packed beer garden next to the campsite which spilled over with noise and people.

'Oh my God!' I whispered. There, marked vegan on the menu, was schnitzel.

It was like the vegan deities had taken pity on us after our pastry mistake that morning. Piles of steaming chips, salad and two cutlets each of soy-based schnitzel arrived and we devoured them. It was an unexpected treat to be able to enjoy a full meal in a beer garden. Basking in the sun, we sat and people-watched.

Back at the campsite, we were met by the owner: a short man in his late sixties. He peered out from thick, wire-rimmed glasses, his long grey hair tucked behind his ears. He walked over to us, sporting a classic combination of socks and sandals. He seemed very pleased we were going to be staying. We paid and were presented with a key. After more garbled attempts at German and English we gathered that the key was for the gateway at the bottom of the campsite, a private pathway which led to the river. Our very own key to the Rhein.

Lili

Day Nineteen, Gotterswickersham

In the grey early morning, I cycled through fine drizzle into the town centre of Voerde. When we were first dating, Abi called me the hunter-gatherer. In Voerde, without a smartphone to rely on, I followed tracks like a forager, watching for an increase in density of people and looking at what carrier bags they had. I located the church (the centre point of most towns) and then, working outwards, passed the brutalist town hall onto a shopping street. I found a Lidl, and in the mall beside it, a large supermarket I didn't recognise. Walking up and down the aisles, I stopped in one and tried to process what I was seeing. *Vegane.* The whole aisle *and* the one beside it were full of vegan food – sausages, schnitzel, cheeses, salads. Budget in mind, I took a film of it on the iPod to show Abi back at the tent.

At the checkout, I couldn't work out how to weigh an onion. My face flushed hot. The cashier grunted in annoyance as I frantically tried to figure out this new system. I froze, overwhelmed.

At home, my social anxiety centred around not understanding how a place works. Often, this left me going to the same places over and over. I couldn't or didn't want to tolerate the uncertainty of going somewhere I didn't know how to navigate. I slowly inhaled through my nose, exhaled through my mouth and shuffled along to pay. A loud machine swallowed my change. I jumped at the noise. The cashier laughed.

When I left the supermarket the rain had stopped, leaving only a faint dampness on my bike. As I cycled back, I started pushing the speed. Beneath the residual tiredness of yesterday, my legs felt strong after two weeks of riding with panniers. I pedalled faster, harder. I wove around obstacles, leaned into corners. I allowed my body to take control. My attention walked a tightrope; my focus was wider than the immediate path, which disappeared under my wheel faster than I could comprehend, but I didn't look so far ahead that I missed what was straight in front of me. I loved this feeling of balance. I loved the way my brain and body felt like one whole. Underpinning this whole trip was how much I loved cycling.

I'd never considered myself a 'cyclist' because cycling seemed an unremarkable part of my day-to-day life. I suppose this is based on what activities we do or don't consider 'cycling'. The Tour de France: Yes. Riding to school: No. People in Lycra on a Sunday ride: Yes. Pedalling home from the pub through empty streets at 2am: No. Unlike Abi, who had stopped riding years before I met her, there hadn't been any significant periods in my life where I didn't have a bike. Cambridge can be a nightmare to ride in; for a city which has such a large cycling population there is some very questionable cycling infrastructure. Regardless, cycling is always visible in the city, people riding on roads or pavements, bicycles crowded at stands outside supermarkets and train stations, locked to lamp posts, scattered in front gardens. I hadn't known anything else. While local government seem to have limited or vested interest in facilitating it, other characteristics of the city mean that Cambridge still consistently ranks highest in statistics around cycling. When I was figuring out how to get somewhere as a child, biking was always an option. As an adult, my mental health meant I would have been denied a driving licence if I had learned to drive. Without a car, I was thankful to have cycling in my repertoire of travel choices.

Abi

Day Twenty, Gotterswickersham

My early feelings about the campsite had changed. The green patch of grass felt like home. I lay in the morning sun under an ancient oak tree. The only sounds were the twittering of birds and the gentle whoosh of the Rhein. The campsite was a relic from another era, but it comforted me to imagine all the lives which had played out in this spot. I imagined all the people who had laid under this tree before me and everyone who would lay under it after me. Lili bundled on top of me, and fell to my side, demanding my attention.

At midday, I levered myself from our idyllic rest spot. Even on our rest days there were always things to do. I needed to plan our route, but first I had to connect to the Wi-Fi that appeared on the iPod. We asked, but our neighbours didn't know the password. Braving another conversation with the owner (and because it was my turn) I walked over to the house. He and his son were busy painting an old garage.

'Hast du Wi-Fi?' I tentatively asked.

Blank stares.

'Uh die . . . internet? Errr . . . W-Lan?'

Day Twenty

'Ah, yes, yes,' the owner replied, and suddenly I was being rushed into his private house, down the stairs and into his basement where he pointed me to an ancient desktop computer. He sat me down.

'Zuerst öffnen Sie den Browser.' He navigated the mouse to the internet explorer button.

After 15 minutes, Lili's head popped itself into the door-frame.

'Um, everything ok here?' Lili asked, concerned after watching me disappear into a stranger's basement.

'Yes, I think he's just showing me the internet,' I replied. I was too polite to explain that I didn't need to use the inter-net for anything too specific. Taking the iPod out, I turned to the owner and showed him the göwicamping Wi-Fi which appeared on the screen.

'Password?' I asked, hoping that this was one of the many words which might easily translate between English and German.

'Ahhhhh, Passwort! Nein, nein,' he said, whisking me back upstairs to a confused-looking Lili.

'Passwort!' he explained to his son.

Understanding now, the son turned and, matter-of-factly, told us, 'We do not know, sorry.'

'I thought you were gone forever!' Back at the tent, Lili laughed.

'I just didn't know how to tell him I didn't want to use his ancient PC,' I said. 'Plus, he seemed so excited to be explain-ing the internet to me!'

Sitting down on our tarp, I had a flash of intuition. 'Let me just try . . . YES!'

'What?'

'I'm an actual genius.' I performed a small dance in cele-bration. 'We have Wi-Fi!'

Lili gaped. 'How?'

'I tried "gowicamping" as the password,' I explained, jubilant.

Later that day we cycled into Voerde looking for a place to print a map for our next day's travels to Essen. The town, like so many others, had been hit hard economically, the high street empty, the market selling knock-off products and cheap clothing. Unable to find an internet cafe we stumbled upon the local library. Walking in we were sent upstairs to the three computers with printing facilities.

We clearly hadn't learnt our lesson from the Netherlands, and we printed off a Google map of the route to our Warm-showers host in Essen. While I route planned, Lili sat looking through the leaflets and resources for newly settled refugees on the table next to us.

We had left the UK amidst the media storm surrounding refugees and migrants; the dominant message being that individuals and families who risked their lives to try and escape war, the devastation of climate change, or who simply wanted a better life for themselves and their children, were scroungers. The media had given particular meaning to the word 'migrant'; allowing it to be used as a political tool which separated 'worthy' from 'unworthy', buoyed far-right parties, and justified sitting back as people, as children, drowned in the Mediterranean Sea. Much of this hate had fuelled the political catastrophe of the Brexit referendum, from which we were both still reeling.

We were silent as we left the library. I was sharply aware that our freedom to move through Europe stood in stark contrast to the terrible journey these people were being forced to make. I tried to disentangle my thoughts and feelings. On this tour, it was easy to forget about anything but your immediate needs. It was, in many ways, an entirely selfish pursuit. Freewheeling along the paths and roads of Europe was only made possible through our whiteness, our Britishness, our class. Stepping into nature was an act of self-care, even self-preservation, but it had removed us from the pressures and oppressions and problems that structural inequality caused. It had taken us away from politics and activism.

I had wanted to make my travel as ethical as possible, but was it responsible to leave our world behind? Could travel ever be truly ethical?

Abi

Day Twenty-One, Gotterswickersham to Essen

'I can see the route!' I exclaimed, peering through a locked metal gate which blocked the only footbridge over the river. 'How the hell are we supposed to get there?'

We'd been cycling since early morning towards Essen but were now at a standstill. The route had started off relatively easy, along the Rhein to Walsum, then a short path through fields to Oberhausen where we joined a tributary of the Ruhr river. We'd pedalled along the water, past stadiums and an incongruous sea life centre. We'd turned onto a suburban path leading into Essen. The illogical route created by Google Maps had only caused minor difficulties. Once on the outskirts of Essen we had joined a local route called 'The Wasser Route' which led straight to our host's house. An hour in, the route was cut off by a tall, impassable chain-link fence. A gateway stood mockingly on one side of a short footbridge over the stream we had been following, padlocked shut and blocking the rest of the path which continued on the other side.

'We don't even have maps of this area,' Lili moaned, resting their head on their handlebars in exasperation. They steadied themselves. 'Guess we're gonna have to find our way around.'

Day Twenty-One

We began riding up the road running perpendicular to the stream in the hopes we would find a detour sign or, at the very least, another sign towards the Wasser Route. We were travelling through a suburb of Essen, the roads busy with traffic.

We turned onto a main road which we guessed ran parallel to the route. Lili led the way. Their navigation skills were getting better, but I couldn't help but worry we'd end up lost again.

'It's called the Wasser Route for a reason, we just need to find the river,' Lili shouted optimistically, taking a sharp left down another road.

'Sure, darling, I trust you!' I reminded myself we could always buy some mobile data if we were desperate.

'There!'

A bump in the tarmac indicated the road crossed water. We were back on the route, signs pointing us in the right direction. Looking behind, I could see another padlocked gate on this side.

'Well done, babe!' I shouted, gleeful that we had found our way around an obstacle. 'Just another 5km now!'

The rest of the path stretched on through parks and suburban streets. Ascending a small hill, we rode along an elevated cycle path which followed an old train line running over canals, streams and, at one point, a very smelly drainage ditch. We passed a massive slide going down from the path to the forest floor below. As tempting as it was, the walk back up looked less fun. Besides, we were nervous about getting to our host's house. Our strict and self-imposed schedule was the only thing which controlled the growing anxiety.

Reaching the turning to Tommy's house, I looked up in disbelief. An almost vertical hill shot up before us. The path was a dirt track. It was only a short distance, but it was also very, very steep.

We got off to push. My shoulders strained against the full weight of my bike. We were both gaining strength on the tour, but I had a significant weight advantage on Lili.

'SHIT!' Lili ground to a halt. 'I can't push it any more! I'm stuck.'

'Ok.' I looked back to see Lili desperately leaning against their handlebars, squeezing hard on their brakes. 'Let me get mine to the top and I'll come back and help, can you hold it there?'

'Probably, but you'll have to hurry!'

Mustering my strength, I heaved my bike up the final incline. I stood it against the nearest tree and, after double-checking it wouldn't roll anywhere, I ran down to a red-faced Lili.

'Here, let me take it.' I grabbed the bike off them, taking its full weight against me. 'I've got this, would you go check mine's ok?'

Images of my bike freewheeling down past me filled my head as I watched Lili stagger up the hill. I heaved the bike up the last ten metres.

'Probably best we don't do that again on the way back.'

'Agreed,' Lili added.

At the top of the hill, we found ourselves on a wide street lined with tall townhouses and ivy-covered five-storey apartment buildings. Trams ran down its centre and roadworks blocked one side of the road creating a complicated one-way system we struggled to understand. After running a red light and possibly making an illegal U-turn over the tram tracks, we were outside Tommy's building. We knew that he lived in a flat, but this building only had a doorbell, as opposed to the intercom systems we were used to. Confused, I put it down to an oddity in German apartment buildings.

I rang the bell and a young man opened the door.

'Hallo, uh, Tommy?' I asked.

Day Twenty-One

The man looked us up and down and, visibly confused, answered, 'Nein . . .'

Shit.

'Um, number 52?' Lili asked, panic causing them to forget all German.

'Ahhhh, no, no,' he answered, gesturing over the road. ' Forty-seven here.' With a grin he shut the door.

I shrugged. 'At least we got the right street.'

We made our weary way across the road to another apartment building. This time, a set of buttons which indicated separate flats gave us slightly more hope that our host lived here. Ringing, a man answered on the intercom and buzzed us in.

Lili propped the door open with one foot. 'You want me to go?'

Normally we wouldn't leave the bikes unattended, but I didn't want to send Lili up to a stranger's flat alone, who knew what he'd be like?

We climbed the stairs and a tall man came into view. He was in his late thirties, had long hair and a short goatee. He wore a low-cut T-shirt, a knee-length cardigan and rolled up grey jeans. His feet were bare.

'Hi, er . . . Tommy?'

Lili, dressed in a sports bra and short cycle shorts, went in for a handshake.

Tommy looked at Lili's outstretched hand and shook his head. He launched in for a hug. I looked on in horror as, without time to refuse, Lili awkwardly embraced this stranger. Escaping, Lili looked back at me with concern as I was gathered into Tommy's arms.

'Lili and Abi, yes?' Tommy asked, stepping away and smiling at us. 'Welcome to Essen, please come upstairs.'

'Um . . . our bikes are outside. We need to get them in first,' I explained, still unsure what to make of this overly friendly man.

'Ah, let's put your stuff in my basement, then I will get you a cup of tea!' Tommy bounded downstairs.

Lili and I followed him, descending into yet another strange man's basement, frantically trying to telepathically communicate on the way. Tommy didn't seem dangerous, just odd and weirdly friendly. I decided to wait it out.

Downstairs, we locked our panniers away and chained our bikes to a lamp post outside. Heading up, we found ourselves in a pleasant two-bedroom apartment. Cups of tea made their way into our hands and we sat and chatted with Tommy about his ex-wife, his children, veganism and the round-the-world cycle tour he had completed several years ago.

'Ah,' Tommy looked at his watch, 'I must pick up my children now. We are going to a lake close by. It is famous! You must come with us!'

I looked at Lili and we both nodded. Why not?

We held on for dear life as Tommy swerved in and out of traffic, loudly chatting with us in English while his children looked at us with curiosity.

Arriving safely, we walked along a footpath to a garden bar. We sat on a long row of seats, looking out onto the glittering lake where boats lazily floated, sails dancing in the wind. The garden was a popular spot. There were beds hung from chains to create oversized swinging hammocks, and beanbags sat slumped around. Young professionals lounged about, their craft beers in hand. Tommy's youngest was curious but wary of us. Bravely he decided to make friends and handed us a storybook, only to realise we didn't understand German. Our attempts to read aloud sent him into fits of giggles and he soon felt comfortable chatting away in German while we nodded our heads in agreement. The eldest was not happy about sharing her precious dad-time with two foreign strangers. As soon as she had stepped into the car, she had decided not to speak to us. She sat slowly swaying on the swing-set, giving us her best death stare.

From the moment we had arrived I had been growing hungrier and hungrier. I was used to getting to a campsite and eating almost immediately, and the change of routine meant I was ravenous. We looked at the few coins in our purse and the expensive prices at the hipster bar and eventually settled on a cone of paprika-covered chips and a strange rosehip drink, enough to keep us going. Carbohydrate, sugar and salt had never tasted so good.

Tommy had offered us two options to stay: either his living room on the sofa bed or camping in his garden (which was more like a UK allotment). We opted for the garden. As soon as we were alone, our conversation turned to our host.

'I wasn't sure I wanted to stay. He seemed so intense.'

'I know! But he has kids, so how bad can he be?'

'He didn't mention that he was divorced from his wife in the profile.'

'I think he's fine, just lonely.'

'I guess so . . . still, there's something odd about the way he looks when he's chatting to you.'

'Hmm.' Lili thought for a moment. Their eyes widened. 'I know what it is! He doesn't blink!'

Lili's impression of Tommy sent us into fits of giggles. In the garden, we decided to split the tasks so Lili went out to get food, while I prepared the campsite. I laid out the tent and slowly threaded the poles through, using the pegs to hold it down and create tension. I inflated my mat and laid out the sleeping bags in the inner tent, as well as the clothes bags we used as pillows and our torches. I retrieved our camping stove from one of the bags and set it on the table next to the small summer house in the garden. Finally, I set about filling buckets of water from the neighbour's garden so we could flush the basic toilet during the night. I stood back to admire my work. I felt confident and I was pleased at how quickly I had mastered camping.

Falling asleep later that night, with stomachs finally full of vegan sausages and sauerkraut, we heard somebody open the garden gate.

Instantly alert, I tried to prepare myself to fight off the intruder. I waited for another noise.

'Abi, Lili?' Tommy's voice drifted through the tent. 'I just thought I would check you're ok. I have picked up two boys from Ukraine who are couchsurfing. They are staying in the flat tonight.'

'Uh, ok, sounds good!' I replied, confused, relieved, but not hugely surprised by the announcement.

A tentative hello came from one of the boys.

'Ok, goodnight, we're leaving now,' Tommy added. The gate lifted again, and they were gone.

'God, I'm glad we stayed in the garden now!' Lili laughed.

'Yeah, those boys don't know what they're letting themselves in for!'

Lili

Day Twenty-Two, Essen

The day before, Tommy had invited us to join him for breakfast. We came through the front door to find him stirring a large pot of porridge in the galley kitchen. The two boys were packing up the last of their things from the sofa, and the table was set for the five of us.

'Who's going to help?' Tommy asked, sticking his head out the kitchen door.

I volunteered as tribute.

Tommy and I carried over the huge saucepan of porridge, and then every variety of topping: fruits, nuts, chia, agave, till the table was laden. I sat down, and Tommy went to the digital camera he had set up on the bookcase opposite the table.

'I'll take a photo.'

Setting the autotimer, he hurried back to his seat, and the result was a family portrait with porridge. He played mum with second helpings.

We talked about travelling and our plans. The Ukrainian lads were at university but had a holiday and had decided to hitch-hike for a while. They described the trip so far. As they talked enthusiastically of nights under motorway bridges or in underpasses, Tommy nodding along, I noticed how little consideration of personal safety was a factor. Not all of that could be attributed to our experiences as 'women', or as queer people. Cultural and class differences were also important. But I think their physical self-assurance played into it hugely. Watching them chat across the table, these two boys seemed confident and certain in themselves in a way we weren't. I didn't know how to articulate our fears without seeming like I was worrying about nothing.

'You have to go to Zollverein, the coke monument,' Tommy extolled. 'It has the biggest escalator in Europe. Here, I will draw you a map.' He started sketching on a piece of paper. 'I'll walk you down to the tram. You should go too.' He gestured at the Ukrainian boys.

They nodded, not wanting to offend their host.

'But first I will show you Bredeney!'

Tommy led the way out of the apartment and through to a small square. He climbed the first steps of a broad, stone flight of stairs, leading up to the imposing entrance of the town hall. From there, he turned to regard the buildings that bordered the square.

'The Krupp family built all this for their workers – they led the way in workers' rights.'

The four of us dutifully nodded. At the tram stop the boys attempted to get out of the enforced trip by not having tickets. Tommy paid for them and sent us all off. On the tram, we told the boys that they didn't have to stay on, and we wouldn't tell, but they seemed committed to the journey now and we chatted more freely out of the strange atmosphere of Tommy's apartment. The tram wove through the streets, heading north through Essen and out the other side. We disembarked at the stop scrawled on our handwritten map.

First built in the 1800s, and expanded since, the sprawling industrial site of Zollverein (formerly a coal mine and later a coking plant) was amongst the largest in Europe, and now houses the Ruhr Museum. We crossed from the tram stop and approached the towering structure of Shaft 12 – marked with 'Zollverein' in large white Gothic lettering. Opened in 1932 the shaft has earned the reputation of 'the most beautiful coal mine in the world'. The building itself was made up of several blocks of minimalist red-brick, built in the Bauhaus style, with narrow strips of windows along its length. It was a hulking monument to fossil fuels.

Towering above the tallest central block was a huge rust red structure. Four large wheels, their spokes strangely spindle-like amongst the large iron struts, were supported by four legs that splayed out in a truncated pyramid over the building. These formed a pulley – the head frame for Shaft 12, which like the tip of an iceberg, signalled the deep mine-shaft beneath it. The escalator up didn't disappoint, taking us three quarters of the height of the head frame and into the Ruhr Museum. The four of us were unwilling to pay the entrance fee. So instead we walked around the interior of the first floor, stripped down to bare brick and iron tresses. The boys headed off quickly, we said our goodbyes and continued to walk around, staring out the window at the sprawling site behind the museum, the geometric red-brick shapes, the hollow earth beneath them.

Returning to the city centre, we searched a bookshop for the maps we'd seen other cycle tourers carrying. Breaking up the whole Rhein Radweg into stages, and resembling a flip book, this map also identified campsites on the route (saving our legs the ascent from the Rhein in search of somewhere to sleep). Successful, we looked round for somewhere to sit for the afternoon.

We found a Starbucks. For the cost of a cup of tea, we plugged all of our devices in to charge, logged onto the Wi-Fi and found a quiet anonymous corner, with a toilet easily accessible, to sit and rest from the bombardment of heat, noise and people on the streets outside. We were meant to be going out for dinner with friends tonight, but I felt totally worn out. My words were garbled, and every sense felt amplified.

Going to Starbucks while you are 'travelling' is read as a clear signal that you're reluctant to really experience a place, that you're willing to fuel the increasingly globalised tourist trade. The reality is not that simple. In a chain coffee store, I'm supporting a global capitalism that commodifies and homogenises, that destroys communities: at home, in Germany, wherever. At the same time, we were living our lives in public, and with public spaces increasingly privatised we were having to make choices that balanced our immediate needs, as travellers, as disabled people, with our knowledge and values.

It is vital to look critically at the challenges globalisation brings, and at the environmental and social impact of 'travelling' and tourism, especially as a White British traveller. It is equally important to disentangle how judgements about how to 'travel' are often underpinned by ableism, classism and racism. Teasing out what it is to 'travel', and whether there is a way to do it that doesn't reinforce existing inequalities, or make the world a worse place, is complicated. Cycle touring didn't exempt us from these questions.

Brigit and Ben were friends of friends who had moved back to Essen, where Brigit grew up, after finishing university. We got in touch with them to see if they wanted to take us somewhere vegan. Brigit drove us all to a vegan pub where we ate currywurst, chips and mayo. Chatting to them was like talking with old friends.

'Sure, workers' rights.' We'd told Brigit about our tour of Bredeney. 'But they also used huge amounts of slave labour in the Second World War. The lake you went to is called Baldeneysee.'

'Sea?'

' "See" means lake.'

'Ah.'

'And the manor house by the lake is Villa Hügel,' they continued. 'It belongs to the Krupp family who owned the Steel Works before and during the Second World War.' They took a mouthful of currywurst.

'The Krupp family received money from the NSDAP, the Nazi party, to swing the vote in Hitler's favour in the Ruhr area, which had traditionally been socialist, as Essen used to be predominantly working class. Essentially, the Krupps were war profiteers.'

'Jeez, Tommy didn't mention that.'

'Yeah. It's not just history. The company still exists today. It's actually expanding in the city centre again.'

Brigit drove us all back slowly through dark streets. We were sad to part ways and lingered in the car as long as possible. Before we met, Brigit had asked if we'd needed anything. We'd both finished the books we were reading, and so asked if they had any they were willing to part ways with. We spent the last few minutes going through the huge stack of books on the back seat while Brigit and Ben offered advice, synopsis and recommendations. They both got out of the car to hug goodbye and we took a terrible selfie of the four of us, where the flash made us look like happy and exhausted ghosts.

Lili

Day Twenty-Three, Essen

Tommy was sitting opposite us, unblinking.

'How did you feel about your parents' divorce?' he asked intently.

I took a breath, unsure whether this was a rhetorical question.

Tommy went on. 'My ex-wife, she just wants all this,' he gestured to a photo collage hung on the wall, 'to be in the past.' He looked up at the clock. 'Oh, I'd better go.'

I tried not to let my relief show.

'If you leave, just put your key through the letterbox,' he added. 'You are welcome to stay here all day if you like.'

At the sound of the front door closing, I stood up to examine the photos hung in a simple glass frame. I regarded the face of the woman cycling beside Tommy. It seemed the rift with his touring partner came when they had different ideas of what came next. For her it had been you adventure, travel, cycle tour, and then move onto the next stage of your life, leaving it behind as a desire maybe to be picked up again when you retire. I didn't want our lives to be divided into before and after. At the same time, after years in and out of psychiatric hospitals, I both wanted stability, normality, and I felt it was demanded of me. I felt like I had a debt to pay back. The NHS had invested time and money in me to 'recover', and what clearer marker of recovery was there than stable employment?

It wasn't something Abi and I had ever talked about explicitly but sitting facing Tommy, as he talked about the challenges his relationship had faced when they'd got back from their tour I was starting to ask – was having a 'normal' life, and cycle touring two separate things? And would we lose one if we had the other?

We hadn't been able to decide whether we were going to leave for Düsseldorf that day. I'd burst into spontaneous tears twice already that morning and I didn't know why. Neither of us felt like we had really rested yet in Essen, and part of this was about Tommy.

'I think maybe we're too hard on Tommy,' Abi mused as we sat side by side, debating staying or going.

'Yeah, maybe?'

'I mean he *is* creepy but it's not threatening, it's just . . . I think maybe he's just trying to validate some of his life choices that contrast so strongly with his ex-wife's.'

'Yeah, but it's hard when you have an odd feeling about someone, especially a man, having to quantify that, or like, interrogate it.'

'Yeah, is he weird and harmless *or* weird and a murderer?'

'You can't figure out why you feel it's one and not the other, and you're worried you're making a terrible call which you will come to regret.'

My period started in Tommy's bathroom, which was probably why I was crying so much that morning. It was settled, we'd delay and leave tomorrow. While Tommy was out, we both showered, and watched the next episode of *Bake Off*. Then, before he returned, we headed back to the garden to prepare for the ride to Düsseldorf.

Gears for Queers

While Abi cooked dinner, I cycled over to Tommy's one last time to return the keys. He opened the door with a child on his hip. Tommy was wearing the tiniest and tightest pair of pants I've ever seen. He insisted on hugging me goodbye, a mirror of our first meeting except this time he was the one who was half-naked.

Lili

Day Twenty-Four, Essen to Lörick (Düsseldorf)

To reach Essen we had followed the Wasser Route away from the Rhein. Poring over maps in Tommy's flat, we identified a better route back – by following the Ruhr to Duisburg, we could meet the Rhein at the intersection of the two rivers. The route was straightforward from Tommy's garden, taking us winding through the streets of Essen to the well-established Ruhr cycle way. We joined the smooth tarmac path alongside the quiet river. Here, the Ruhr was smaller and more bucolic than the Rhein. The water was lined with trees, the tips of low-hanging boughs brushing the water. The bank was verdant. We were free of the city, free of Tommy, and I basked in the sunshine. Still, cycling on a period proved difficult. The Ruhr cycle route seemed characterised by its use of unnecessary bridges criss-crossing the river. I could have done without these steep ups and downs while bleeding profusely from my uterus.

Before we left, Abi had taken me through the steps of using a menstrual cup – an environmentally friendly period product that, provided I had access to fresh water, promised to make life easier on the road as I would not need to source or dispose of tampons or pads. Riding a bike with one in took some getting used to. It wasn't in itself unpleasant, but since it was only my second time using one, I was too afraid of it somehow getting sucked up inside me to cut off the small length of plastic that extended from the base and could be used to hoik it out. This was now making an uncomfortable amount of contact with my saddle. I glanced jealously at Abi's saddle, with a hole in its middle, and carried on pedalling. Halfway to the Rhein, I had to stop. It had been several hours, and it was the second day of my period, so I was going to need to find a toilet.

Toilets fundamentally affect the accessibility of public and outdoor spaces. Their absence impacts some groups, including disabled people, older people, and folks who menstruate or who have given birth, more than others. In Amsterdam, we struggled to find a free public toilet. While most folk with penises could use the free urinals, we were left paying a euro a time for the pleasure of sitting down to pee. In our time on the road, it seemed unremarkable for most cyclists with a penis to whip it out to pee on the side of the road. So far, we had to wait for tree cover or dense bushes to wee out of sight.

There was no tree cover. We passed a block of public toilets, all urinals. Things were becoming increasingly urgent. At some unattended roadworks was a Portaloo with the 'male' symbol on the front. Opening it, expecting a urinal, I discovered a perfectly serviceable toilet, although the floor was plastered with wet toilet paper. I crouched over the loo to remove my Mooncup. Fumbling, I slipped.

'Fuck-shit-wank-bollocks.'

Menstrual blood flew all over the tiny cubicle. I rinsed the cup out in the sink and reinserted it. Using toilet paper, I tried to remove the worst of the spill, but it was a hopeless battle without wet cloth. Stepping out, it looked like an inexpertly covered-up murder scene.

Periods are a messy business.

*

Cycling without a GPS, mobile data – or, in this instance, a map – required an acceptance of wrong turns and dead ends. One of the books we'd picked up in Amsterdam was *Zen and the Art of Motorcycle Maintenance* and we had adopted the notion of gumption to describe our energy to problem-solve. Pirsig fails to identify the main drain on gumption: being on your period. Reaching the end of a long path along a canal, to find it opened to a viewpoint and a dead end, I burst into tears.

'I can't afford wrong turns today, I just can't,' I sobbed.

Abi looked at me and both of us knew what a ridiculous statement this was. If I didn't want to take a wrong turn, I should have spent money on a map of the Ruhr route.

Meeting the Rhein in Duisburg I felt relieved; I triumphantly pulled the map we had bought in Essen out of my bag. We turned off away from the Ruhr and cycled down a main street, past the grand town hall and imposing tower of St Salvator church, its spires blackened with soot.

The city's urban landscape had familiar echoes. When I was 18, I lived in Coventry for six months. I had just dropped out of university and couldn't hold down a job. I ran obsessively through its streets lined with post-war buildings, exploring the sense of interruption, a break in continuity. Like a new branch grafted onto an old tree, something had fundamentally disrupted the organic growth of the city.

Duisburg, like Coventry, was heavily bombed in the Second World War, and now had the disjointed feeling of a city totally rebuilt. It remained heavily industrial, but it was also growing and changing. We cycled through an area of old workers' housing in Hochfeld, into the Rheinpark, a sparse concrete desert reclaimed with meadowland and trees as part of a broader regeneration planned for the length of the city. There were no other bikes on this segment of cycling infrastructure, and it was impossible to know the context that it emerged from. Did a cycle path belong here, and who did it serve? For a long time, I felt unequivocally positive about new cycle paths, because I was only looking at them in the narrow frame of how they served me. I had only recently begun to consider how cycle paths are often a symbol of, and a tool of, gentrification. They sometimes only serve communities who cycle for leisure or sport, rather than those who choose or have no choice to use cycling as transport. They sometimes aren't built for the communities they pass through.

We followed the path around the steelworks, the huge blast furnaces blocking our view of water, and re-joined the river on the other side. The tall chimneys slowly disappeared behind us. Outside of Duisburg, we began to see day trippers riding or walking on the path, enjoying the sunny weather. Turning towards the river, I started to freewheel down to a small quay.

'Hold up,' I said, braking. I wasn't sure this was the right way; I couldn't see a path that turned off before the river's edge. I couldn't face another wrong turn, and I didn't fancy going all the way down only to come back up again.

Abi had already committed to the downhill. I felt a hard thud at my rear, sending my bike nearly shooting out from under me. I steadied it to see Abi grappling her own. She looked up at me, helmet askew.

We turned at the sound of heavy laughter, and realised we had an audience of three elderly German men sitting on a bench directly facing our slapstick comedy moment. With an embarrassed nod of the head we were off again down the hill, where a sign emerged pointing us right, along the shore of the river. I was grateful not to have to cycle back past them.

I wheeled my bike onto the small ferry which crossed the river to Meerbusch. The flat rectangular deck was crowded with

Day Twenty-Four

foot passengers and cars. We landed at the entrance to the campsite we'd planned to stay at and wheeled up to reception.

'I'm sorry but we have no pitches.'

This break from script threw me.

'It is the biggest campervan exhibition in Europe here this weekend,' the attendant explained, as if this was something I should have known.

I stepped out of the little hut. I felt totally devastated, like something had cracked and every ounce of motivation had flowed out. I choked out an explanation to Abi.

'So, we keep going,' she said.

We had no choice: I got on my bike.

I felt inconsolable. The only thing I could do was keep cycling. I narrowed my vision, and instead of thinking about my anxiety over where we would sleep that night, I focused on my bike. I allowed the familiar noises to soothe, the motion of the pedals, the spinning of the wheels. As I calmed down, my vision began to widen again, and I started to look around me. There – a spot perfect for wild camping. There – a sign for a town. The next campsite marked on the map was a further 15km away in Lörick on the outskirts of Düsseldorf, and by the time we arrived there I was confident that we would be able to camp somewhere back along the route if needed.

We were greeted by an older woman, who smiled and said there was plenty of room. She set us up in a pitch beside two small caravans with the distinctive smell of pot thick in the air.

Abi

Day Twenty-Five, Lörick (Düsseldorf)

'Painkillers, painkillers . . .' I muttered to myself, fumbling around in the dark tent. Lili snored lightly. I switched the headlight on and shone a beam right into their eyes.

'Sorry, sorry!'

They stayed fast asleep.

Locating the painkillers, I swallowed a few and tried to doze. Having suffered with migraines since I was two years old, it was a familiar routine. I was surprised I hadn't gotten one sooner; heat and exercise are both triggers for the pain. In the dark, close confines of the tent I settled in for a fitful few hours.

Lili woke up as the sun rose and cooked porridge. I stayed in the tent, my migraine ensuring that today was a rest day. The remains of the day came in the fragments between sleep; Lili reading in the sun as I took more painkillers; Lili writing in their journal as I threw my head out of the tent to get some air.

'What do you fancy for dinner tonight?' Lili quietly asked at 4pm, poking their head through the door.

'I don't know, bread, I think, maybe some hummus?'

'I'll get some crisps too, yeah?'

Day Twenty-Five

'Thanks, baby.'

Lying back down I stared at the orange tent ceiling. Even after 25 years I still found it hard being limited by pain which was impossible to control. Being forced to have a rest day felt different from choosing to have one. I turned onto my side in an attempt to block out the light. This was not an optimum migraine environment. Where usually I would seek darkness and coolness, I was stuck in heat and light. I rubbed my eye and tried to relax; my natural urge to scream and flail would only make the pain worse.

Lili arrived back with bread and crisps for dinner.

'It's a Sunday,' they said, throwing down a small bag of food.

'And?'

'All of the shops are closed so I had to go to a garage. Apparently shops in Germany still close completely on Sundays.'

'That seems weirdly religious. Oh well.' I fumbled through the food bag. 'This will be fine, thanks. We better keep it in mind for the future though.'

The bread and salty crisps eased my migraine, and I started to feel a bit more human. We enjoyed the last hour of the day in the failing sunlight.

As we settled into sleep, Lili turned to me.

'Abi?'

'Yeah, babe?'

'I'm feeling pretty rough.'

'Oh?'

'I think I'm getting sick.'

Abi

Day Twenty-Six, Lörick (Düsseldorf)

Lili was very ill.

'I couldn't sleep all night,' they muttered, crawling out from the hot tent onto the sticky tarp outside. 'I think I have a cold or the flu or something.'

I wrapped them up in my sleeping bag and set them up with a book and some water. We knew we were going to get sick at some point, but Lili couldn't help but bemoan another day off so early in the tour.

As I sat reading, Lili dozing beside me, a middle-aged woman wandered over from the caravan next door.

'Hallo?' I said. Lili opened their eyes.

She gestured to Lili and then to the cup in her hand. Lili took it, trying to decipher what tea it was from the label on the teabag. The woman watched expectantly.

'Es ist gut für Erkältungen.'

Grabbing the iPod, I attempted to translate. 'I think she's saying it's good for colds?'

'Danke, danke,' Lili mumbled between sips.

The woman smiled and wandered back to her caravan. Under a small porch she lit a joint and disappeared into her home.

'What is it?' I asked Lili.

'I'm not sure. Try some?'

I took a sip.

'It reminds me of that rose hip drink we had at the lake.'

'You're right. It's nice though, a bit bitter.'

Lili sipped some more. A wave of panic crossed their face.

'You don't think it's poisoned, do you?'

I laughed. 'If she's put anything extra in, I doubt it's gonna poison you. Might make you relax a bit though.'

Lili raised one eyebrow. They finished the rose hip tea, then lay down to sleep again.

That afternoon we walked slowly down the road towards town. Lili had convinced me that a walk might do them good, and I was grateful for the company on the way to the supermarket. We found a Lidl and stocked up on the basics we usually carried – spaghetti, tomato puree, cheap vegetables, crisps and chocolate soy milk. Happy now that we wouldn't go hungry, we headed back. Lili was quickly losing strength and arriving at our tent they collapsed back on the tarp.

I set up the stove and started cooking some spaghetti. We'd chosen the pasta arbitrarily based on the cute chicken image on the packaging. Staring at it as it boiled, I had a moment of dreadful intuition.

'No, it wouldn't . . .' I turned the packaging over. In bold, the word 'Ei' stood out like a sore thumb. 'Fuck.'

Lili stirred. 'What's the matter, babe?'

'This pasta has egg in! Dry pasta with egg!'

I was pissed off. In the UK we rarely checked dry pasta packaging because it was always vegan. We'd assumed it would be the same everywhere.

Lili and I stared at the pot. The pasta was almost cooked, and we were both starving. The shop was a 30-minute walk away.

'I hate wasting food.'

'I just don't fancy it any more though.'

The pasta stared at us.

'We could eat it and throw the rest away.'

'I really don't think I can go back to the shops or wait for us to cook again,' Lili added, their face pale white.

It was settled. We ate the pasta and threw the rest of the packet away. It felt wrong to chuck perfectly good food in the bin, but there was no way Lili and I could eat it again. We barely made it through that meal.

Lili was struggling to sleep. Being outside in the air all day seemed to have aggravated their cold. They lay in the tent, coughing. I tried to comfort them, feeding them Strepsils and keeping them topped up with painkillers and water. By the early hours of the morning, it became obvious that something more needed to be done.

'Lili, maybe we should book a hotel?'

'No.' The expected reply. 'For one, we can't afford it.'

'We can. We may have to cut down a bit. We have the money that Claire gave us. But right now, I think you need a rest, and you're not resting in this tent.'

This seemed the perfect time to use the money Lili's boss had gifted us specifically for this purpose. Lili didn't see it that way.

'I know it's hard,' I started.

'It feels like giving in.'

'Look, there are no rules to doing this properly. Give yourself a break.'

Lili pursed their lips but wasn't arguing back.

'Ok, I'm going to book a hotel.'

Looking online I booked the cheapest hotel within a 2-mile radius. It was still painfully expensive, 100 euros a night, but it wouldn't involve riding very long. I booked two nights.

Day Twenty-Six

Knowing we were staying in a bed tomorrow night seemed to calm Lili a bit. We popped some David Attenborough on the computer, and they cuddled into my arms as we dozed off.

Lili

Day Twenty-Seven, Düsseldorf

The tent was getting smaller and smaller. Every sensation was intolerable. I drifted in and out of sleep without anchor. Only the voice of David Attenborough and Abi's soothing reassurance punctuated the haze and distracted me from the intense all-body discomfort. My sleeping bag was damp and cold with sweat. At 11am I crawled out of the tent and watched Abi pack up. I bent double over the bike, snot dripping straight from my nose onto my handlebars. I followed her onto the main road into Düsseldorf, subsumed in the self-pity only a bout of flu can afford.

There was nowhere to put our bikes outside the hotel which, located in the financial district, catered for businesses. We locked them either side of a huge white column at the entrance and decanted our panniers into the lift, much to the bemusement of the receptionist. The room was cavernous. Everything in it was shiny. I pulled my boots and socks off. The texture of the carpet felt strange under my bare feet. After four weeks living in the tent and three weeks on the road, being in an environment that was completely artificial, so completely insulated from the outside natural world, felt strange. We'd been living our life in public for the last month, with our only moments completely to ourselves within the confines of the inner tent. I stripped down to my pants. Abi looked me up and down, and then glanced at the crisp white bedlinen behind me.

'Let's shower before bed, eh?'

Finally clean, I crawled into bed. Part of me expected someone to walk in at any point. My sense of public and private space had completely shifted. It seemed strange that this huge expanse of room was just for us.

'Abi,' I called out to the bathroom, but was met with only the sound of the shower. I sighed. What was the point of feeling so ill if I couldn't elicit pity from those around me?

I felt around for the phone.

'Mum,' I croaked in my most pathetic voice down the line. 'I'm sick.'

'Oh, sweetie,' she cooed, 'it could be so much worse.'

Lili

Day Twenty-Eight, Düsseldorf

I couldn't bear the idea of visiting Düsseldorf and not seeing any of it.

'I'm feeling so much better,' I whined at Abi, who looked at me with one eyebrow raised.

'I'll take it really slow and come straight back if I feel ill,' I lied.

We cycled down from the hotel to the centre of Düsseldorf and locked our bikes on the broad promenade by the Rhein. Beneath the oddly contorted spire of the Sankt Lambertus Basilika, we squeezed through the narrow quiet streets of the Altstadt; the bars and pubs that occupied nearly every building wouldn't be open for several hours.

'Shall we go in?' Abi pointed through the archway of a church.

I shook my head.

'Are you feeling ok?' Abi asked.

'Yeah, yeah, fine. I just want to walk around the city a bit more.'

At the Kunsthalle I stood and stared up at a sandstone sculpture; the four giant women were the gable figures of the original building and stood in sharp contrast to the blank concrete of the newer brutalist construction. They were meant to represent the fine arts. The towering figures wobbled. I admitted defeat.

'Home?' I croaked.

Back in our room I ran the hot tap and dropped a cherry blossom bath bomb into the tub. Abi's old workplace, Lush, was a ubiquitous presence in every city we'd visited. I climbed in. Soon, I had to hoik my feet over the edge. The combination of the heat and a fever was making me feel faint, but I wasn't willing to sacrifice this moment of bliss, suspended in clean hot water. I sat and read until the water got cold, and then Abi and I changed places and she ran her own bath while I sat in bed sneakily eating biscuits and surreptitiously wiping crumbs off the clean sheets.

'Do you need to stay an extra night?' Abi asked as she lay beside me in bed.

I weighed it up. I wanted to stay: the bed, the food, the bath, the privacy, but I was feeling better. I missed our tent and the simplicity of our life on the road. We had budgeted to allow ourselves a fixed number of nights in a hotel or hostel – if we were sick, or needed a break, or were scared. I wasn't willing to use up more money for the luxury of another night. In this hotel, I felt a widening gulf between us and the world outside – being able to just dip in and out of it felt like I was experiencing the city out of context. It had thrown into sharp relief what it felt like to travel by bike, and why we had chosen to camp on top of that. From our hotel room, I felt like I was looking out of a small plane window as the landscape passed us by.

'I think we should head off tomorrow.'

Lili

Day Twenty-Nine, Düsseldorf to Merkenich

A dull ache spread down my legs as soon as I started pedalling. Were the bags always this heavy? We retraced the trip we'd taken from the Rhein route several days earlier, clattering off the high kerb and navigating the busy roads of Düsseldorf in the early morning rush hour. I was struck by how cycle paths permeated the city, even if occasionally cars or lorries making early morning deliveries would park in them – hazard lights flashing. Once we reached the river, we headed south towards Köln (Cologne when anglicised). My legs had started to ease up and it felt good to be on the move again, and back outside. We sat and ate our lunch on a stone wall, bathed in sunlight. I felt lucky, if still a little fragile.

From Düsseldorf the route passed through Dormagen, where an old windmill, constructed with a mishmash of small red, black and white stones, still stood as part of the city walls. The black skeleton of its sails was still. On the other side of the medieval town, we arrived at the Rheinaue Worringen-Langel, a nature reserve on the banks of the Rhein.

'Abi, look!'

I pointed to a triangular sign, edged in green, with a silhouette of an eagle.

'Beware! Eagles!'

Abi laughed. The path turned into the nature reserve. Since there were no cars, I took my helmet off to enjoy the breeze, hanging it from my handlebars.

'It's typical of Germany really,' I joked as we pedalled, 'to have an eagle as the symbol for nature reserve. So bloody dramatic.'

I turned a corner and, out of the bushes directly in front of me, a huge bird of prey swept out across the path, its feathers turning from black to brown to gold as it flew away from the shadow of the trees and into the sunlight. A flash of beak and talon.

'Fuuuucck!' I swerved and screeched to a halt. 'Did you see that?'

Abi caught up with me. 'Oh my God, are you ok?'

'That was the biggest bird I have ever seen.'

I fastened my helmet back on my head.

'Beware, eagles.'

Directly on the route, sandwiched between the road and the river, was a simple campsite, with a restaurant closed for the season, and a paper sign directing us to an adjacent house. We followed the arrow up steep stone steps to the front door. An elderly German man answered.

'Hallo?'

'Hallo, hast du ein platz für ein Zelt und zwei Personen für eine Nacht, danke?'

I could make out from his reply that it would be 15 euros with an additional amount for the toilets, a deposit that would be returned. My German had improved enough to hold a basic conversation, but only if it was about arranging a camping pitch. Still, I was lacking in some basic nouns.

'Ich habe keine . . .' I held up the cash I had: a five-euro note. 'Ich habe . . .' and I held up a bank card.

'Was?'

'Ich habe keine . . .' I held up the cash, 'Ich habe . . .' and I held up the bank card again. He looked blankly at me, then barked something down the hallway. An older woman appeared.

'Hallo?' she asked me.

'Wo ist die . . . ATM?' I mimed putting a card in a machine, entering a PIN . . .

'Der Geldautomat?'

'Ja ja! Der Geldautomat,' I replied, grateful that she had triggered my memory of the German word for cash machine and interrupted my pantomime.

It was straight down the road in the nearest village. Unloading the panniers from my bike, I went to check I had my bank card in my bumbag.

'It's not here.'

'What?' Abi looked up.

'My bank card, it's not here.'

'What do you mean?'

'I had it, I had it literally just now when I was talking to the woman. Maybe I dropped it.'

I scanned the stone steps. I knocked on the door again and, to the bemusement of the woman, swept the entrance. Nothing. I came back to Abi.

'They must have taken it. They've taken it.'

'Lili, what on earth would an elderly German couple do with your debit card?'

'I don't know, but they're evil, I know it.'

I was in a full-on spiral of panic and paranoia. I have always hated losing things. When my mental health deteriorated as a teenager, I began to experience extended periods of disorientation and dislocation. I would do things I couldn't remember. My world would descend into chaos. It had a profound impact. At home Abi was used to something as simple as not knowing exactly where I put my keys leaving me inconsolable, sobbing profusely until she inevitably found them, usually in my bag or in my pocket.

'Ok, so when did you last have it?' Abi asked, playing the game my mum used to play with me.

'When I was explaining to the woman that I didn't have cash.'

'Are you sure? Could that have been my card?'

'I don't know, I thought I saw my name on it.'

'When did you have it before then?'

'I guess when we paid in Lidl on our way here . . .'

A few visual memories came back to me; paying at the checkout, putting my card down to pack our bags, walking away.

'Oh.'

'Ok, so use my card to get cash, and we'll call the bank and cancel your card, ok?'

The ride to and from Rheinkassel took ten minutes. After paying and pitching, Abi retreated to the inner tent.

'I feel totally exhausted.' She sniffed.

Abi

Day Thirty, Merkenich to Rodenkirchen

Turning over in the night, I felt my hip dig into the hard floor.
  'Shit.'
  My airbed had deflated. I checked the time – 3am. Groaning, I began to re-inflate it, hoping it would last till morning.
  'What are you doing?' Lili shuddered awake.
  'My airbed is flat.'
  'You want to try and mend it?'
  'No, I'll just keep pumping it up when I need to. We're gonna have to buy a new one soon.'
  'Ok. Tomorrow.' They turned over and fell straight back asleep.

The North Rhein-Westphalia region is the most populated region of Germany and heavily industrial: it makes up a quarter of the total economy. The evidence of this was obvious along this part of the river. Large power plants and cargo ships spilled dark smoke into the skies as we pedalled towards Köln. It wasn't the most inspiring landscape. Lili and I tried to kill time by chasing ships along the river, inevitably losing as our path turned off on a detour through another tiny village.

Day Thirty

We entered the industrial area on the edge of Köln and began carefully navigating the larger vehicles and potholed roads. These areas seemed to sit on the outskirts of all big cities in the region and were my least favourite to ride through. Even on cycle paths, the fast traffic made me nervous. A passing lorry was loud and unbalancing. I could feel the sheer bulk of each one, even when they passed on the other side of the road. I swore loudly at lorries which came too quickly or too closely, an attempt to drown out my fear with righteous anger.

To drive a lorry through Cambridge or London, you legally must complete a cycling proficiency course. This gives drivers an understanding of the vulnerability felt by cyclists on the road, as well as a view to how cyclists move, turn and think. When we completed a basic bike maintenance course in Cambridge, we spotted a group of lorry drivers wobbling off onto a busy road. It was reassuring knowing that they would experience cycling alongside vehicles like the ones they drove, that had so much power to damage. They might begin to understand that what they perceived to be safe in their cab wasn't actually safe for the cyclist; that a safe distance and speed wasn't the same as a comfortable and respectful distance and speed. I pedalled, focusing on each metre of road ahead, pushing hard on my handlebars to stop from veering from the edge of the pavement. I wished that all drivers had to attend these courses. I wondered how much safer the roads would be if they did.

Soon we found ourselves on the riverbank again, this time moving through the suburbs and then straight into the heart of the city centre. The promenade was thriving with tourists who crowded the bike path. My eye couldn't focus on the bombardment of sites. Spires, sculptures, fountains, ancient and ultra-modern houses and behind them all, glimpses of a magnificent cathedral.

'It's beaten us again!' shouted Lili, pointing at the river cruise boat we'd been racing since the beginning of the Rhein. 'Damn you, Celtic River Cruises!'

I laughed and shook my fist at our retiree transporting nemesis.

'Shall we have a look round now?' I asked, spotting a sign to the chocolate museum.

'How about we get to the campsite and then we can come back to explore,' Lili suggested, jumping onto their bike to weave expertly through the crowds.

The campsite we'd chosen was to the south of the city and sat opposite a large pastel pink mansion. Its defining feature: a life-size zebra on its balcony. We grabbed the best pitch we could, in the shade of a tall van and a larger tent.

'How are you feeling?' Lili asked.

I had been sniffling on and off for a few hours, trying to clear the sudden onset of a blocked nose. 'I'm fine, though I might not want to cycle back in.'

Lili nodded, we each grabbed a rucksack and headed out.

The tram platform was crowded with jostling, shouting teenagers. The eye of the storm was a boy with a bloodied nose. Intimidated, we let them pile in first and found a place to stand by the door. The tram snaked slowly into Köln. Lili closed their eyes and inhaled, battling their inevitable motion sickness. The stifling heat of the tram car no doubt adding to the nausea.

Steaming bowlfuls of pho, noodles, spring and summer rolls arrived at our table. We were sitting in the sun outside a vegan Vietnamese restaurant, hidden off the main square on an unremarkable residential street. The heat of the chilli cleared my sinuses. I relished the crisp refreshing crunch of fresh vegetables and mint leaves wrapped in rice paper. I dipped them greedily into the thick peanut sauce, scooping out more than my fair share and hoping Lili wouldn't notice. I'd been feeling really ill when we sat down but, belly full, I leaned back in my chair and looked over at Lili with a satisfied grin. Everything tasted better after weeks of campsite food and countless days of cycling. Neither of us moved. I surrendered to the feeling of contentment, the day's tasks forgotten.

'This feels like a date,' Lili remarked.

'Yeah, except we're both ill, smelly and covered in sweat.'

They laughed. 'Seems about standard for us.'

The waitress came to take our plates, and we reluctantly walked back into the city centre to look for camping mats. What we found was the camping store of our wildest fantasies.

Walking into Globetrotter in Köln is like walking into heaven (if you really like outdoor adventure stuff). Five floors of wall-to-wall camping equipment, walking maps and guides, a small swimming pool on the bottom floor for trying out kayaks before you buy, a large climbing wall for trying shoes and harnesses. I knew we weren't getting out of there quickly. We methodically explored each floor looking at maps and clothes. The expensive padded shorts called to me, but we had to stay on mission. Eventually we found the camping mats. We tried a few out on a variety of rough, bumpy surfaces and settled on the larger Thermarest. Grabbing two, I turned to Lili to see them frowning.

'Lili. Seriously.'

They pursed their lips.

'You need a mat. You're already complaining about your hip.'

'I know . . . I just think the foam mat I have is fine and . . . I just kind of want to get out of here now.'

I knew that protesting would only make Lili even more stubborn about their decision. I understood that the shop was overwhelming them and that this, coupled with a general anxiety about money, was stopping them from making the most sensible choice, but there was nothing I could do about it. Popping one back on the shelves, I headed to the till and then straight onto the busy street.

I've always had a fascination with old analogue photobooths, the kind that were all but replaced with the generic passport picture booths during the digital photography revolution. A new wave of enthusiasts in Berlin had remade and refurbished some of these original booths and had begun to get them back onto the streets of Europe. We had pictures from one in Brighton and another in Amsterdam, and I planned on searching out as many as possible. In a small shopping centre, downstairs and hidden away by the toilets, we found it. It was 3 euros for a strip of experimental pictures. We gleefully jumped in, changing poses after each flash and then waited for ten minutes listening to the sounds as the machine dipped the paper in various chemicals and popped it out. The result: four black-and-white snapshots of two bedraggled cycle tourers. We tucked it in the back of Lili's diary.

To finish our tour of Köln we headed towards the twin ornate spires of the cathedral which towered into the sky, dominating the city that lay around them. Churches in Britain didn't measure up to the sheer ornateness of this. The cathedral was free to enter, so we headed inside. Lili, a staunch atheist, lit a candle for their nana as part of the ritual they'd been following since she died ten years prior.

'She used to pray for me every night. I like to think of all the places she's been remembered in.' They shrugged.

Walking around cathedrals as somebody who never went to church as a child is an odd experience. I didn't feel any link to a God, and I didn't feel any comforting nostalgia for my childhood. There was a sense of wonder, but a wonder at the work which went into the building. There was also a sense of calm that derived from the silence of the cathedral. It made sense to me why people believed in God, especially in places like this; especially historically, when churches held grandeur which was inaccessible to many people. I was never going to find faith, but I enjoyed the stillness of the cold, ancient stone. The ceiling arched high into the building; oversized stained-glass saints stared down at us.

'Let's go,' I whispered. 'I'm feeling super rough.'

Back at the campsite, I finally accepted that I'd inherited Lili's cold. I crashed down inside the tent, desperately downing painkillers and Strepsils and coughing heavily. As I was falling asleep, strange German techno music began to drift nearer and nearer to the campsite.

'Lili, help. The noise,' I called out, disorientated.

Lili popped their head in the tent. 'Don't worry, it's just some sort of party boat.'

I crawled out. Looking at the mirrored waters of the Rhein, we watched as a large passenger boat floated by, blaring music and spilling coloured lights onto the surface of the river.

Lili

Day Thirty-One, Rodenkirchen

We'd been lying side by side in the tent for a while. Neither of us felt like moving. Eventually my morning coffee habit proved enough motivation. I shifted up from my sleeping bag, and a pain shot from my hip down the length of my leg.

'AOOOHHH.'

'You ok, babe?'

'Mmmmhmm . . .' I dug my fingers into my hip to release some of the pain.

'Why didn't you buy a mat in Globetrotter?'

'I don't know, I wasn't ready, this is fine,' I said, wincing as I shifted my weight from one hip to the other. Once out of the tent, the pain subsided the more I moved about. I didn't fancy lying down again in a hurry. I'd been nursing this hip pain for nearly a year until I'd gone to see a physiotherapist. A lovely Geordie woman, she'd caused me unimaginable pain releasing some of the tension, before informing me the issue was my piriformis, a flat band of muscle in my butt, at the top of the hip joint. She'd sent me off after a few sessions with some exercises, and some techniques to ease it if it kicked off again. These mostly involved rolling around like an upended turtle. I dreaded to think what she would say about my sleeping arrangements.

As I shook the pain off, Abi sat up and gently moaned.

'I'm sick.'

I dragged a shivering Abi into the shower and helped her wash before wrapping her back in her sleeping bag and zipping her in the inner tent. We needed more paracetamol, and it was a Sunday tomorrow. On top of this, we didn't have any food.

'Maybe I should cycle to Köln, I could go to Globetrotter too and get a mat . . .'

From the cocoon of sleeping bags, Abi gave me a wry look.

The ride into Köln was beautiful, and though my legs were tired, I enjoyed following the now familiar cycle path in the sunshine. It flowed alongside the river, taking me into the city through an arch made of the same dark stone as the cathedral. I locked my bike on the wide promenade and took a moment to use the Wi-Fi available in public spaces to message my mum. Then I started climbing the steps to the city centre. The ride in had taken longer than expected, and the city was crowded with people. I had totally misjudged how tired I was, and my ability to deal with the throngs of Saturday shoppers. Swinging into DM where we had bought tofu tortellini the day before, I stocked up on food and painkillers. Then I went to a supermarket for bread. I thought about walking to Globetrotter but couldn't face it. Hauling my pannier back out of the city centre, heavy with shopping, it was a relief to be back on my bike and away from the sea of people.

They thought I couldn't see the looks they gave me. I pedalled faster and faster along the river path. I could. I noticed the double take as shop assistants, or the women behind me in the queue, assessed the scars on my arms and legs. I spotted the second, and third, glance shoppers gave me in the street as they tried to figure out whether I was a boy or a girl. I'd unthinkingly cycled in shorts and a T-shirt, without bringing a long-sleeved top. I didn't have Abi to focus on and, overwhelmed by the density of people and general tiredness, feeling so self-conscious was wearing me down. Riding my bike, I found myself letting go of tension I didn't know I was holding. I wanted to ride so fast, no one would be able to see me, I'd just be a blur to them. I slammed my feet down on my pedals, faster and faster.

How much of this cycle tour was driven by not wanting to be perceived, not wanting to be judged, not wanting to be gendered? I felt so different living in the tent, away from people and cities, riding on quiet cycle paths with only Abi for company. How much of that was about not having to consider the ways my body was being read by people around me?

Lili

Day Thirty-Two, Rodenkirchen

I hung up the phone to my mum and lay back on the grass, still damp with dew.

Back home, she still texted me goodnight, every night, a hangover from times when she never knew if I was safe, or whether the late-night phone call would be from me, a hospital ward or a police station. I didn't think other cycle tourers called their mums. I felt hit by a sudden pang of guilt; that I still demanded support from others to achieve a selfish whim, something as navel-gazing as 'travelling'. When you are disabled, you often find that support is only offered to facilitate things other people have decided you should do. You often come up against the expectation, filtered through society, that you earn the right to travel, to leisure, to the 'rewards' of independence, of adulthood. Disability support is often structured along these lines. Leaving the UK for more than three months, I forfeited receiving the ESA that had allowed me to live, working a manageable 16 hours a week. It felt like a huge risk, but I had the safety net of support which made it possible.

There are many barriers to travelling as a disabled person. Aside from physical accessibility, welfare and support dictates what we should be working towards, or doing with our lives, energy, our daily spoons. Austerity policy made it harder to challenge this. People are fighting every day for just the support to stay alive, but we don't just want to live. Disabled people, as much as anyone else, want to thrive, explore, experiment, try new things, and fail.

In the late afternoon we ventured down to the river's shore, bringing our maps and a Sharpie with us. We began marking campsites at rough intervals, approximating the time it would take us to reach Basel, Switzerland, when we would reach the end of these maps and leave the Rhein behind. We were 17 days away.

Facing us on the other side of the river was a large white panel with the black numbers 681. The campsite was called Camping Berger, but the merchandise was all branded with 681, mirroring these numbers. We'd spotted the numbered boards along the route already, and they'd been counting down. We'd been at 800 in Gotterswickersham. We guessed this was some measure of the river and looked it up when we got back to the tent. Since 1 April 1939 the Rhein had been divided into kilometres – the Rheinkilometer – with a zero point in the middle of the old Constance Rhein Bridge (at the source) and the end point, Rheinkilometer 1038.20 west of the Hoek van Holland. We had joined the Rhein south of Rotterdam at about 1000 and we'd be leaving it behind at about 50. I sat and stared at it for a while, considering this literal measure of our progress on two wheels along a single river.

Lili

Day Thirty-Three, Rodenkirchen to Mehlem

I sensed a shift in Abi's movement and breathing that meant she was awake. I turned towards her. She was lying with her eyes open, looking up at the ceiling of the inner tent.

'How you feeling?' I ventured.

'Better, I think. Good enough to get going.'

While she packed up, I gave our bikes a once-over – checking the bolts on the pannier racks, the brakes and the tyres. I wasn't an expert; all I could do was to check things looked the same as they looked every other day. Nothing looked too out of place. Using the small handpump, I inflated Abi's rear tyre and set the wheel straight in the frame. As I did so a man emerged from his caravan to observe my labour. He walked over to me.

'Willst du eine Fußpumpe?' he said, gesturing at my pump and moving his arm up and down.

I shook my head.

'Nein, danke.' I made the gesture of feeling the tyre. 'Das ist gut.'

He disappeared back into his caravan and reappeared wielding a large standing bike pump. Clearly, I must have misunderstood, why else would I have refused his offer? He proceeded to show me how to attach the bike pump (not realising it was set up for a different valve, common on mountain bikes). Before he did some serious damage, I took it off him and reversed the pump by unscrewing the front and turning around the two inner parts. I attached it to the already perfectly inflated tyre. He triumphantly pushed down the pump, looked at the gauge and said, 'Ah, das ist gut, nein?'

'Ja, ja,' I said, frustrated that politeness meant I felt I had to waste time sitting back and witnessing this man's unnecessary help.

The landscape was gradually shifting as we travelled down the Rhein. In Holland we had ridden along a wide river, tamed by canals, through agricultural delta. Though there were moments of beauty through Duisburg, Düsseldorf, and Köln, the river was dominated by industry. Now, it was opening up to a large valley. The same water flowed beside us, giving the ride a sense of continuity. At the same time each day brought us up close with the different communities that shared the banks of the river.

As we cycled I looked out for the signs marking the Rheinkilometers. They proved a frustrating indicator of our progress, as the twist and turns of the cycle path didn't always translate to a great stretch of river travelled. Instead, I started counting the castles and stately homes which had started to appear, nestled among trees in the valley's side.

'Can we just sit here for a bit?' Abi asked as she pulled up to a bench on the path. It was the second time we'd stopped since lunch. 'I'm feeling really rough, I don't feel like I can do this.'

I sat down next to her. 'I know, darling, but it's just in your head.'

She looked hurt. That wasn't what I meant. I just didn't have the energy to both acknowledge how Abi was feeling and to keep going myself.

Day Thirty-Three

I have a huge capacity for switching off when I'm focused on a task or goal and turning down the dial on thirst, hunger, pain, even needing the loo. Sometimes I don't know I'm doing it. Other times I use it to keep going. Abi was allowing herself to dip into it, to feel sick, to rest, to wee, and I couldn't stand it. I felt like so much energy was being wasted stopping and starting. We didn't have any choice but to carry on until the next campsite, so why drag it out? Still, we were going nowhere while I was being hard-line about it. I tried to relax and reached my arm around Abi to give her a half-hearted hug, tolerating the feeling building inside of me.

We pushed on in silence and, after an hour's ride, reached a campsite which was separated from the river by a thick band of trees. A narrow path overgrown with brambles led to a small beach. Across the water, a castle was perched high atop a hill. The reception, housed in a dark wooden cabin, opened soon after we arrived. Peering in, hundreds of glass eyes peered back at us from the gloom. The walls were lined with taxidermy of various German forest animals – badgers, foxes, a giant eagle swooped from a corner (the twin of the one that had startled me the day before). Any empty space on the bare wood walls was filled with pelts, mostly the black and white stripes of badgers, and huge branching antlers. Taking it in, we approached the snarling fox at the counter and organised a pitch with the woman behind.

Abi climbed inside the tent. 'I don't feel like you were very fair to me today.'

'I was just tired and stressed,' I said, dismissively. 'I'm going to go get some food.'

I emptied a pannier and cycled towards the church in town. There was a small supermarket next door where I bought ingredients for dinner. When I came back, Abi was asleep in the tent. I sat on the ground.

Sitting in the grey shadow of the trees, the low light stripping the bark and leaves of colour, I eased my frustration out of me, softening it from hardened and justified anger into compassion. She was ill, I had been unkind, and I loved her.

Abi stirred in the tent. 'Lili? Is that you?'

'I'm sorry, I . . . I wasn't very kind, I just wanted today to be easy and it wasn't and I took that out on you, and it wasn't fair and I'm sorry.'

I was met by silence.

'I was just anxious and worried that if we let the feeling in, we'd be stuck there.'

I heard the tent door unzip.

'You can come inside if you want.'

I crawled in.

'You got to stay in a hotel when you were sick, and I didn't, and it's ok but it was hard, and I still feel ill and . . .' The words tumbled out of Abi's mouth between sobs.

We lay side by side for a while, and I stroked her hair and listened.

Before it got dark, we walked down to the river. I took off my sandals and waded out into the cool shallows, easing off some of the soreness of the day. As they soaked, I stared at my feet, their outline crisp in the clear water, my toes wrinkling and the hard skin on my soles starting to soften.

Abi

Day Thirty-Four, Mehlem to Koblenz

Cycling was feeling better than yesterday. The only remnant of my cold was an upset stomach. The route became more beautiful with each kilometre pedalled. Curling green vineyards climbed vertically upwards as the river carved its way through the canyon. Rocky cliffs rose and fell on the opposite bank. I was getting used to the unrelenting sun, but the temptation to throw myself into the river to cool off grew as we descended into the valley.

We took a break on a bench overlooking a small pier. A passenger boat was winding its way towards us on the far side of the river. I clumsily shovelled large handfuls of peanuts into my mouth, smacking the salt from my lips with satisfaction. I couldn't get enough. The boat sped up and we watched, mouths gaping, as the captain pulled a perfect handbrake turn, skidding sideways across the river. His command of the boat brought it to a perfect stop half a metre from the walkway. Lili and I burst into applause. I felt privileged to be privy to this small moment of joy.

At Remagen we rode beside the blackened towers of the Ludendorff Bridge. This bridge had been crucial in the final weeks of the Second World War when it was captured by the

Americans, as it was the only Rhein bridge remaining after the systematic destruction of all others by German forces. The capture helped to end the war, as, without it, the river would have been incredibly difficult to ford.

The bridge was destroyed ten days after its capture. Now only the towers on each bank remained, one serving as a museum, the other as an occasional performing arts space. We continued through the yellow hayfields of the Golden Miele, enjoying the view of the hillsides opposite and chatting about nothing in particular.

My bladder was uncomfortably full and, seeing signs for a little town called Bad Breisig a kilometre away, I decided to wait and enjoy the comfort of actual indoor plumbing rather than my usual squat by the river.

'Abs, the toilets are really close to the Roman Baths. Shall we have a look?' Lili was examining a tourist map.

I was wary of the time, but we'd barely stopped at any sites so I agreed to take a detour, not knowing what to expect.

When we reached the site, we were confronted with a modern-looking spa.

'Oh my God, I think these are the baths. Shall we?' Lili looked at me. They knew there was no way I could pass up the chance to swim in geothermal baths. We read the sign in the gardens outside the spa and learnt that the area had previously been part of the Roman Empire. They had exploited the natural heated springs, but it wasn't until 1914 that the baths were rebuilt as leisure pools. In 1958 the town of Breisig got its name Bad Breisig ('Spa' Breisig). There was, however, one problem with entering the spa: our huge amount of luggage.

Lili wandered in to see if there were locker facilities, as well as how much it would be to bathe there. I waited outside. A few locals coming in and out of the baths glanced at me and our overladen bikes. I had gotten used to being an unusual sight in small towns. Lili arrived back out.

'It's cheap, and they do have lockers, but I don't think we'll fit all our stuff in. We'll have to leave some outside.'

I made a face. I wasn't happy about this, but the pull of the cool water was too strong. Was it really that likely that someone would attempt to steal a load of smelly camping stuff and two second-hand bikes?

Looking at our bags we grabbed the essentials – our tent, the pannier which contained our stove, towels and swimming clothes and our small bag of electronics, passports, money and maps, and the ukulele. At least if everything else was stolen, we'd be able to get back to the UK (and play some music on the way). We locked our bikes together to the bike stand with our heavy combination locks. We threaded our longer chain through the top loop of the panniers we had left and padlocked it closed. It was as much of a deterrent as we could manage.

In the spa, the woman looked at our stuff with a curious smile as she pointed us in the direction of the changing rooms, politely ignoring the mud we trailed down the polished white tile floor.

'Oh my God, look at me!' I turned to Lili. I'd seen myself in a full-length mirror for the first time since we started the tour.

'What?'

'My body looks so different, I didn't realise.'

After a month of cycling, looking at my swimsuit-clad body was a surreal experience. My calves were huge and well defined. My stomach, hips and waist had shrunk. I was still fat by most people's standards, but my body had changed considerably.

I would have thought I'd be happy, but it just felt odd. I felt out of place in this new body. I knew before the tour that I'd lose weight cycling for six hours a day, and secretly part of me had wanted that. It frustrated me that even though I felt happy with my appearance most of the time, I still internalised the messages society fed me: I needed to lose weight to be a better person.

Staring at my reflection, I was conflicted. I hated the idea that when I went home people would only comment on my body and not the things I'd achieved on the tour. I had been trying hard to change my subconscious goal of losing weight into a desire to be stronger and fitter, and I hoped this tour would help me openly love my body. In the mirror, all I could see was a slightly thinner me that people would be happy to see, as if being thin was a major accomplishment.

'Come on, I wanna get in!' Lili tore me away from the mirror.

Floating on my back I felt the warm water rush under me, heated by the earth's core. In the water I felt reconnected to my body. I forgot about the anxiety I attached to my size, to the numbers on the scale, to other people's opinions. I stared up at the bright sky and counted the fluffy cumulus clouds as Lili swam a few lengths away.

'Isn't it just perfect. I can't believe we almost missed this.' Lili waded over and grabbed me, lifting me into their arms in a way that was only possible when I was buoyant. I allowed myself to be carried along, the embrace reminding me that not everyone wanted my body to change.

Suddenly they threw me up and dropped me into the pool with a loud splash.

'Really?' I spluttered, surfacing and snorting water from my nose. I tried to hide my wide smile with a faux stern expression.

Lili laughed hysterically as I raced to catch them.

After the baths, I felt refreshed and cleaner than I'd felt all tour. Neither of us was good at breaking the rhythm of our cycle rides, but the baths had served as a timely reminder why stopping was so important.

The water evaporated from my hair as I cycled, cooling my head and neck, breaking the rising heat. We stopped to have lunch by the river: sandwiches with vegan pâté, squeezed from cheap supermarket tubes, and crisps. As we climbed back on our bikes, I was struck by terrible pain.

'Lili, hang on, come back!'

Lili cycled back to me. 'What's up?'

'My stomach is cramping, I need the toilet, quickly.'

Lunch, coupled with all the exercise, the heat of the day, the remains of my illness and my generally irritable bowel had seriously upset my stomach. It felt like my colon was twisting into a ball. I frantically checked the map.

'Oh God, the nearest town is miles away – I can't wait that long.'

The path was on the riverside, elderly cyclists passed regularly, waving happy hallos as they went. There was nowhere to hide.

'What about down there?' Lili pointed to the sparse vegetation beside the river. 'I'll distract anyone who comes if you want to go quickly.'

I was halfway down before they'd finished speaking. Crouching on the riverbank I saw a cyclist coming towards us. I looked up at the path. Lili was flailing their limbs and singing a Disney song at the top of their lungs. It was definitely distracting.

Sweating, I dragged myself back up the bank and threw myself on the bench.

'All good?' Lili asked.

'Not really.' I grimaced.

The cycling became harder the closer we got to Koblenz. My stomach was still churning and I was feeling light-headed and dizzy. Not wanting to stop again, I powered on up tough inclines onto bridges which passed over motorways and main roads. I was feeling fitter; my legs kept going regardless of how the rest of my body felt.

At Andernach, in Rheinanlagen park, I finally asked if we could stop again.

'It's not long now, babe.' Lili looked at me with concern. 'You probably need some salt. How about some peanuts?'

I gagged. 'I really don't think I can eat right now, but I'm dying for some more water . . .'

We'd run out of water an hour ago and had been cycling on fumes since. Looking around, Lili noticed a garage not far down the road.

'Just hang on here and look after the bikes.' They smiled, off to hunt and gather once again.

I sat in the shade watching day tripping cyclists pass by. The river gleamed in the afternoon sunlight.

'Here.' Lili handed me two bottles of electric blue Powerade. 'You should drink one now, it'll give you back some of the stuff you lost.'

We sat on the bench as I weakly sipped the drink, feeling better by the second. After half an hour I was ready to get going again.

'Thanks, babe, I really needed that.' I gave Lili a quick kiss, nearly toppling both our bikes as I leaned too far to reach them. 'Not long now!'

As we approached Koblenz, we were overtaken by increasing numbers of men in Lycra. They sped past on racing bikes, at double the speed we could manage. Sometimes I wished we could travel unencumbered, but though our pace was slow, it worked for both of us.

The campsite was huge and expensive. We were directed to an area the size of three caravans where there were already five or six tents pitched. A chain-link fence bordered one end of the pitch, separating the campsite from a busy path and train tracks behind it. The earth was bare and parched. Borrowing a mallet from a nearby camper, we fought to get the space we needed as two more groups of tourers arrived; all of us had been allocated the same small area.

A man in head-to-toe Lycra sat in his tent porch watching us put up our tent.

'Where are you from?' he asked, eyeing up our bikes.

'The UK, we're heading to Spain.'

'I've come from Amsterdam. So far it has taken me four days, how long have you been cycling?'

'Uh,' I laughed, 'about four weeks. We're pretty slow.'

'Huh! How many kilometres have you cycled today?'

'Um, I don't know . . .' The man went quiet, clearly uninterested in any other aspect of our tour.

I turned away. 'Guess, we're not good enough for him, eh?' I whispered.

Lili shook their head.

Three male British cyclists arrived. They'd been doing a charity cycle ride and this was their sixth day down the Rhein. Their bikes were carbon fork racing bikes, unladen save some empty water bottles.

'Our van's going to bring our stuff in a bit,' they explained cheerfully to the man in Lycra. Laughing together, they began chatting bike specifications, route mileage and the assortment of tech they had with them. Lili and I were invisible to them; we weren't *real* cyclists.

We walked away to sit on the green grass across the river from a monstrously huge statue of a man on a horse. It seemed a fitting symbol for the day: a huge male figure overwhelming the landscape, boasting his achievements.

'I hate men in Lycra,' I said, downing half a pint of chocolate soy milk. 'They're so fucking arrogant.'

'Try not to let it bother you. They're just a type – at least they're cycling.'

'They're a type, all right! Bikes are becoming the new midlife crisis sports car.'

Lili laughed.

'I just don't see the point in doing this route if you're not going to see anything! You might as well be cycling in the gym,' I continued.

Lili looked at me as if to remind me that today was the first day we'd really stopped to do anything. I didn't care. I was in full rant mode.

'The amount of money all that kit must have cost. I guess it's because they're *real* cyclists, they need to shave off those seconds with the tightest Lycra possible.'

The man in Lycra on his brand-new racing bike was as alien to us as two queer people on second-hand bicycles were to him.

Lili

Day Thirty-Five, Koblenz to Spay (Sonneneck)

I didn't want to stay on a narrow stretch of baked earth, bathed in the glow of a streetlight, for another night. After I cooked breakfast, we took the time to clean our bikes. Much of the wear and tear of long-distance riding can be avoided with proper maintenance. Certainly, the chain set – the combination of chain rings, cassette, chain and derailleurs that make up the gears – sustains a lot of wear because of the way the grease picks up dirt. It was dry and sandy riding, and we were using an all-purpose bike oil. This was a middle ground viscosity, a compromise between a wet bike oil that risks being washed off with the first rain shower and a dry oil that is thicker but immediately picks up dirt. After a week or so riding on the dusty roads and bike routes our chains were getting clogged up. We'd packed basic cleaning stuff – a brush, an old toothbrush, and some rags. I set about filling a Tupperware with water and washing-up liquid to clean down the chain and gears. We checked the brake and gear cables, and once everything had dried we reapplied some oil to the chain and ran through the gears, with the rear wheel up in the air, to distribute it across the cassette.

I used some duct tape to tidy up the loose cables running along my frame. The cyclists camping around us slowly disappeared, and we were the last to leave. We cycled along the river, past a huge statue that sat on the confluence of the Rhein and the Moselle. Across this narrowed point of land, the sky was cut by cable car wires which took visitors across to the ancient town of Koblenz – its buildings and fortifications chiselled from the hillside.

At the bottom of a bridge that crossed the Moselle river, I veered off the route. Abi followed behind me.

'We need to turn off back there.'

'I know, but I thought I'd get a sleeping mat.' I pointed at a camping shop.

'Hallelujah.'

I exchanged my roll mat for a Therm-a-Rest, and we were off again, speeding along the path and following a sweeping route down the valley. Over the last two weeks, the route had snaked on and off the Rhein, detouring around factories, towns, fields and lakes, but now it clung tightly to broad sweeps of the river which cut deep through the valley. The hills were etched with lines of vineyards which stretched out, up and over. We sped along the path, caught up in the flow of the water, surging downwards, cascading through the valley. I felt a rush of excitement to be riding through this epic landscape: carving the same path as glaciers.

We raced each other, and other cyclists, until Brey where we spotted the campsite. The reception was closed and the site eerily quiet, populated only, it seemed, with shop mannequins, draped in strange clothes, hats, sunglasses and rubber gloves. One was propped up in a phone box.

'What do you think?'

It horrified me. 'I don't have a great feeling about it.'

'We could keep going to the next one. We have plenty of time and we can always come back here.'

I looked over at the blank face of a mannequin. We weren't ever coming back here.

The path cut a thin line between the water and the light stone wall of the town, built high against the Rhein. The sun was rising further in the sky. On the tour so far, we'd always been conservative with distances and chosen campsites that were realistically in reach. I always felt as if I needed to keep something in reserve, *just in case*. It felt exciting to keep going, both a risk and an exercise of freedom.

We passed through allotments, in their centre stood a miniature dark brick church, straight out of Salem. I laboured up the steep hill to the main road, Abi crunching her gears behind me. Cresting over the top, breathing heavily, my back drenched in sweat, legs protesting loudly, I peered down at the campsite where a large rectangle of blue shone.

'Oh. My. God,' I said.

Glinting beneath us like a jewel was a swimming pool.

We flew downhill and through to the reception where we secured a pitch. We set up the outer tent, unloaded our panniers and cycled back together to Brey to locate the supermarket. The cold water beckoned, but it was drowned out by the hunger in my stomach.

Supermarkets and food shops seemed to be in one of two places in most German towns, which was generally decided by how big the road running through the town was. Smaller shops were on the high street (which was normally identifiable by the church). Large purpose-built supermarkets would be found on the town's outskirts, usually only accessible by car. We cycled down beside a railway line and did several laps of the church with no luck. Instead we headed out of the town and reached a Lidl after a hairy ride along a main road.

When we got back, sweaty and exhausted, we threw on our bathing suits and sprinted to the poolside. There, the older population of the campsite, decked out in floral swim-wear and speedos, watched in bemusement from sun loungers as we threw ourselves into the cold water. I jumped about like an ecstatic seal. Abi lay floating, bobbing happily up and down. We spent the afternoon laying side by side on deck chairs, letting the hot sun evaporate the water from our skin.

As the sun set, we wandered over to the beer garden and sat opposite a German couple who were devouring a huge plate of ribs. The waitress walked over.

'Guten Abend.'

'Ein bier und . . .'

Abi was scanning the menu.

'Ein Riesling?' she ventured.

'Trocken, halb-trocken oder Suiss?'

Abi looked at me. Hedging her bets, she replied, 'Halb-trocken?'

We sat and watched the sun set over the Rhein. The water reflected the deep oranges and reds of the sky. With the light fading, I thought of the hours we'd spent cycling to get here. These were the moments we cycled towards.

I leant back in my chair and watched the high valley, the vineyards, houses, and river disappear as the sun finally fell behind the horizon. I could just make out Abi, tracing the familiar profile of her face in the darkness. I wasn't in a hurry to get anywhere.

Abi

Day Thirty-Six, Spay (Sonneneck)

The pool was calling me like a siren as I woke to the sun beating into our tent. I heaved myself up and turned to Lili, snoring loudly next to me.

'Babe, I'm gonna get into the pool.' I prodded them gently.

'Wha?' they snorted awake.

'I'm going to get into the pool.'

'Ok.' They paused and then turned to me with a sweet smile. 'Would you mind doing the washing first?'

I sighed. 'Sure.'

Gathering up our clothes I gave them a tentative sniff and instantly recoiled. It had been a couple of weeks without access to a washing machine. I walked over to the large clothes washing sink near the sanitary block and filled it with hot soapy water. Plunging the clothing in, I realised I had no idea how to hand-wash anything. I tried to remember the times I'd asked my mum or nan to wash something delicate for me and attempted to recreate the process. I scrubbed each item against the enamel washboard of the sink and hoped for the best.

Lili had awakened by the time I arrived back, and we threw the wet clothing haphazardly on the top of the tent to dry.

'Pool?' I asked.

Lili nodded.

I waded into the cold water. My whole body sighed in relief. I lowered myself slowly, thighs, waist, chest. I could feel the heat and pain of four weeks' cycling ease out of my muscles. I dipped my head underwater, the sharp shock of cold instantly releasing all my tension. Underwater I completely relaxed. I counted the seconds, seeing how long I could hold my breath. I was resisting the inevitable return to the surface, to the brightness and heat and colour of the world above.

Lili jumped in beside me, their legs unmistakable by their unusual cycling tan: thighs cut in half, light brown up to the line of their cycle shorts, then a stark white. I swam up to meet them.

'It's perfect.' I pulled Lili towards me and gave them a kiss. 'It's like we're on a real holiday.'

Lili laughed. 'Ah, yes, as opposed to the hellish nine-to-five we've been labouring away at?'

I looked at them. 'You know what I mean.'

We read and chatted, swam and slept. The older occupants of the swimming pool, who lay roasting on deck chairs, didn't give us a second glance.

I spent the day desperately happy, feeling overwhelmed by our luck.

Abi

Day Thirty-Seven, Spay to Mainz

The air felt cooler as we packed up the next morning. A group of Scouts had arrived late the night before, and I took pleasure in taking down our tent in a few swift movements – showing off and enjoying the minor ego boost that came from being slightly more competent than these teenagers at dismantling a tent.

For the first time, the route was mostly downhill. We zoomed towards Mainz, enjoying the ease. The path traced the river's edge. Quickly, we passed Boppard, Bad Salzig, St Goar, Oberwesel, Bacharach: the names of each town blurring into one as we raced along the path. We counted 13 castles. Cycling was beginning to feel second nature. The pedals and the frame had become an extension of my body. Any saddle sore had been soothed by our two days' swimming. With each push I felt the new strength in my legs – we still had a long way to go, but right now I felt invincible.

The perfect path made it easy to push my speed. I took a huge amount of joy in amping up the gears and feeling the rush of adrenaline as I hurtled down the gentle hills. I felt a sense of complete freedom moving under my own steam. We passed cyclist after cyclist. It seemed nobody wanted to miss out on the bright sunshine.

We crossed the river on a small boat at Bingen, aiming for a campsite marked on our maps. The Rhein cycle path runs on both sides of the river for much of the route, leaving it up to the tourer which side they want to travel on. Our maps were in German, and although they seemed to offer advice as to which side was easier we couldn't decipher it. Our decision was usually based on the number of campsites or nature reserves one side had – the more the better.

We arrived at a small tent-only campsite in a grassy area shaded by trees. It sat on the banks of the river. The setting sun turned the city of Mainz across the water into a silhouette, the outlines of the roofs, cathedral and spires cut out from the pink sky. The tent field was populated by a few other cycle tourers and we chatted as we prepared dinner, scoping out their tents and touring set-ups. We'd been cycling for 30 days, and Lili had spent 30 days complaining about the cheap case that was attached to their crossbar, and which hit their thighs every turn of the pedal.

'Abi, look.' They pointed jealously at one of the other tourer's bikes. 'They've got the Ortlieb handlebar bag from Globetrotter.'

It was reassuring to be surrounded by other tourers with as much luggage as we had, travelling at a similar pace. Even though we had invested a good amount of money in our luggage, opting for a mix of Ortlieb and Vaude waterproof pannier bags, our other kit was a mismatch of second-hand items and gear bought from bargain sports shops. It was another reason to question our identities as 'real' cycle tourers, but right now, we felt part of the crowd.

That evening we donned jumpers for the first time in weeks. I took Lili's hand and we walked over to a wooden bench overlooking the still river. The city was lit in a golden

Day Thirty-Seven

light which spilled a mirror image onto the water, its buildings glittered in the dark. The fresh, cold air felt good against my face. I cuddled closer to Lili who draped their arm around my shoulders and rested their head against mine.

Lili

Day Thirty-Eight, Mainz to Beibesheim

'I'm bored. Bored, bored, BORED!' I shouted.

The valley had fallen away and we had been on the same low, flat roads for miles, cycling the other side of a high bank to the Rhein, the weight of water palpable through the earth. Just as back home, I was aware that it was only the will of man (and the efforts of capitalism) that meant the ground beneath my feet wasn't submerged. The landscape was all straight lines; the cycle path zigzagging between squares of endless furrowed fields. We could see our route criss-crossing before us. I was jealous of the birds who flew overhead able to take the most direct routes. The sweeping valley behind us, we played games to keep entertained.

'Answer as quickly as you can, how many European capital cities can you name?'

'Er . . . err . . . 12.'

'Go.'

'Berlin, Brussels, Paris.' I paused. 'London, for now.'

Abi laughed.

'Budapest, Madrid, Vienna . . .'

If I didn't make 12, I lost. If I did and Abi was able to name one more, she could steal the win.

Day Thirty-Eight

'Geneva, Dublin, Bucharest, Stockholm, Copenhagen. Is that 12?'

'Yes,' Abi confirmed. I smiled before she continued, 'Warsaw, Helsinki, Sofia . . .'

'All right, all right! Show-off.'

'And the capital of Switzerland is Bern.'

I could never win at the geography ones.

We stopped at the edge of a track marked un-cyclable on our map. I looked down at the path which was littered with huge rocks and was inclined to agree with the cartographers. Climbing off our bikes, we pushed them along half a kilometre, until impatience had us back riding, wobbling around potholes and apologising to our wheels when we hit them.

At the end of the track was a long and narrow campsite. Caravans rested on a strip of bright green grass. A sign at the gate informed us that the campsite was closed until later that afternoon. We propped up our bikes against the hedge and climbed the fence to see if there was anyone about to chat to. Met with a strange quiet, we wandered about. There was a square fenced off area marked *zeltplatz*, overgrown with waist-high long grass, and overhung by trees, which painted sinister shadows across it.

'Do you think there's snakes in it?' Abi asked, looking concerned.

'Noooooooooo.'

We climbed the gate out of the campsite and walked towards our bikes. Abi turned to me, a grave look on her face.

'I really don't have a good feeling about it, I don't want to stay here.'

'I think we should get some food.'

It was lunchtime, we were hungry, and sometimes a gut feeling can be just that. There was a supermarket just along the road, and we bought bread and sandwich filling, lemonade and crisps and demolished them on a bench. I wiped the last crumbs from around my mouth and wrapped up the remainder of the food hoping this would dissuade the wasps that buzzed around me.

'How you feeling?' I asked, hoping that Abi's worry was down to low blood sugar.

'I want to find somewhere else,' she said firmly.

'Ok,' I replied gently, unsure why she'd taken such an intense dislike to this campsite, which was basically indistinguishable from all the others we'd stayed in.

'I just want to look around the town and see if there's a hotel, on the main road maybe. I just have a bad feeling, and I want to know we have options.'

'That's fine, we can look.'

We cycled out from the town along the main road, past deserted office blocks. There was one option: an old and dark house, a lopsided sign the only indication that it was a hotel. I walked into the dining room, decorated with brown patterned wallpaper and crowded with deep mahogany dining chairs, and asked how much a room was.

Too much.

'Look, we'll just ask at the campsite and see what they say, and if you've still got a bad feeling we leave it and find somewhere else. You know the rule. But I think it's worth checking out.'

Abi nodded reluctantly.

We returned to the campsite. The gate was unlocked and we wheeled our bikes in. Greeted by a young German man, we were shown our pitch – a small area of bright green mown grass, beside the shower block and a wooden shed with a bench and table.

'Is this ok?' I mouthed at Abi.

'Yes, yes.'

Day Thirty-Eight

The man left.

'Are you sure you're ok with this?' I asked again.

'Mmmhmm,' Abi replied sheepishly. Then she spilled out in one breath, 'I was just really worried we would have to camp in that long grass full of snakes.'

Abi

Day Thirty-Nine, Beibesheim

I awoke to pounding rain. We stumbled out of the tent and straight into the dry room for shelter. I took the time to clean out our cheap plastic bottles which had grown green mould in them thanks to Lili's morning soy milk coffees. Lili played ukulele and I sang along.

That afternoon we played Ludo; Lili kept rolling sixes.

'I'm just saying, you always win, and you always will, because you always roll a six! You're lucky like that,' I said, sulking a bit.

'There's no such thing as luck, Abi. It's random.'

'Oh, so you're just randomly rolling three times as many sixes as me and I'm just randomly only rolling ones?'

'Yes!'

'Just admit you're lucky and that's why you always beat me at games.'

'No! Look, let's prove it. Let's play so that the number one now counts as six and vice versa. You keep rolling ones, so this should even it out and prove that it's just random.'

I rolled the die. It landed on six. I sighed, exasperated.

Day Thirty-Nine

I knew exactly what was about to happen. Expectantly, I passed the die to Lili.

Lili rolled. It was a one.

I threw my hands into the air. 'I rest my case!'

Abi

Day Forty, Beibesheim to Mannheim

Field after field created a monotonous landscape. Outside a barn three huge figures made of hay bales stood: a groom, a bride and a baby, the only landmark on an otherwise boring ride.

It had begun to get colder, and the chill had seeped through my thin cycling layers. The grey sky wasn't helping my mood. Some days riding felt effortless. Today it felt like pulling teeth.

'I think there's a dog up ahead, if it chases us, we might have to kick it,' Lili called back.

'Great,' I replied. Loud barks punctuated the silent landscape. They were either coming from a farmhouse up ahead or the path. I desperately hoped it was the former.

Lili began to quicken their pace and I followed suit. I'd read stories about wild dogs attacking cyclists in Romania and Turkey and I couldn't help but picture a pack of rabid wolves encircling us as we desperately fought them off with whatever was at hand: a pannier bag, a water bottle, an umbrella. As we neared the farmhouse a large dog barked at us from behind a tall fence.

'Thank God for that!' I shouted. I eased up on my pedals.

Day Forty

'I wouldn't speak so soon!' Lili answered, picking up speed. They pointed ahead to an open gate. The dog had started to chase us along the other side of the fence.

'Sp-rrriii-nnnttt!'

We both set down on the pedals. I was in a head-to-head race with the dog: a blur of brown fur and teeth glimpsed through the wire fence. If I could beat it to the gate, I could probably outrun it.

Adrenaline pumping, my legs pushing down like pistons, I zoomed past the gate. A month of cycling had increased my strength and stamina considerably. Looking behind me, I cried out in victory, enjoying my sudden burst of speed.

We arrived at a red-brick tower: the entrance to the bridge into the medieval town of Worms. The tower had originally been one of a pair; the other had been destroyed in the Second World War. Crests adorned the brickwork and a gold clock glinted in the sun. The road ran beneath the arch and was busy with traffic.

The city was a detour from the route, but I was desperate to break the repetitiveness of the morning's scenery. I had the vague whisperings of my old history teacher ringing in my ears and the knowledge that something significant relating to Martin Luther happened here, but I couldn't remember the details.

'Which way should we go?' Lili asked.

We were stuck at a crossroads.

'I'm not sure, I think it's this way.' I pointed straight down a small street. My intuition told me it was a shortcut which led to the centre.

'I'm pretty sure we should just follow the signs.' Lili pointed to a sign directing bicycles to the left. The German words beneath it didn't make it any clearer where it led.

'Why ask me if you've already decided?' I replied curtly. Lili didn't respond. 'I think we should go my way,' I asserted. I was fed up of taking wrong turns spearheaded by Lili. This time I was going to make the right decision.

We headed down the narrow road which turned from pavement to cobblestones. I slowed down, the uneven path rattling my body. Lili rode ahead in silent anger. We turned a corner and stopped. A line of traffic stood stationary, waiting at a temporary traffic light. The road ahead was a patchwork of compacted earth, potholes, broken tarmac and gravel.

Lili looked back at me, their face red with fury. The light turned green. They pushed off, riding fast over the path that was being resurfaced. Suddenly they pulled hard on their breaks and rolled onto the pavement. I followed them. Their bike was making a terrible banging noise.

'Shit!' Lili bent over their handlebars. Their front pannier was lolling to the side. The rack had come loose, and movement was making it reverberate off the wheel spokes. It was missing a vital screw. They dismounted, and let their bike fall against the wall.

'For fuck's sake, I knew we shouldn't have gone this way.' Lili paced the pavement, ranting angrily.

I stared at them, barely containing my own anger. I was pissed off I'd made the wrong decision, but I was also pissed off with the way Lili was reacting. After all, Lili had made a lot more navigational mistakes than me.

'I'll try and find the screw,' I offered.

I searched for a few minutes, but it was hard work. The path was littered with detritus, and I was being intermittently forced to the pavement by oncoming traffic. The screw was lost.

I turned to Lili. 'We're gonna have to find a hardware shop, or a bike repair shop. Sorry.'

Day Forty

Lili gave me an angry look then, huffing, pulled the pannier bags off the front of their bike. We each hung one around our shoulders and walked to the repair shop marked on our maps in furious silence.

An elderly man in blue overalls greeted us. He was helping a sharply dressed middle-aged man with a brand-new hybrid bike – fixing a pannier rack and new leather seat. The middle-aged man took a cursory glance at our dirt-covered bikes and selves and returned his attention to the new bike. We waited as he headed off on a trial run. Lili gestured to the problem. Wheeling the bike into his small courtyard, the mechanic pulled out a large toolbox of various nuts, bolts and screws. Quickly finding the right tools, he attempted to adjust the rack to its original position as it had been bent out of shape by the weight of the falling bag. Distracted again by the new-bike man, who had come back and stood hovering above us, he handed us the tools and the screw and Lili set about fixing the rack.

I watched the mechanic take a new pannier bag, which he then unfolded and placed on the man's bike. The man stared at his phone, tapping his feet. Meanwhile, Lili aligned their rack, carefully screwing it into place. The mechanic traipsed back through the courtyard to get something else for the other man. Looking down at Lili, he noticed that they had fixed the rack back into place. He patted Lili on the shoulder and smiled. 'Sehr gut! Sehr gut!'

I looked down at Lili. Their frustration was gone and now they beamed with pride. I recognised the joy of competence. I looked over again at the man with his new kit. It was sad that he'd probably never experience the joy of fixing his own bike.

The repair man wanted nothing for the screws, he just praised Lili some more and sent us on our way. We ate lunch in the Heylshof Gardens, the former site of the Bishop's

Palace. A plaque on the floor reminded me that Martin Luther had once defended his theses here, leading, eventually to the schism of Protestantism and Catholicism. Lili wasn't interested, they were too caught up by the day's events. Instead, we chatted about bicycle repair, about how we wanted to learn more, about how there was something radical and joyful about learning how to fix such a simple machine – one you could break down to its smallest ball bearing and then build back up again.

'I guess *this* time it's a good thing I took us the wrong way!' I laughed as Lili batted me on the arm.

We headed back along the Rhein towards Mannheim. The city was set out on a confusing grid system, much like I imagine American cities are, and contained an abnormal number of one-way streets. It was nicknamed 'The City of Squares' and had been designed to fulfil Renaissance ideals of beauty. Right now, it felt like it was designed to confuse cycle tourers.

'I think we want road 12C or maybe 12D.' I stared at the incomprehensible map, willing it to reveal the way.

We cycled up and down until, finally, we got off our bikes to walk. It was easier to navigate on foot as we didn't have to obey the one-way systems. We walked through a large university complex and then arrived onto a wooded route. Riding into the campsite, we were offered a tiny pitch sandwiched between a hedgerow and a path. We'd run out of credit, and it had been five days since I'd spoken to someone other than Lili. I hoped the campsite might have Wi-Fi so I could Skype home, but the campsite owner shook her head and walked away.

'We passed a hostel on the way in, sometimes they have cheap bars, we could go see if we can get Wi-Fi there?' I suggested.

Day Forty

Riding without panniers was freeing. I enjoyed the cool air and the feeling of lightness. The hostel bar was only open to guests, but they gave us a map with a Starbucks marked on the grid system and we headed back into the maze of Mannheim.

After Skyping our families, we finally set up the second phone we'd brought with us with a giffgaff SIM. We'd now be able to keep in contact when apart. It had only taken us a month.

Lili sat swilling the dregs of coffee in their cup. The call home had left us them feeling particularly homesick.

'Hey, Lils.' They looked up. 'Did you see the vegan sign at the buffet next door?'

They gave me a wry smile.

We filled our plates high with salad and enjoyed a bit of comfort. It had been a while since we'd eaten so many vegetables at once. We finished with a cake each and cycled back to the campsite.

We passed a man riding a mountain bike. The path continued to twist and turn, undulating satisfyingly through the forest. A cyclist pulled up beside me and then, in a burst of speed, overtook us. It was the same man, on the same mountain bike. He swerved in front of us, out of the way of oncoming cyclists, and slowed down considerably.

Throughout the trip, we'd often been overtaken by men who accelerated past us, only to experience 'overtaker's regret' and, realising their new pace was unsustainable, slow down. To begin with, we would slow down too, unwilling to face the awkwardness of overtaking them mere moments later. It quickly became clear that if we didn't change our strategy, we'd spend the whole of the Rhein trailing insecure men in Lycra. We found that if we stuck to our pace and naturally overtook them again, they wouldn't bother to rush past us a second time.

This time we weren't laden with bags. I wanted to see how fast I could go. I overtook the man. Lili followed, reading my intentions. As I pulled level with him, he sped up. I started amping up the gears. How quick was this man willing to go to save face?

Racing through the trees it was clear he was willing to go quite fast. His breathing became more ragged as I enjoyed the benefits of having cycled for five weeks straight. I was barely breathing heavier than usual. Still he wouldn't relent. Lili and I looked at each other and hiked our bikes into the highest gear. We pushed forward, flying through the forest, the man far behind us and out of sight.

Exploding out of the woods we turned into the campsite, triumphant that we'd won the race.

Lying in the tent that evening, I opened my eyes to see a large dark shape on the outside of the fabric just above Lili's face.

'Fuck! Lili!'

Lili jumped out of sleep. 'What?'

The shape had scampered away at my shout.

'I'm sorry, it's just, outside the tent, there was a huge animal just balancing over your face. It was outside but on the inner tent lining.'

'Did you see what it was?' cried Lili, looking desperately around.

'I dunno, it's gone now, it looked like a ra—'

'Don't say it!' Lili clenched their eyes shut.

'I mean, it was probably a, um, a vole?'

'Yeah, a vole. Ok, just a nice friendly vole.'

'Yeah, just your average, run-of-the-mill, huge, long-tailed vole . . .'

We looked uneasily at one another. One thing was for sure: we'd wouldn't be staying here another night.

Lili

Day Forty-One, Mannheim to Philippsburg

After the rat incident the night before, Abi and I left Mannheim as quickly as we could. We rode through the flatlands. Across the river we could see the sprawling medieval city of Speyer. The huge twin towers of the Kaiserdom cathedral looked like a castle perched on the bank, its light blue roof blended into the sky. The river spilled out into floodplains and we ambled around the irregular border of wetlands.

A large heron landed 100 metres ahead of us, blocking the path. We cycled closer. It didn't move. At ten metres away, I started frantically ringing my bell. It tilted its head to the side to look at me with one prehistoric eye.

The heron was right in front of me, completely blocking the path. I pulled on my brakes and slowed to a crawl. I wasn't sure what we'd do if it didn't move. I felt struck by a sudden panic – nature was unknowable and unpredictable and definitely out to get me. I felt pathetic, pinging a piece of metal, unable to scare this very, very large bird out of our path. If it didn't move, that would be it, the end of the cycle tour. No, that would be ridiculous. We'd just have to retrace our steps and take a different route. Just before I pulled to a complete stop, it took off into the sky in a flurry

169

of wings. I let out a sigh of relief. It landed 100 metres down the path.

Behind a Lidl and through a car park filled with packed up circus trailers, we came to a still, wide lake, and a campsite. We pitched tent on the banks beside a small beach with a children's play park. The temperature was dropping, and I put on layer after layer to keep warm. We sat on a picnic bench drinking beer and Riesling. Giddy with excitement and the kind of cold that you become slightly manic in, we played on the rocking animals. I tried riding an unwieldy wooden dolphin and fell off. We laughed, relaxed.

We decided to take a walk arm in arm around the campsite, still laughing and talking loudly. Rounding a corner, we were confronted by a large Confederate flag hanging from one of the caravans. When we had talked with Tommy, I had described our surprise at the large number of German flags, or those of particular regions, which we saw wherever we stayed. I explained how the English flag (the red and white St George) was often just a low-key way of saying 'I mask my racism/xenophobia in a more socially acceptable nationalism'. The Confederate flag isn't low-key. It was a stark reminder that feeling safe somewhere was a privileged experience.

Abi

Day Forty-Two, Philippsburg

I could see my breath condensing in the air. The weather was finally turning. I called another rest day. Lili agreed. We weren't sure what the next campsite would bring, and I was a little hungover.

We'd paid to have electricity in our tent as we needed to charge all our devices. Prior to the tour we had invested in a power pack and solar charger – designed to be outside and suffer the blows of cycle touring. We'd spent the heatwave charging our devices as we cycled – the solar panel bungeed to the front pannier racks. It was a great technique while the sun was out, but as the days got shorter it had become less effective.

With electricity and Wi-Fi, we ended up spending most of the day comatose in the tent, watching reruns of *Friends* on Netflix and endlessly scrolling on Instagram. Before we'd left, we had started following other cycle tourers. At the time it had been a source of inspiration. Now, it was a stick to measure ourselves against, and we always came up short. We didn't look like these people; we couldn't do what they did. A lot of our cycle tour so far had involved one of us crying: in a tent, on a bench by the Rhein, on our bikes. They made travelling look effortless, but it wasn't – it was messy and complicated and hard. Even our joys and triumphs couldn't measure up to theirs. I felt a huge amount of pressure to live up to the slick social media image of perfect bodies in perfect places.

I posted a picture of us lying wrapped up in the tent, looking like death. If I couldn't be perfect, I may as well be honest. I waited for the likes to crawl in, staring at the screen like a zombie. It felt like I was being held hostage by social media.

Abi

Day Forty-Three, Philippsburg to Plittersdorf

'Who the hell thought gravel was a good cycling surface?' I stopped and stretched my fingers back one by one, trying to coax some feeling into them.

Lili shook their head and stared at the never-ending path of tiny white pebbles. We had been cycling for less than 10km and I was already getting tired. The rattle of the stones was driving me insane. The Rhein route is famous for being the first EuroVelo route to be completed, but apparently 'completed' did not mean 'completed to a rideable stand-ard'. I finished stretching my fingers and they instantly bent inwards again, turning my hands into claws.

I began cycling. With each kilometre pedalled my body cried out for me to stop. Instead, my mind searched for anything to distract me from the painful and monotonous path. I imagined being back in Cambridge, arriving home to a fanfare of my family and friends, thin, confident and with hundreds of stories to share. I would spend my days painting and learning how to build eco-houses. I would get a job in an environmental charity. I would move to Scotland with Lili and climb all the Munros. We would get married and adopt four children and Lili would get a rescue dog called Pepper.

'I think when we get back, I'm going to take up Roller Derby again,' Lili announced. I laughed; it seemed I wasn't the only one indulging in fantasy.

A big yellow sign and a barrier stopped us in our tracks.

'Um-lei-tung,' I read aloud.

'It's a detour sign.' Lili hung their head, resting their forehead on their handlebars.

'That's ok.' I was determined to stay positive. 'At least it's paved.'

We headed into the nearest town, following the bright yellow detour signs around the centre and out again. Forty-five minutes later we were back on the path, barely a kilometre from where we left it. We could even see the section we'd been on.

'Well, that must have added a good 10km.' Lili sighed, steering their bike back onto the gravelled path. 'I'm so glad we followed the ridiculous detour.'

We kept cycling, frustration at the poor path turning to joy every time we neared a town or city and it became, briefly, paved again. We had 70km to cover today, which was at the top end of what I felt confident doing. It had now turned into 80.

The path split into two routes and we faced a choice: continue on the gravel or follow a paved path which rose and fell at steep intervals beside the riverbank. We opted for the latter. My hands were struggling to brake or change gear and, as much as I hated any incline, a reprieve from the bumpy surface was much needed. We'd chosen steel-framed bikes because they were older, cheaper and easier to mend. However, unlike aluminium or carbon fibre they don't really absorb any of the shock from the road. I was beginning to understand why they were nicknamed 'Boneshakers'.

'Unnecessary hills, make me want to die, on this cycle ride . . .' Lili sang loudly to the tune of The Dresden Dolls

Day Forty-Three

'Coin Operated Boy'. It had been our cycling anthem since the Ruhr route. I could feel my patience for the path fraying.

Ten kilometres along, we hit another detour, the yellow sign bright against the grey path. I felt my frustration rising. I took a deep breath. Throwing a strop wouldn't help anyone. We headed off along farmland lanes except, this time, the yellow signs stopped, sending us nowhere. We were flung off the route, with no idea where we were, no signal on the phone and no idea how to get back on track.

Lili pulled our OS map from a pannier bag and together we tried to identify landmarks in order to plot our route. Every road we took was blocked by works. We cycled by a small roadside orchard, busy with locals knocking apples into wicker baskets. We kept cycling.

'How are we here again!' I screamed.

The two of us flung our bikes down, exhausted and confused. I watched the same people pick apples from the same trees which lined the same country lane. I let myself be engulfed in a wave of hopelessness.

Lili hugged me and handed me my water bottle. We each took sips. They re-opened the map.

'The path is here, but this road is blocked here and here.' I pointed at a few useless lines on the paper. 'But, if we take this trail here, the one we spotted, we might end up further down the road and that *should* take us to the path.'

'If it's not blocked too,' Lili added gravely.

We cycled down to check out the trail. It was heavily wooded with dense undergrowth. We would have to push our bikes along it. I grappled my handlebars and man-oeuvred my bike down the narrowing path. Nettles stung my legs and thorns tore at my clothes as I wrestled my bike through.

'It shouldn't be much further,' Lili called ahead to me. 'Is it doable?'

'I think so, as long as it doesn't get much worse.'

We were lucky. Pushing through the last of the bushes we made it to the road. I was scratched and battered. I desperately hoped I wasn't wrong about this route. We rounded a corner.

'No, please, no!' I shouted.

Another dreaded yellow diversion sign.

The path we needed was blocked by a short barrier and ran through a quarry which was full of building works.

'Abi?'

'Yeah?'

'There's no one working today, we could just take the path? We can see where the building works end, after all . . .'

I looked ahead. Two hundred metres away the newly tarmacked road continued onwards, a yellow detour sign marking the end of our detour (or the start of some other cycle tourer's hell).

'Ok, let's do it.'

We pushed our bikes around the barrier and onto the path, cycled the short distance and squeezed through a gap between some trees. There was no way I was taking another detour.

'How much farther do we have left?' I asked Lili.

'Probably 20 or 30km.'

I frowned. I wasn't sure how much longer I could keep going. We'd already ridden an extra 30km thanks to the terrible detours, and my legs felt heavy. I cycled behind Lili, matching their rhythm. I knew I wouldn't have been able to do this tour without them. Their stubborn desire to stick to our schedule, to keep on no matter what, was the drive I needed to keep going. I worried that my lack of independence was yet another thing which separated me from the cyclists and adventurers I admired. Could I ever be a real cycle tourer if I so heavily relied on somebody else?

'Let's just hope the path improves,' I muttered to myself.

It didn't. At Karlsruhe harbour a not-so-helpful sign told us that the path continued on the other side of a small footbridge. The footbridge was elevated, with around 70 narrow steps to the top. Even if we could carry our bikes, we weren't sure they'd fit through the tiny enclosed bridge. I was furious.

'How is this a fucking cycle route? What actual idiot thought this was acceptable?'

Lili let me rage as we began the long detour around the harbour.

'I guess it's fine, if you're a strong man, with a carbon-framed bike and no luggage!' I ranted.

Lili nodded, knowing better than to argue.

'I mean, this is supposed to be family-friendly. This is supposed to be an accessible route. GAHHHH!' I let out a last howl of frustration and fell into angry silence.

Five kilometres later, we emerged on the other side of the footbridge.

'Well, that was worth it,' Lili said glumly. 'At least it was well signed.'

I looked up at the other side of the footbridge and pushed down hard on my pedal.

We were back on a gravel path, but this time a road ran parallel to us. Fed up and eager to make some progress, we decided to risk it.

Lorries raced around me, leaving only inches as they overtook. Road riding was tiring in a different way. It was mentally draining. I couldn't drown out my awareness that I wasn't the one in control. If a driver made a mistake, I would take the damage.

We cycled in silence, picking up our pace. I concentrated on each metre of tarmac and sped up around corners in the hopes that cars wouldn't make the foolish decision to overtake me. My nerves were in pieces by the time we headed back onto the path, but we'd managed to make good time and only had a few more kilometres left before I could collapse and rest. I felt totally and absolutely at my limit.

Lili

Day Forty-Four, Plittersdorf to Kehl

I winced at every push of my pedals for the first half hour of
our ride. I could feel the intense tiredness of yesterday
ebbing in every muscle, my body too exhausted to acknowledge individual aches and pains, just the low hum of fatigue.
Since Philippsburg the temperature had been slowly dropping and we were aware of an increased urgency to our
journey south as we chased the last of the summer. We put
our heads down, and while ordinarily the busy roads that
made up the days ride would have made me anxious I was
too tired to feel concerned. I was going to make it to
Strasbourg, or I was going to die under the wheels of one of
the huge lorries steaming past me en route. Either way I'd
finally be resting.

From the campsite we re-joined the route: the same gravel
path along a high dyke which we had been riding for the past
few days. It was mid-September, and we skirted fields
burdened with crops ready to harvest. From out of a thick
band of trees we arrived back onto the banks of the Rhein.
A dam immediately ahead split the river, and the water which
passed us rushed downstream, white and grey. On the other
side of the dividing line, the water was still, frozen with

potential, restrained by the large concrete barricade. Gravel crunched beneath my wheel as we laboured in silence along the water's edge.

There, in the far distance along the river, I could pick out the faint outline of a city: Strasbourg. It was a straight ride, and after several hours of riding through treacle we were only about 15km away.

'I need to take a rest,' Abi blurted out, and stopped cold.

I swung off my bike, sighed, and wheeled it back to the bench where she now sat, dejected, looking out across the water. I sat beside her. My tiredness was turning into frustration and anger. We always seemed to be stopping for her, when I needed to keep going. What was the point in stopping and wallowing, when we could be moving and making progress?

'This is awful, this whole tour has been awful.'

'Well, I don't know what tour you've been on, but I've had some lovely days,' I said, angry that this momentary hardship was casting a dark cloud over the whole endeavour.

'It's just relentless, I just can't do it.'

'Well, we have to.' I tried to coach her. 'We don't have another option.'

'No, I'm not carrying on. I'm not doing it.'

'So, you're just going to stay here?'

'Yep, you can go on without me, it's fine.'

'So, I'll just leave you here and cycle off without you?' I was increasingly desperate.

'Yes.'

'Fine!'

I was furious. I sat next to her and fixed my gaze on the surface of the water.

Our presence on the bench brought two swans over to us. They dipped their long necks beneath the water, creating strange mirrored objects, indecipherable until they came up, gulping down some reeds or insects or whatever it is swans eat.

As I watched them, I let my feelings crash over me. They peaked at the height of anger and sadness and desperation, and I was full of them and I remained still, and then they ebbed out and created space, enough space to remember Abi, and how much I loved her, and feel compassion.

I noticed she was crying. I reached my arm around her and she didn't pull away.

'We're going to take it 5km at a time, ok?' I said. 'You can do 5km, it's not that far.'

She nodded.

'And we're going to stop every 5km and have a break and eat something. Ok?'

She nodded again.

We set off and stopped 5km later. I thrust a handful of peanuts into my mouth. If stopping was the price I paid for getting there, it was worth it.

'I was really ready to give up,' Abi admitted, swigging straight from the carton of chocolate soy milk.

'I know. That's what scared me so much.'

We stopped again, 5km later, and followed the same routine. I straddled my bike and wiped the remains of chocolate milk and salty peanuts from my mouth. These scheduled stops weren't so bad.

'Only 5km more,' I reminded Abi.

The campsite at Kehl, across the river from Strasbourg, sat next to an eerie empty waterpark, closed now autumn was upon us. It had been hard but we had made it.

At the supermarket neither of us could decide what to eat.

'What about fajitas?'

Abi's eyes lit up. We'd been eating the same things over and over again – things that didn't need a lot of prep or cooking time and were cheap and used bulk carbs like rice or spaghetti or sliced bread. The idea of something spicy and fresh, in something as decadent as a tortilla wrap, was exciting. We prepared our food on a bench in the campground and ate messily, relishing every bite.

I felt safe when I denied my basic needs, for food, rest or water, because to need something is to be vulnerable, and I did not want to be vulnerable. I chewed on a mouthful of tortilla. I felt safest when I denied physically existing at all.

I looked at Abi appreciatively. She stopped to look after herself. This wasn't a display of weakness. We weren't protected from hunger or tiredness or all the things I was afraid of on this tour because I refused to stop for a drink. Fajita juice dripped between my fingers onto the bench. I felt my belief, this magical thinking that my own self-reliance would keep me safe, start to loosen.

Abi

Day Forty-Five, Kehl

I stood on the modern bridge, one foot in Germany, the other in France. In Great Britain, with the sea defining our borders, it was easy to forget how artificial they truly were: invisible lines drawn, and redrawn, down rivers or across mountain ranges. It was the first time I had stood across a border between two countries, a feat made easy and possible for me by the EU and freedom of movement. It felt symbolic of some of the things we were losing through Brexit. I looked out at the still water and at the padlocks which spanned the rails of the bridge, each a tiny moment of love, of friendship, of unity. I was furious with the people who had lied and tricked and cheated others into believing that the UK was better off on its own. I was furious that racism and xeno-phobia had once again been such an effective political tool – one that overshadowed everything else; one that continued to protect a system which only cared for the rich and powerful. This move towards fortifying borders, rather than dismantling them, was a step towards a terrible future. Borders were a mechanism of capitalism, colonialism, war, slavery, genocide, pain and death; this was obvious enough to anyone who had ever studied British history.

Gears for Queers

I felt a deep sense of powerlessness, of hopelessness and sadness rise, peak and wane. I tried to shake it off. I moved my left foot across and walked into France.

I wasn't used to the slow pace of being off my bike. Despite my sore feet, the long walk into the town was enchanting. We passed through the greenery of Le Jardin des Deux-Rives before following the main road into the centre. We passed flowing canals and broad thoroughfares. I hummed the opening song to *Beauty and the Beast*, excited to be exploring a French city and pleased that its picturesque scenery met all my expectations. We were lucky to quickly find an English language bookshop where we eagerly grabbed our next long reads.

The historical centre of Strasbourg is a chocolate box of narrow cobbled streets and ancient wooden houses. The cathedral, one of the tallest in the world, peaked out from the alleys and over the rooftops of the buildings. Its unusual stone gleamed pink in the sunlight. We took photos, capturing the Gothic frontage and large round rose window and enjoyed being tourists. Cycle touring had its ups and downs, but travelling slowly like this allowed us to see so much more of the countries we travelled through.

I pulled Lili over to a glass shopfront. Beautiful French patisserie enticed hungry tourists inside. I looked at Lili and pulled an exaggerated sad face. It would have been lovely to try some.

'C'mon, I'll take you somewhere vegan.' They grabbed my hand.

We began marching to a far-flung suburb. An hour later and I was beginning to get tired and irritable; my legs could only take so much exercise on a rest day.

'This better be the best vegan restaurant we've ever been to.'

'It'll be worth it. Trust me.'

Day Forty-Five

We arrived at *Velicious*; a small, modern-looking restaurant nestled deep in the Jewish quarter. Inside, the walls were covered with quotes from prominent vegan celebrities.

'They do a *vegan* charcuterie plate?' I stared in disbelief at the menu.

'I know! And they make their own cheeses!'

Lili and I looked at each other in amazement and ordered two platters.

The food did not disappoint. My annoyance at walking so far was soon forgotten as I tore into a selection of vegan meats, cheeses, figs, salads and dips.

'This is the best vegan restaurant I have ever been to,' I extolled through a mouthful of bread.

Lili looked at me smugly.

In the chilled counter, intricate tarts and gateaux stood in perfect symmetry. I was amazed. I'd never seen vegan cakes like them. I couldn't resist my favourite Black Forest gateau and Lili tucked into a tropical fruit tart.

'I think this is the best cake I've ever had.'

'I know, I'm starting to panic that the cream is real!'

The flavour of the cake was intensified by my hunger and by the bland camp stove fare we were used to eating. I could taste every element. The sharpness of the black cherries, the sickly sweetness of the jam, the rich chocolate sponge all amplified. We sank down into our seats and watched people pass by, enjoying our first glass of French wine.

Abi

Days Forty-Six and Forty-Seven, Kehl

Our second two rest days passed in a blur. I felt both agitated and exhausted – a strange mixture of wanting to get on with the tour and wanting to sleep forever. Lili was ovulating, hormonal and in pain. They spent a lot of time napping in the tent while I lay on my sleeping bag in the cool outside air.

We would be in Basel soon and still hadn't found cycle maps of Switzerland. We'd downloaded the *Swiss Mobility* app, which had maps of all the national and regional cycle routes across the country (as well as less helpful roller-skating, canoeing and sledging routes). These were broken into stages and info pages providing distance, total incline and decline, and a grading from 'family-friendly' to 'hard'. Useful, but it was only detailed if you could connect to the Wi-Fi. I spent the day screenshotting parts of the route we planned to follow, hoping that the signage alone would get us through.

At the end of the second day I was excited to get started again. The long rest had relaxed my claw hands and I was no longer struggling to do up my trousers or hold a cup. As I flexed my wrist back and forth, I noticed a large bump had formed at the centre of the joint. Dr Google diagnosed a ganglion cyst – a build-up of fluid that would go away after a few weeks out of the saddle. I sighed. That wasn't going to happen anytime soon.

Lili

Day Forty-Eight, Kehl to Neuf-Brisach

As Abi was packing up, I scrolled through our emails. 'Fuck.'
  'What?'
  'Apparently you have a £1,300 unauthorised overdraft.'
  'WHAT?'
  'There's an email here from your bank.'

Abi grabbed the iPod off me. Logging into her online bank account, her eyes widened.

We'd been slowly paying off the overdraft on Abi's student account, chipping away at it before we went away. Now, exactly a year after she'd left her PGCE, her student account had been changed into a current account with no overdraft. The letters intended to warn Abi could be in one of any number of short-term rented flats. Thirteen hundred pounds of very manageable debt had suddenly become a £1,300 unauthorised overdraft which would accrue an impossible amount of interest and associated charges.

Our tour was over: this was the full sum of money we had left.

  'What are we going to do?'
  'Call the bank first, see what your options are.'

Day Forty-Eight

Apparently because it had been clearly written into the terms of the account, Abi should have known this was happening. Abi was convinced this was further evidence of her inability to be an 'adult'. Our options were: pay it off in full or enter into a repayment plan with the bank which would wreck her credit history, incur extortionate interest and send us home.

'We could call your mum or dad?'

Abi shook her head. 'They haven't got the money to pay off that much at once. Plus, I'd feel terrible even asking them to while we're just fucking about in Europe. It wouldn't be fair on Tom or James or Char—' Abi was on the verge of a full-blown panic attack.

'Ok,' I said, trying to calm her. 'Ok. Call my mum.'

'We can't call your mum!'

'Look, let's just call and ask her advice. We need to talk to an adult.'

My mum took the money out of her ISA to pay the overdraft off, giving us a grace period to finish the tour and pay her back.

Travel culture makes sweeping statements about what's possible. Quit your job, hit the road, explore, live in the moment. What is in the background of all those statements is the safety net afforded to the majority of middle-class and upper-class people. Abi and I always had a home to come back to – even if it meant squeezing into old childhood bedrooms. We were never going to find ourselves stuck somewhere without the resources to get home. Cycle touring was a cheaper way of travelling, but it wasn't free. Beside the cost, the freedom to drop everything and leave is a privilege not everyone has access to. It's easier to take risks when you're never going to lose everything.

Leaving Kehl we crossed the bridge into Strasbourg. Its railings were lined with the ubiquitous padlocks that glinted in the morning sun, sending a percussion of light playing across the path. We cycled through the public gardens and out onto the main road. There we joined one of the busy cycle highways that ran alongside it and into the historic city. I knew we needed to turn left and was scanning the signs for anything that pointed towards the Canal du Rhône au Rhin. Strasbourg was buzzing in the middle of the day, and as we cycled along a narrow tributary of the Rhein we weaved through crowds of teenagers and adults on their lunch breaks. We crossed the water, and circled back again, crossed it at a different point, circled back, until we found a small turn off the road, leading down to the path beside the canal.

Despite the midday sun, it was cool and dark, the sky hidden by trees. Daylight occasionally crashed through the thick cover of leaves, striking the still surface of the water. The path was tarmacked, and silent, and we began the ride. We had 75km to go. The path was unnaturally straight, and so I couldn't distract myself from the ride by navigating, or kid myself that our destination was around the next bend. The featureless canal bank left little to focus on but the very slight and relentless uphill. We stopped for lunch early, both already craving a break in the endless pedalling, and wolfed down our sandwiches. We had left later than planned, so knew we had to make good time to get to the campsite in Neuf-Brisach before it closed.

Our first day riding in France became an endurance race. We watched the signs:

Breisach – 30km . . . Breisach – 29km . . . Breisach – 27km . . . Breisach . . . 29km? The illogical progression of these drove us both mad, as they were the only marker of progress along the unchanging canal.

Breisach – 15km . . . We stopped to take a swig of chocolate soy milk. Breisach – 10km . . . A handful of peanuts.

Breisach – 5km . . . With the end in sight we pushed the speed. Breisach – 7km . . . We stopped for another drink.

At about 6pm we reached the campsite and wheeled our bike through to the dedicated section for cycle tourers. There we pitched tent next to a couple from Germany, who were cycling with their two-month-old baby.

'Maternity leave is good in Germany, and we didn't know when we would get the chance again,' the mother explained.

'Wow, it must be hard work.'

'He is mostly very good, we just have to travel at our own pace, we only really like to cycle on paths without cars.'

'Yeah, totally.'

'We are going to head across France, it's green way the length of our route, so completely car-free.'

We cooked tomato pasta as we watched the couple change the baby's nappy and set him up to sleep in a small cot in their tent. Maybe we didn't have to get all the cycle touring out of our system before we had a family after all.

In the washing-up area, I scraped our plates after dinner and paid heed to the informative tri-lingual sign pasted above the sink:

PRESENCE DE RENARD RANGER VOS PROVISIONS LEBENSMITTEL GUT VERSTAUEN, DER FUCHS LAUERT TO YOU SHOPPING FOX RANGER.

I walked back over to the tent and handed Abi the pans.

'To you shopping fox ranger,' I intoned in a serious voice.

Abi looked at me as though I was having a psychotic break again. 'Huh?'

Abi

Day Forty-Nine, Neuf-Brisach to Saint-Louis

We decided to stay on the German side of the Rhein as we headed towards Basel; it was a fitting end to our time in Germany. The map indicated this was another easy path beside the river, as opposed to a more snaking route through France.

'I can't believe we've finished Germany,' Lili mused, as we cycled side by side along the path. 'I'm a bit nervous about Switzerland—'

'I'm a bit nervous about the hills!'

'—and the fact we have no maps.'

'And the weather!'

We glanced at each other and smiled. As nervous and as unprepared as I felt, I was also excited to be in a new country.

'Um, hang on, do they use the euro in Switzerland?' Lili asked.

I couldn't believe I hadn't thought of this. 'No, I don't think so.'

'Guess we'll just have to wait and see!'

I was determined to get to Basel, and not even the call of the spa towns we passed could pull me from our mission. I felt calm and meditative. We wound through the nature parks which lined the river, the smell of wildflowers drifted through the air. My legs felt strong. My breathing was even and steady. We were averaging about 10km every 40 minutes and only had around 60km to travel today. Compared to the beginning of the tour, when 50km took six hours and left me feeling broken and drained, this pace was a huge accomplishment. I felt masterful and confident in my body's ability to keep pushing on. I inhaled deeply; I wasn't sure life could feel any better than this.

'How are you feeling?' Lili was pedalling beside me.

'Great!'

'Yeah? Even after yesterday?'

I frowned. Did they have to remind me? Yesterday had been a hard day. Hidden beneath the feeling of competence was a knowledge that all of this was only possible because Lili's mum had been able to bail us out, to bail me out. I wasn't ready to probe this too hard; I wasn't sure what to do with the feelings of guilt and shame.

'You know my mum doesn't mind.'

I was silent. The voice in my head was bombarding me, reminding me of the ways I was useless, incompetent, selfish. I tried hard to transform my guilt into gratitude. I knew I was lucky to be in this position, and that every part of this trip relied on the support of others, visible and invisible.

'Look!' Lili pointed excitedly at the sign. I glanced up.

'Only 10km to Basel,' I acknowledged.

Lili launched into a rendition of *Les Misérables* 'One Day More', replacing the lyric 'one day' with '10k'. I laughed and joined in. Singing at the top of my lungs, I drowned out the negative voice. I sped towards Basel, leaving the overdraft behind me.

*

Gears for Queers

I could tell we were getting closer to Weil am Rhein as the trees and fields gave way to large warehouses and commercial units. The cycle path into the city was clearly marked and we pedalled through lanes of traffic which increased in density. We reached a roundabout and spun round it, stopping just east of the Three Countries Bridge. About 200 metres in front of us was the border between Switzerland and Germany. We weren't planning on entering Basel today. Instead we headed west, crossing the bridge into France.

The campsite was in Saint-Louis, the French equivalent of Weil am Rhein, across the river border. My inner geography geek was wildly excited to be on the border between three countries. Where most tripoint borders in the world were illegal to walk through without going through border control, this one was slap bang in the middle of Weil am Rhein and could be walked through easily. Or, at least, the real border was in the middle of the river, a symbolic line dividing the water into three, and the three countries could be walked though in less than ten minutes.

When we reached the campsite, the owner was friendly and welcoming. Unlike a lot of the campsites we had stayed at, there was a large concentration of cycle tourers. Basel was the point of convergence of several cycle routes: the Euro-Velo 15 (Rhein Route), the EuroVelo 6 from France, and the EuroVelo 5 from London to Rome (and beyond) as well as other, local, routes. We set up our tent on a large patch of grass near the toilets and sat in the sun sipping our drinks and watching as other cyclists pedalled slowly onto the site. A grey-haired, diminutive woman with a huge touring set-up rolled into the campsite. Her bike was laden with panniers and bags, and her face was set in steely determination. We had passed several cycle tourers on the route, but few had been single women. I had Lili to lean on, to talk to, to help me feel safe, to comfort me when things went wrong. I was in awe of any woman who could do this alone.

I nodded hello to the female tourer as we left to go shopping in Germany. The Rhein Center shopping mall was frequented by people from each of the three countries, as indicated by the various licence plates which spilled out from the car park. We headed straight to the large supermarket, set in the back of the mall. It was the first time I'd found myself in such a large commercial space for a while, and I readied myself for the bombardment of brightly coloured signage and advertising. In a space so radically different from the outside living we had gotten used to, I felt myself clam up. The noise, the lights, the colours and the bustle of hundreds of people combined to make me feel like an alien.

Back at the calm of the campsite, a few of our fellow tourers had emerged from their tents and were sitting on benches at the covered food area. We decided to join them.

The female tourer was sitting alone, chopping vegetables. Karen was from New Zealand and spent most of her time touring different countries. She was heading the opposite way up the river. Lili and I looked at each other. The maps we had bought in Essen were almost past their usefulness; we'd be leaving the Rhein route just past Basel.

'Would you like our Rhein maps?' Lili asked.

Karen's face broke into a wide smile. 'Only if you're sure?'

We walked back to the tent to get the maps. Lili turned to me. 'You don't mind, do you?'

'No, I was thinking the same thing, we won't need them after all.'

I felt that giving away our maps was an important way of being part of this haphazard community. Offering Karen the maps felt like a small way we could offer her some of the support we received day to day from each other.

'I love your bike,' Lili remarked to Karen as we sat back at the table.

'It's beautiful,' she conceded. 'It's a Surly made specifically for touring. It even comes with a front fork with suspension that you can swap in for more off-road stuff.'

Lili's eyes shone with desire. We loved our bikes, but we could feel ourselves straying when presented with such a gorgeous machine.

'How much was it?'

'Nearly 2,000 dollars.'

I didn't need to know the exchange rate to know this was way out of our budget. Patti and Paula would do for now.

The sun was setting earlier and earlier and as we sat undercover in the gloaming, I spotted small shapes flitting through the sky.

'What sort of birds are they?' I asked Lili.

'They're bats,' Lili replied, drawing my fleece around their shoulders. 'Let's get to bed, I don't want to be bitten.'

I'd never seen bats in the wild. Their tiny bodies flitted from tree to tree, swooping occasionally to catch invisible insects, then reeling back into the sky. While Lili hurried, I walked slowly to our tent, totally enamoured by their frenzied dance in the moonlight.

Lili

Day Fifty, Saint-Louis

I spotted them as I was cooking porridge for breakfast. I'd
clocked their bikes the evening before: two expensive-
looking touring set-ups leaning up against a tree. The Brooks
leather saddle and shining wheel hubs engraved with an
elaborate logo screamed they had money to spend – but I
hadn't put two and two together. It was only after several
furtive glances I realised we'd been following their journey
on Instagram since before we left: another couple who were
cycle touring together, from Austin, Texas. Thin, vegan and
capable of being everything we weren't: adventurous, spontaneous, effortless. It wasn't really their fault I'd taken an
irrational dislike to them – social media generally, and Instagram specifically, is not an accurate lens to judge people
through. But this didn't stop me from shaking my fist in the
sky and shouting their soy-based Instagram handle, Just-
TofuOfUs, like a Scooby Doo villain every time we were
confronted with a way we didn't measure up.

Now, here they were in the same campsite as us, the
embodiment of our failings. They sat either side of a bench,
completely oblivious to their symbolic role in my psyche, in
cycle shorts and caps, sharing a baguette.

'Lili? The porridge?'

I looked back to breakfast which was currently burning to the bottom of the pan. 'Shit, shit. Sorry!'

We left the campsite on bikes, crossing the bridge across the Rhein which took us from France to Germany. Reaching the other side of the river we turned right, climbing the short distance up the main road towards the border between Germany and Switzerland. Cars were stopping at a set of cream-coloured booths. Anxious, we dismounted and walked our bikes. We crossed the border uninterrupted. Other people were stopping, answering questions, presenting papers and passports, receiving stamps. We were again exercising the privilege afforded to those with British passports. Borders are lines designed to specifically include and exclude, and to that end they served us more than most.

We got back on our bikes and cycled the 5km towards Basel's Altstadt (old town). The route wound through quiet residential streets, alongside train tracks, plywood scrawled with graffiti, and then onto the banks of the Rhein. A dense tapestry of buildings sat on the water's edge on the other side of the river. We crossed the first bridge and locked our bikes at an intersection busy with trams. The city appeared to tower above us.

Basel felt an impossibly old city; construction of the Münster, whose red-brick twin spires stood out against a bright blue sky, was started in 1019, but the original settlement had been pre-Roman. We wandered through the city streets. Basel was a blur of old, traditional Swiss architecture and newer, expensive-looking shops. We passed the ornate Rathaus. The town hall had a bright red facade, painted with heraldry and yellow figures picked out in light blue, and rectangular windows. 'Hie Schwiez Grund und Boden' (Here Lies Swiss Land) was inscribed on the balcony; the town hall was built as an important symbol of Basel joining the Swiss Cantons in the 1500s. From there we climbed up the streets to the Münster.

'Shall we go in?' Abi asked.

'Let's not bother.'

I grew up in Cambridge, a city known for its old colleges, towering spires, bridges, quads and tall light stone buildings with stained glass, towers and turrets. I felt totally alienated from the scenes pictured on postcards at newsagents. To me, Cambridge's architecture was rows of post-war houses, the twin chimneys of Addenbrooke's Hospital, the hideous grey and blue fronted Travelodge, the sleeping giant under the hill at the Gog Magogs. I used to love cycling along the river from town, not through the backs of the colleges inaccessible to the public, but through the tall grass, dodging cowpats, to Grantchester. I and most of my friends worked in town, we didn't live there. I learnt that grand buildings were not built for me, and even as a legitimate visitor I was always afraid of being found out.

'I'll rephrase it. We're going in.' Abi took my arm. 'I'm never going to understand your irrational reluctance to actually enter buildings. It's a wonder we see anything.'

Bypassing the large stone archway at the front, guarded by sandstone figures and a knight whose lance pointed threateningly to the dark and ornate wooden door, she marched us through a small side door. The structure inside was nothing like the cathedrals we knew. Instead we found ourselves in a light cloister, with a lawn garden in the square at its centre. The sunlight glinted off the brightly coloured tiles on the roof, which combined to create a geometric pattern: diamonds of red, yellow, green and white. This cloister led us into the main body of the Münster, which was more familiar – a cool dark stone interior. I took great pleasure in the strange small faces, human and animal, carved into the dark wood between segments of the pews.

Rounding the corner, we found ourselves at a large pink marble slab, upright, with letters engraved and offset with gold, and at the bottom 'Erasmus Von Rotterdam, 1536'. Erasmus, defining scholar of the humanist movement in Europe, had died unexpectedly on a trip to Basel and so was buried there.

Daylight poured through a round window, set within it a Star of David. Like much of Europe, when you dig beneath the surface, Basel had a history of violent anti-Semitism and a wildly oscillating relationship with its Jewish population, who seemed only allowed to be benefactors or scapegoats in the story of the city's history. The Jewish population had contributed heavily to the building of Basel's Middle Bridge in 1225. For hundreds of years this was the only permanent bridge over the river between the sea and Lake Constance. Then, in 1349, over 600 Jewish people were murdered in a barn on an island in the middle of the Rhein; the Basel massacre was a result of the Jewish population being scapegoated as the cause of the Plague. Less than two decades later, after the Basel earthquake of 1356 they had been fundamental to the rebuilding of the city, their city. These historical buildings often obscured their own history.

We sat outside the Münster to eat our lunch, enjoying the view over the low stone wall out across the broad river. The skyline was made up of layers like those of old-fashioned theatre sets – traditional Swiss buildings in the foreground, tall modern office blocks behind them, and in the background the lines of mountains.

We returned to the campsite where Karen was sitting poring over the new maps on a bench. We sat for a while chatting to her, but I only had one thing on my mind.

'We're just going to do our inventory,' I said abruptly, standing up.

Day Fifty

'Your inventory?'

'Yes, I like to know exactly what's in each bag and just check everything is all organised.'

'Oh, sure.'

'We'll only be—' I looked at Abi '—20 minutes or so?'

If you've ever had sex in a tent, you'll know the sudden post-coital realisation that there has only been a flimsy piece of fabric between you and the rest of the world, as well as the awkward, sweaty emerging from the tent door into the cool air, trying not to look too guilty or like you've obviously just done the deed. We pulled on extra layers, grabbed the jumbo bag of mini Austrian wafers we had picked up at the supermarket and walked back over to Karen, who was now chatting with a couple.

'Inventory all done?' she asked.

'Yeah,' I replied sheepishly. 'Wafer, anyone?'

We spent the rest of the evening talking with Karen and the Swiss couple, Ruth and Matteo. When cycle tourers are put together, it seems only a matter of time before maps start being pulled from bags or panniers, unfolded, examined, compared to information online, stories told, lessons learnt shared.

'The Rhône route from Geneva is ok,' Matteo hesitated, 'but it's mostly one busy road, lots of tunnels.' He pointed to the small yellow line that snaked across the border from Switzerland into France on the map in front of us. 'It's an incline, obviously.'

'Yeah . . . we're not so sure we'll be able to do it with loaded bikes . . .'

'You just have to go into a low gear and keep pedalling. One foot in front of the other.'

Abi and I looked at each other. Matteo made it sound so straightforward.

'Well, we've got to get through Switzerland first.'

'What route are you taking?'

'The Rhein to . . . Waldshut, then the Aare.'

'Oh, you *have* to visit the Rheinfall!' Ruth pitched in.

'The what?' I asked, through a mouthful of wafer. We'd bought this pack on the false economy that it would last a while, but I was powering through them.

'The Rheinfall. It is the largest waterfall in Europe. If you are cycling all the way to Waldshut on the Rhein, it would be silly not to go a little further to see it.'

Ruth pointed to Waldshut on the map, and then traced her finger 40km east along the Rhein, tapping the point.

Abi and I shrugged at each other. 'Why not?'

ABI'S BASIC SALTY CHILLI POTATOES

Essential Ingredients
Potatoes (chopped into wedge sized chunks), Oil, Salt and Pepper, Chilli Flakes, Wholegrain mustard

Additional Ingredients
Chickpeas, Radishes, Lemon juice, Tomatoes, Basil, Cucumber, Avocado

Method

1. Cut and boil potatoes till soft enough to poke a fork through easily.
2. Whilst the potatoes cook, you can prepare an additional salad. For this we mostly chose cheap, seasonal veg. Our perfect salad included cucumber, tomatoes and avocado cut to chickpea size pieces, mixed with chickpeas and sliced radish.
3. Tear basil and throw into your salad. Mix up a quick dressing of two parts oil to one part lemon juice, a tsp of mustard and some salt and pepper, whisk well and liberally coat salad.
4. Once potatoes are cooked, drain them, then stir through a tbsp of mustard, a huge glug of oil and salt, chilli flakes and pepper to taste.

SERVE AND ENJOY!

Switzerland

Lili

Day Fifty-Two, Saint-Louis to Möhlin

I'd spent 24 hours moping around the campsite at the mercy of my period. Although the worst was over, I wasn't looking forward to the day's ride. We packed up and left the campsite, waving goodbye to Karen, Ruth and Matteo. JustTofuofUs were nowhere to be seen. There were numerous cycle route signs, all deep red arrows pointing in every direction. A light blue square, with a large white number 2 and small Swiss flag, marked the Rhein route. My thighs burned up the hill through Basel's streets and out of the city.

'If that's not a good omen, I don't know what is!' I called out, pointing to the huge statue of a diplodocus inexplicably across the path from us.

We continued away from Basel, joining a smaller road that snaked off and around the busier one. It was our first day in Switzerland, but I was already aware of how much closer the cars were passing us. By the second corner where I had watched helplessly as a car rushed past me at speed, I hardened my vulnerability into annoyance. I shifted my position away from the kerb, holding the centre of the lane. The more I posed a significant obstruction, I reasoned, the less drivers would feel they could just speed past me. If I was going to be overtaken in a way that was dangerous, I wanted them to really feel they were overtaking me. I hoped that Abi would follow my lead, I knew she was a less confident rider.

Safe is the bare minimum of what I want to feel when riding my bike on the road. Safe passing distance is the bare minimum to ask of drivers. I also want to ask drivers to be considerate, compassionate, empathetic: to think about how unpleasant it is to be overtaken at speed and close distance. The cars passing me were loud, and substantially bigger than me. Their drivers separated from us by glass, metal, experience and power. I suddenly felt very exposed – aware of the wind whipping around my unprotected body.

I was glad to weave away from the main road again. My back hurt from riding hunched over (as if I could somehow protect the vulnerable parts of me with a hard shoulder). We swept down to the banks of the Rhein. A large hydroelectric dam stretched out across the river. A third of the way across, past the lock for boats where the water was boxed in, stood a long, pastel pink building with tall windows and a roof tiled with solar panels. This housed the machinery of the dam. I looked around to the incline above us. It put the small hills of the Netherlands, and steady slopes of Germany, into perspective. We started heading up, clicking our gears down and down.

The gears on most bikes work like this: there are three cogs (small, medium and large) where the pedals are, and then some number of cogs (often 6–8) on the hub of the back wheel going from smallest at the front to biggest at the back. The chain loops between these two. When the chain is on the smallest cog at the front, and the biggest one at the back then the wheel turns a small number of times for each turn of the pedal. This makes it feel 'easier' because it does not take as much effort to turn the wheel. As the gears get higher, one turn of the pedal equals increasingly more turns of the wheel, so at a high gear one push on the pedals generates lots of turns of the wheel (and therefore lots of power and speed).

Gears are there because it doesn't make sense for one turn of the pedal to equal one turn of the wheel, and the ability to change gears transformed cycling. In Cambridge, I rarely changed gears. So far, I'd stayed in the same range of six gears on the tour. To continue up the hill I realised I was going to have to use the lowest six gears in my repertoire. I needed to move my chain down from the middle cog on the set of three at my pedals, to the smallest. I cranked the gear lever with my right finger, which loosened the wire and sent the front derailleur (the metal guide which the chain threads through at the front) down a level, theoretically bringing the chain with it. I couldn't remember ever being in this gear. The chain grated against the derailleur for several painful turns of the pedals, and I had to yank again on the gear lever before it finally switched. Relieved, I cranked up the rear gears, searching for a rhythm that I could sustain up the hill.

I stopped halfway up, panting, legs burning. I took a gulp of water and looked around for the first time. It took a while to register what I was seeing. We'd left behind the small town and were in the middle of fields. Opposite me was a model of a man. He was dressed in a rough hessian toga, frozen, engaging in some sort of activity. I gave Abi a quizzical look. We continued up the hill. We stopped again in front of a low square building, with terracotta tiles, and columns holding up the lip of roof that extended over, creating a walkway all the way around. To our right lay a collection of jutting abstract structures of dark and light brick, that at some point must have formed a large building. An information board filled us in on the details. To my surprise, we were passing through Augusta Raurica, a huge Roman archaeological site and open-air museum that was home to the best-preserved Roman theatre north of the Alps. It was testimony both to my appalling geography and the selectiveness of the English history curriculum, but I had never considered how far north the Roman Empire had stretched, nor that there would be Roman remains in Switzerland. We had visited the baths in Germany, the Roman Empire had taken the same journey on the Rhein as us in reverse, so it made perfect sense.

I cycled on autopilot, following the blue signs until the town of Rheinfelden. There I turned a corner and rode straight into a large crowd. The narrow street of the old town was filled with people, stalls and the smell of food cooking. We both dismounted and started pushing our bikes through the bustle, over the cobblestones, enjoying being caught for a moment in the festivities. The houses that lined the street were all uniform, three stories tall and stacked next to each other. The bottom floors were small cafes or shops with painted facades. Each building was rendered in a different colour, with contrasting wooden shutters thrown open: cream, pink, cobalt blue, moss green, shades of terracotta with a pop of colour from a window box spilling with bright pinks or purples. At the edge of the market, we approached a white tower, edged in large terracotta bricks, which the road passed under through a narrow archway.

On the other side of the town, we rode through the dense green of the Möhlinward forest where we followed a network of gravel paths to a campsite. It has been a short day, but the skies were quickly filled with clouds, heavy and dark with rain, and I was nervous about how far it was to the next campsite. We pitched the tent as the first few drops fell and retreated to the campsite's dry room. Equipped with free Wi-Fi and a hob, I cooked dinner and we read and played cards until well past dark. I had gotten used to the sunset dictating our bedtime, so I was fighting sleep by the time we decided to go to bed.

We stepped out of the bright artificial light into the dark of the forest. As my eyes adjusted a figure seemed to material-ise from the night. Sitting on a bench outside the dry room was a large man in a smart suit, with a huge handlebar moustache. I couldn't see his eyes for the bowler hat that cast the whole top half of his face into shadow. Protruding from his mouth was the polished wooden shaft of a large pipe, tobacco embers glowing, smoke swirling into the night. It was overwhelmingly sinister.

'Gute Nacht,' he intoned in a low voice as we passed.

'Gute Nacht,' I replied, my voice several pitches higher than usual.

Abi and I lay in silence side by side in our sleeping bags.

'I think he might have been the Dev—'

'Don't say it.'

Some things are better left unspoken.

Abi

Day Fifty-Three, Möhlin to Waldshut

The next morning, no devil in sight, we packed up. The owner of the campsite was a hulking man with wispy white hair and as we paid, we fell into splintered conversation.

'Where you go?' his broken English once again much better than our broken German.

'Um.' We pointed to Waldshut on a map.

'Ah, do not go Switzerland. Go Germany.' He pointed out a bridge on the map which crossed the river back to Germany. 'Is gut, is sehr gut.'

'Ah, danke, danke.'

Lili continued to chat while I used the loo. Swinging our legs onto our bikes we headed towards the bridge, keen to follow the campsite owner's advice.

'He told me we should go to Bad Säckingen,' Lili relayed.

'Oh yeah?'

'Yeah, I think he said something about a bridge. It's maybe the oldest, or the longest, or the longest oldest? I'm not really sure.'

'Sounds good to me.' I laughed.

First, we had to cross the river over a long concrete footbridge over the top of a dam. I dismounted and walked across, a meshed metal railing the only barrier between me and the dark water. I set my head down, slowly counting my steps until I was back on solid ground. Forests sprung from the German banks, and after the bustling city of Basel it felt good to be back in nature again. Grey clouds blanketed the horizon. We started cycling.

'I'm glad we followed his advice!' I called back to Lili. The Swiss route had followed a busy road towards Waldshut but in Germany, we found a tarmacked cycle path stretching on before us.

Ten minutes later, it began to rain. I pulled on the only waterproof I had – a florescent yellow number. It had been almost impossible to find a cheap pac-a-mac which fitted me before we left for the tour. In the end, I had taken an old high-vis waterproof from Lili's mum's house. It was designed for a 'male' body, so didn't fit around my hips properly, but did fit just enough to keep out the worst of the weather. Apparently, outdoor clothing companies didn't believe fat people existed or, at least, didn't believe fat women existed. Certainly not fat women who wanted to go outside.

I struggled with the zip and pulled it up over my hips. I would just have to let my legs get wet. I felt self-conscious in the bright yellow but had resigned myself to looking silly. At least I'd be visible.

The 15km to Bad Säckingen passed quickly. It was the first time we'd really cycled in rain, and it felt good to feel the cool water on my face. We entered the town on cobbled streets, sandwiched between tall, wooden beamed houses. The old buildings which lined the river looked like they'd sprouted naturally from its waters. The narrow streets dropped and dipped, creating momentum which allowed us to fall through them. In the centre of the town we arrived at the entrance to the possibly oldest, possibly longest bridge.

'Well, it's definitely pretty old,' I said, admiring the bridge. It was completely wooden, with a tiled roof. It sat on three wide stone plinths over the river. Inside, the ceiling was gabled, and large wooden beams criss-crossed the construction. Small rectangular windows opened at various points, allowing a view over the Rhein. Along the bridge was a recess with a large wooden statue of St John of Nepomuk, the patron saint of bridges, covered in huge white cobwebs. At the midway point we stepped back over into Switzerland. An aluminium plaque which covered a floor beam allowed us once again to place one foot in either country.

'So apparently it's the longest *roofed* bridge in Europe,' I knowledgably informed Lili after reading an information board on the riverbank.

'Ah, that makes sense. No wonder I couldn't translate "roofed".'

The sun was breaking through the clouds. Hills and vineyards sloped up into the distance and covered the banks of the river. As the clouds dispersed, the sun illuminated the scenery.

We followed the path away from the water and through endless repeats of the same picture-perfect Swiss villages. Turning a corner, we found ourselves on a grassy spot with benches and a sweeping view of a bend in the river. The sun was shining brightly, and we shed our wet-weather clothing. It was a perfect picnic stop.

'Why don't you set up the food? I'm just gonna pop for a wee.'

I grabbed a loo roll from my basket and looked around. There was a small beach down a steep path to my right. It was enclosed by trees on all sides. Even the opposite banks of the river were shielded from view.

I stumbled down into very wet sand. Taking two steps towards a more secluded spot I sunk up to my ankles.

Day Fifty-Three

Growing up on the North Norfolk coast, I had gotten used to sinking into the muddy sand of Heacham Beach when my dad took me cockle picking. I was also familiar with the cautionary tales of children drowning in quicksand.

I pulled my feet out slowly to release them from the mud and stepped back. There was stable ground around the edge of the beach, and I squatted to wee, hoping that the extra liquid wouldn't sink me further into the ground and then watching in horror as it slowly did.

'What the hell have you done there?' Lili asked as I plonked down beside them on the bench.

I looked at my feet and calves, covered in thick, sandy mud and probably urine. 'I got stuck.'

Lili laughed and handed me a crisp and pâté sandwich. 'I just hope there are showers wherever we end up. I'm not going to let you in the tent like that.'

The route got hillier and we pushed on. We began an ascent. I started pushing the speed, desperately trying to climb as quickly as possible. My strength started to fade. Pushing on the pedals felt like lifting weights. I clicked down and down through my gears, my legs getting weaker, going slower and slower until with every push I could feel the whole weight of myself and everything I was carrying: every stupid book, item of clothing, and unnecessary camping accessory. My breathing came out in ragged gasps. I was going to die. My heart felt like it was going to burst through my chest. Sweat pooled in the small of my back. This was never going to end.

I heaved over the top and stopped pedalling, letting my bike idle on the flat while my breathing slowly returned. The view of Waldshut was straight off a postcard. The river was lined with brightly coloured three-storey houses. They leaned towards it as if preparing to dive in. A stone bridge crossed the border to Tiengen in Switzerland. The Rhein was almost luminescent. The whole village was bordered by trees and sloped up away from the river. It stood in stark contrast to the industrial stretches of the Rhineland.

Exhilarated by our glorious surroundings, we raced downwards, across the train tracks and along the river path where walkers and cyclists were out for the warm afternoon. The river was wilder here. Waves crashed lightly against the shore, their motion creating endless ripples of light across the water. We passed a mini-golf course and headed out of the town centre. A large riverside restaurant marked our next campsite: a caravan site with a large grassy pitch for tents.

I was glad we had followed the campsite owner's advice. I sat at the end of a small jetty, looking down into the surprisingly clear, fast-flowing water. Tomorrow we would ride against the current, abandoning our schedule to follow another tip. It felt like an adventure.

Abi

Day Fifty-Four, Rheinfall

'I just can't eat any more porridge,' I moaned from the inner tent. 'Please don't make me.'

'I'm not making you, but you have to give me another option. I can't just magic up a full English.'

'Ugh, I dunno what I want.' I was sick of the same food over and over. 'We have canned mushrooms, right?'

'Yeah.'

I unzipped the inner tent door and smiled sweetly out to Lili who was sitting in the porch setting up the stove outside the tent.

'Mushrooms on toast?'

'Sure.'

'And some fried bread.'

Lili looked at me incredulously then sighed. 'Sure, baby.'

The Rheinfall was 40km away, making it an 80km round trip. The first five minutes on my bike felt a bit destabilising. I had gotten so used to the weight of my pannier bags that I wobbled out of the campsite. I felt vulnerable without the bulk of luggage around me. After a freewheel down a small hill, I began to adapt to the speed and agility of an unladen bike. We began our exuberant race to the falls.

The cycle route took us along minor roads which rose and fell in manageable gradients. After several days of rain and cloud, the sun had started to shine.

Twenty minutes in and I was beginning to feel a bit worse for wear. Ten minutes later and my stomach was in agony.

'Lili! I need to stop!'

Lili pedalled back to me along the roadside bike path.

'What's up?'

'My stomach . . . It's happening again. I'm not sure I can keep going.' I was bent double over my handlebars.

'You've gone a bit grey.' Lili looked concerned. 'Do you need the loo?'

'I'm not sure. It's like radiating up my side. I . . . fuck.' Slowly, I got off my bike and, clutching my right-side stomach just below my ribs, I collapsed onto the grassy verge.

'Just give me a minute,' I managed through gritted teeth.

Lili adjusted our bikes, so they were out of the way of the path and grabbed some water. I took a few sips.

'I might just try to go. It's fairly hidden behind the hedge.'

Lili nodded and handed me some loo roll. I stumbled down an uneven farmyard path, churned up by a large piece of farming equipment.

Squatting again, I was thankful for the loose earth and the bushes which at least half hid me this time.

'Any better?' Lili asked me as I lumbered back over.

'I'm not sure, maybe. There's just so much pain.'

We sat down again. I sipped more water.

'We could go back?' Lili suggested.

'I really don't want to. I've never really seen a waterfall. Not a big one anyway.'

'Ok, let's wait for ten minutes, and see how you go.'

The pain seemed to be coming and going. Just as I thought it had disappeared it would be back, getting worse and worse till its almost unbearable peak, then dying away again. Each peak was getting less painful. I was determined to keep riding.

'I think it's getting better. It might just be muscle pain from riding so much. Let's just keep going.' I stood up and lifted my bike from the grass. 'If it gets bad again, we'll turn around.'

'Ok, deal.' Lili swung their leg onto their bike. 'But I'm never letting you off eating porridge again.'

The pain died down as we cycled slowly. I could feel the tension in my muscles begin to ease. We passed a grey brick building by the side of the road; an old, now unused, border control point. We re-entered Switzerland.

The way was well signed, and we sped through small villages of medieval timber-framed houses and fields of huge sunflowers, dressed in black, heads hung mourning summer. The road was broad and straight and cut through fields, climbing towards dense forest. We reached the crest of a hill looking almost vertically down along the path.

'Jesus, that's steep.'

'It'll be fine, we're so close now, it's just beyond this hill.' Lili smiled and sped off.

Terrified, I picked my feet off the ground and allowed my bike to teeter and then slowly roll down. Within seconds I gathered speed, accelerating uncontrollably. My hands rested tightly on my brakes. I had bought new gloves in Basel and I was thankful for the thick padding, which allowed me to pull the brake levers hard. The natural momentum launched me straight back up on top of another hill. It was followed by an even steeper decline. It felt like a terrible deadly rollercoaster.

Turning a bend, I could see the path ended with a busy road. Lili was a speck waiting at the bottom of the hill. I began to pull on my brakes, trying to reduce my speed. I slowed, but barely. I kept squeezing, tighter and tighter, until I realised, desperately, that I wasn't going to be able to stop

'LILI. I REALLY CAN'T STOP! IS THE ROAD CLEAR?'

Lili looked frantically around.

'It's ok, you should be fine. It's clear. Use your feet if you need to stop!' they shouted back.

I wasn't entirely sure how to use my feet to stop, but I was prepared to hurl myself into the bushes next to the path if need be. Hands clenched on my brakes and slower now (but not slowly enough) I passed Lili and then, with a quick check to make sure I wasn't about to be flattened by a lorry, I found myself speeding along the road. I let out a few short breaths. I wasn't dead.

Pulling into a nearby car park I waited for Lili to catch up. My hands were shaking. The road was full of traffic now.

Lili pulled in beside me. 'You ok?'

'My brakes aren't really working.'

'Yeah, I guessed that.'

'I'm ok though.'

I didn't want to dwell on my near-death experience. We cycled our bikes around the Rheinfall car park and locked them against a lamp post. The thundering sound of water got louder as we walked along the forest path. Each of us was keen to be the first to spot the waterfall.

The forest opened onto a clearing and the ice blue of the Rhein flowed away to our right. In front of us water crashed down, turning white with foam, rolling over jagged black rocks and creating mini falls. At its foot, a boat floated passengers across the pooling water onto a large rocky outcrop. A tiny set of steps climbed up to the top, where people stood in the middle of the falls, spray soaking them.

Lili and I made our way round to the set of stone steps which led to the top of the falls. A light mist dusted our faces.

Day Fifty-Four

Across the river stood the towering grand Altena Castle, the world's first youth hostel. We climbed the narrow steps and competed with other tourists for the best views, stopping regularly to take in the sheer force of the water. At the top we stopped for a cup of tea.

The cafe's tables overlooked the top of the fall. Beneath us was a patchwork of rock ledges, smoothed over centuries by the fast-flowing water. As we looked, three teenage boys jumped the barrier and started hopping from rock to rock.

'What the fuck are they doing?' I was horrified. One slip and they'd be straight off the side of the waterfall.

Quiet fell over the cafe as everyone watched with bated breath. One of the boys, slipping slightly on the rock, slowed and came back. The other two seemed oblivious to their mortality and continued towards the middle of the river.

'Fucking idiot boys,' Lili remarked. Neither of us wanted to watch them fall, but there was a fear that if we stopped looking, they'd be more at risk, like only our anxiety kept them from harm.

They traversed one small rock and then hopped down to the last platform of stone, right in the middle of the river. Triumphantly they posed for selfies.

'Do they not know how dangerous that is?' I muttered. The crowd around us were shaking their heads but no one looked away. Everyone wanted the boys to come back safely.

Unfazed, the teenagers headed back. They scaled the low fence and disappeared quickly into the crowd. There had been no security to stop them and no one to reprimand them when they came back. I didn't want to feel like I was ruining people's fun, but it really did seem to be a stupid unnecessary risk. A foolish act of bravado in the pursuit of Instagram likes.

Despite that, there was, maybe, a small part of me that was jealous. It must have been a magnificent feeling to stand in the centre of all that raw power. What I wouldn't give to have the physical confidence to experience things like that.

Lili

Day Fifty-Five, Waldshut to Brugg

It is hard to overstate how ill-suited Abi and I are to hill-riding in the best of circumstances. Growing up in the flatlands of East Anglia meant we never developed the muscles for it, and the pay-off for a hard ascent – the chilly, eye-watering, whoosh downhill – always felt terrifying and poor recompense. Add to this the weight of fully loaded touring bikes, and at points not even my full weight on my pedal was enough to keep my bike moving in a forward trajectory uphill. It is one thing to admit defeat graciously mid-ascent, and quite another to keep pushing until your matchstick, fenland legs give out on you, and you and your unwieldy bike crash unceremoniously to the verge. Any Swiss readers, or those familiar with this section of the Aare will be shaking their heads in disbelief. True, the 'Fitness Level' for this part of the route on our Swiss map app is described as 'Easy', but we might as well have been trying to climb Mont Blanc.

We left the Rhein and Germany behind us. Crossing at the town of Koblenz (as ancient as its German counterpart), we followed the Aare river south into Switzerland. We cycled alongside the flowing water, past meadows bright with flowers and traditional gabled houses. The Aare was starkly different to the broad Rhein. The water was a crisp, glacial blue. Looking closely, beneath the fast current, I could make out the patterns of the pebbled riverbed, diffracted by the water. We joined a bike path beside the main road and followed it down a steep hill into the small town of Brugg, where we had booked a hostel for the night. It was an autumn day, almost warm in the sunshine. Coming up the paved drive, we were greeted by the large grey stone hostel building, with a roof that zigzagged to a point, mimicking crenulations, and wooden shutters painted with red and white diagonal stripes. We wheeled our bikes around the back. There was a simple garden, its grass lawn bordered by trees and low stone walls. It was a few hours before the reception opened. We unloaded our panniers and tucked them into the wood panelled dining room and cycled back the way we came for food.

Back on the grass at the hostel we tucked into our lunch – an assortment from the Swiss version of the Co-op. Our lunch routine was slowly developing. Today we'd bought bread, crisps, some smoked tofu, tomatoes and our usual can of chickpeas. These I would open, drain and add whatever assortment of flavourings or spices I had available (which this day was some BBQ sauce, salt, chilli and paprika). I would then mush them with a fork in the tin to create a sort of sandwich spread.

I took my boots off and lay on the grass in the sunshine. We took an earbud each to listen to an audio book – a terribly nasal American voice butchering the poetry of Audre Lorde's essays. The sun shined with a quality that sharpened every colour: the green of the grass, the blue of the sky. At home, I felt like I was constantly buzzing, my mind always working to manage noises, smells, tastes, sensations. I did not find stillness restful, as it did nothing to silence the endless hum. All stillness did was unpleasantly focus my attention on the sensations of my body. The complete tiredness of cycling had drowned out this sensory input, and as I rested my head on Abi's chest, I felt a sense of calm. I hadn't ever experienced such profound stillness.

At about 4.30pm, half an hour before the reception opened, I heard the clatter of wheels on the path. I looked up to see a family arrive – grandfather, mother and five children all on bikes. We nodded hello. It emerged that the nine of us were sharing a dorm in the ancient building. We climbed the old stone steps into the wood panelled room. Abi and I chose a bunk by the door – leaving the bulk of the room to the energetic children, who set about unpacking. While the family ate a dinner provided by the hostel, Abi and I sat and cooked beans, mushrooms and pasta in the sheltered porch of the outhouse.

We spent the rest of the evening in a small nook in the castle, nestled in tall dark wood chairs, old German Gothic lettering picked out in gold above my head. We held out as long as we could before going to sleep, hoping that the children would have worn themselves out before they went to their beds.

Abi

Day Fifty-Six, Brugg to Solothurn

'Guten Morgen.' The grandfather from the cycling family greeted us warmly as we sidled down the stone staircase to the breakfast room. 'I hope the children weren't too noisy last night?'

We had fallen asleep quickly after a making a minor passive-aggressive move and turning the light out at 10pm. I'd put earplugs in just in case. To the children's credit, they had gotten the message and we hadn't been woken at all.

'No, not at all. They were very considerate.'

'Ah, das is gut, das is gut.' He picked up some bread and walked over to sit with his daughter and grandchildren on one of the long wooden benches and tables which lined the dining room.

Breakfast was a variety of home-made jams, bread, nuts and fruits. We filled our plates and wandered over to another table next to the family.

'What route are you travelling?' the old man eagerly asked.

'Um, we're planning on following the Aare route and then the Mitterland route. We want to get to Geneva.'

'Ah! The easy routes. They are for families. You should go the Jura route, it's much more beautiful.'

Day Fifty-Six

The man's athletic frame and developed calf muscles betrayed a lifetime of cycling up mountains. I looked at Lili, the sheer thought of travelling over the Jura mountains was laughable, we had barely managed the hills so far.

'I think we'll stick to a flatter route; we aren't very good at hills.'

The children got down from the table and ran off giggling.

'Ah, die Jungen.' The old man sighed.

'Die Jungen . . .' we chorused in an understanding way.

Even at 25 it was odd to be accepted as a responsible adult by this weathered, elderly patriarch, especially when I still felt like a lost kid.

Outside we began our morning checks on the bikes. My back wheel had developed a habit of skewing out of place and rubbing against the frame, which usually resulted in me struggling to ride for ten minutes before I got off to fix it. The steel wheel shunts of my old Dawes frame and the brand-new wheels weren't overly compatible. I checked our pannier racks. The screws which connected to the wheel hub often became loose with the vibration of the path. Several times they had flown out after riding particularly bumpy surfaces. So far, we hadn't lost one of mine. I reached to squeeze my wheel. We had a more pressing problem. My back tyre was flat.

As we sweated to remove the tyre, the family emerged from the hostel, clad entirely in a mix of hiking wear and Lycra; the grandfather's cleats tap tapping on the concrete floor.

'Good luck!' shouted the old man. Gracefully they mounted their bikes and cycled off, the picture of the perfect Swiss family.

We popped a patch on the puncture and re-inflated the inner tube to test it. Immediately it burst.

'Ah, we should have known it would do that.' I pointed to the puncture. The hole was situated on the reinforced rubber which circles the valve, and no quick patch was going to hold. We discarded it and popped my spare inner tube in. After an hour we were ready to tackle our second day in Switzerland.

We continued along the Aare river. Unable to find a campsite which was open, we had a second youth hostel booked in Solothurn, 75km away. Wild camping is illegal in Switzerland and while we were unlikely to be prosecuted, I feared getting moved on by the police. My fear had still not diminished. The Paalkampeerterreinen hadn't been the stepping stone I'd hoped for because even though it was basic, it was a legitimate camping space. I might have felt differently in the mountains but pitching up in a random woods or field risked angry landowners. Growing up in rural Norfolk had given me a healthy fear of those. It also risked bored aggressive teenagers stumbling upon us; once I'd been one of those.

There were other forms of free camping in Switzerland, including a culture of sleeping in farmers' barns but this involved social interaction. I felt paralysed and frustrated by my anxiety. This wasn't meant to be so hard.

Lili was keeping a keen eye on my back tyre. Near Aarau they asked to feel it again.

'I think it's deflating.'

'What? No, let me have a feel.'

It definitely wasn't as hard as it had been when we pumped it up, but if it was losing air, it was losing it very slowly.

'Let's pump it up, have lunch and then see if it's gone down at all. If it has, there's a bike shop in Aarau, it says on the app.'

Day Fifty-Six

I shovelled sandwiches into my mouth as quickly as I could. Lili moved back and forth from the bikes, appearing at the bench wearing another warm layer each time. By the time we went back to check the tyre my hands were numb with cold.

'It's definitely gone down.' Lili looked up at me with frustration.

We crossed the bridge and entered the walled town of Aarau, too cold and annoyed to take in the ancient stone buildings, stacked like a wedding cake, connected by bridges and winding cobbled streets. We cycled through a grand courtyard where flowering window planters towered high above us at shuttered windows. The bike shop was closed for lunch. We would have to wait an hour.

'Oh my God. I just want to get going already.' Lili hopped from side to side.

'I know, I know.' It was infuriating to feel like you'd fixed a problem only for it to haunt you later in the day.

'We need a plan. What if I go and find a nice warm drink somewhere and bring it back? You could be getting the tyre off so it's ready?'

I could tell they didn't want to sit still. Lili wandered off into the centre of town while I once again struggled with the tyre. Inner tube in my hand, I set about trying to find the hole. I held it up to my cheek and turned it. I felt for a burst of air, the tell-tale sign. There was nothing. I needed to find another way to do this. Looking around I spotted a large stone fountain, like a basin, carved into the side of the building. It was filled with cold clear water. I'd noticed a few of these as we had cycled along, and so far, I hadn't worked out what they were for. I knew what I could use it for though. Systematically submerging the inner tube in the water, it seemed there was no hole. Confused, I checked around the valve again, this time plunging the whole thing into the

229

water. Bubbles rose up to the surface. I pulled it out and felt the valve. It was closed. There was no hole, but there was a faulty valve. I pulled out the tube to find Lili arriving back with two massive drinks.

'I need this,' I said, taking a sip of sugary hot chocolate.

'Good. You'll never guess how much they cost . . .'

'I dread to think.'

'Found the hole?' Lili asked.

'Yeah, well, sort of. There isn't one, the valve is faulty.'

Lili picked it up to inspect it.

'Damn, I guess we definitely need to wait for the shop to open now.'

We sat in the cold, hands cupping our drinks, waiting for the time indicated on a handwritten sign in the shop window. Twenty minutes late, a man hurtled down the cobbled street on a moped. He opened and we stiffly walked in, wheel in hand.

'Es is der reifen, huh?'

'Ughhhhhh . . .'

'English?'

'Yes, please. We need a new inner tube,' I said, holding up the old one. 'The valve is faulty.'

'Uh-huh.' He took some pliers and adjusted the valve. Then, after pumping it up, he tested it. It was holding.

'This is fixed now, but you might as well change to a new one and use this as a spare.'

The man grabbed an inner tube down for us and the tyre off me. He began the task of putting the new tube in. Wrestling with the unwieldy tyre, Lili and I winced as he manhandled it.

'Uh, it's a very difficult tyre to get back on, it needs to be done slowly.' Lili looked concerned at the man's method. 'I could . . .'

'It is good.' He popped the inner tube in and started

squeezing the tyre back into the rims with brute force and several tyre levers. Lili did not look convinced.

'I just don't understand why he had to do that. We know your tyre; we know it doesn't respond well to force.' Lili exploded with anger as we left the shop, wheel in hand.

'As long as it lasts, I don't mind.' We let out some air to get the wheel back onto the bike and then pumped it up again. 'Let's get going.'

We still had another 50km to ride and would have to cycle quickly. The receptions at most hostels closed at 6pm in the off season. On top of this, we didn't want to end up cycling in the dark.

Out of Aarau the route snaked away from the river. At points it felt like we were heading on long sweeping detours. It might have made more sense to ride on the big roads, but neither of us felt comfortable about route finding without a map or riding alongside heavy traffic. This way we just followed the endless blue cycle signs.

'Lili, I'm really struggling.' It felt like I was pedalling through thick mud. I just couldn't work out why.

Lili was cycling at a fair pace ahead. I had been complaining for a good hour, on and off, but we needed to get to the hostel and Lili wasn't stopping for anything.

'I need to stop!' I shouted at Lili.

They braked and turned. I stood over my bike and felt round to the tyre. It was completely flat.

'It's flat, Lili.' I was annoyed. Annoyed at the tyre and the man who had brutally pushed the new tube in and annoyed that I'd been riding on a flat for an hour while Lili ignored my complaints.

I was totally worn down. I got off my bike and threw it to the floor. 'I give up.'

Lili wheeled over in stony silence. 'Let's have a break.'

We wheeled our bikes off the path and into a small forest clearing where trunks on their sides created a natural circular seating area. I sat down, put my head in my hands and allowed the hopeless feeling to wash over me. Switzerland had beaten me. The hills were one thing, the cold another, but three flat tyres? There was no way I could keep going.

Lifting my head, I looked around me.

'Were these here when we sat down?'

Lili looked up and started. Surrounding us in the clearing were hundreds of strange wooden gnomes, of different shapes and sizes, who formed a circle with us in the centre. They were on the benches, in the trees, hiding in the undergrowth; if you looked anywhere long enough, one would emerge.

'It's like some sort of weird coven,' I whispered to Lili. After all the troubles of today, it made sense we were going to be murdered by tiny mythical creatures. I looked from one smiling face to the next.

'I feel like they're mocking us.'

We sat, exhausted, in this surrealist nightmare. The sun was beginning to set, and we still had at least 10km to go.

'I don't want to be here when it gets dark.' I half-joked, tilting my head at the gnome to my left which glared back with hollowed-out eyes.

'Let's pump up your tyre and see if it lasts. We can always keep pumping it regularly until we get there.'

I nodded my head. Patti had been rideable for a while after leaving Aarau. I walked over to attach the bike pump and started the laborious process of hand inflating the tyre to 100 PSI. I removed the plastic nubbin. The valve was loose. Clearly, one of us hadn't fully closed it. I side-eyed Lili. Maybe this was the cause of our problems this time?

Day Fifty-Six

With the tyre re-inflated, we cycled out of the demented gnome forest and onto another long agricultural path. I felt miserable. Knock-back after knock-back had left me feeling like I wanted to quit.

Being this drained, both physically and mentally, was something I had never experienced before. I had wanted to challenge myself with this tour, to see if I could push past my limits, but I hadn't known how I'd react when I reached them. What surprised me, as I pedalled on and on, was the deep sense of determination propelling me forwards. There was something there that wouldn't let me stop, something that had grown since the early days in the Netherlands. I felt more confident and more resilient; I felt stronger.

The sun was setting quickly behind the Jura mountains, and I pedalled faster, keen to get to the hostel before night-fall.

We turned onto a cycle route beside the major road entering Solothurn. It was freezing cold and I hated every stop we took. Looking briefly over the map, we knew we needed to take a right turn to reach the hostel. Lili took the first right.

'Are you sure it's this one?' I called forward.

'I don't know. Do you?'

'No. Let's try it for a bit, if we don't hit the town soon then it's wrong.'

We cycled along the smaller road, heading towards the river. Around us the forest thickened.

'Lili, stop, we should have hit houses by now.'

'God damnit!' Lili turned to bark a quick, monotone order, 'Let's get back quickly.'

We cycled back along the road. At least my tyre was holding out, I repeated to myself. It was starting to get dark and

I pushed the button on the back of my helmet, producing a small red light.

We stopped on the main road and put on our full set of lights for the first time all tour. Lili stood sobbing, unwilling to stop and acknowledge all the terrible feelings. Today had been a disaster from beginning to end. With our last inch of stamina, we cycled into Solothurn.

The reception was still open.

'There's two beds left in a girls' dorm, but you'd be sharing with a teenage school group.'

I stared at her. I was desperately trying to find the words that would explain to her why sharing a room with teenage girls might actually kill me. She looked up at us and registering our dark ringed eyes, dishevelled clothes and dejected expressions, typed something quickly into the computer.

'I'll open up a new dorm upstairs for you. I can't promise you won't have to share, but you might get lucky.'

I don't think I had ever felt so grateful. 'Thank you so much, we're so, so tired. It's been a horrible day.'

'No problem, I understand.' The kind receptionist handed us our keys.

'Thanks.' We turned to head upstairs. 'Oh, I don't suppose you know anywhere vegan to eat? Or where the nearest supermarket is?'

It was a long shot, but now I had a safe bed I allowed myself to acknowledge my empty stomach.

'Um, the supermarkets will probably be closed . . . but there is a falafel shop around the corner.'

Our eyes lit up.

'It was voted the best falafel shop in Switzerland.'

Maybe today could be redeemed after all. We headed straight to the little shop. A huge man handed me a pitta

Day Fifty-Six

from across the counter. It was still warm from the grill and stuffed with fresh falafel, handmade pickles and salad. I've never tasted anything better in my life. It really was the best falafel in Switzerland.

Abi

Day Fifty-Seven, Solothurn

Our dorm was on the top floor and had stayed empty through the night. This was a huge relief for two reasons: firstly, we needed all the rest we could get and secondly, the beds in the room were not our ideal set-up. For some reason, each of the four large bed spaces was made up of three single mattresses with no gaps in between. This meant that if the room filled, Lili and I would have to choose who took the middle bed and shared their personal space with a stranger. I felt very aware of my Britishness; terrified at the prospect of making any sort of accidental physical contact with another person. We'd taken the mezzanine level where there were only three spots.

We needed a rest day. The saga of my bike tyre had chipped away at all our resources. We woke up slowly to the sunlight filtering in through the blinds. Downstairs we grabbed our normal Swiss hostel breakfast of bread and jam and sat surrounded by the teenagers on their school trip.

'Thank God we had our own room last night,' Lili said through mouthfuls of bread.

'Tell me about it. It was so quiet, I couldn't even tell that the hostel was full of kids.'

Day Fifty-Seven

With nothing to do but rest we decided to explore Solo-thurn. The Jura mountains overwhelmed the landscape, looming over the buildings and dwarfing the town. The snowy peaks were a stark reminder that we had definitely chosen the best route. We ambled up and down the cobbled streets of the old town, under archways and through gateways, looking for anything interesting. In a large square, we stopped at an impressive clock tower which featured two different ornate clock faces and a small diorama of Death, a soldier and a King. One of the clocks was astronomical and featured a sun hand, a moon hand and 12 painted segments depicting the signs of the zodiac. This was inset into the light grey tower which had a high peaked green tile roof. We were deciding whether to sit outdoors at a cafe when the weather decided for us. Rain came in a thick mist from the ever-present mountains.

We returned to the hostel and lay reading on our communal bed. Lili looked over to me with a contented smile.

'I love you,' they said softly.

'I love you too,' I replied. I put my hand up for a high five. They went in for a kiss and my outstretched hand smacked them in the mouth.

'Ow!' They laughed, rubbing their jaw. 'Did you just try and high-five me?'

We burst into hysterical laughter. I'd gotten so used to restraining from public displays of affection, I'd forgotten we could kiss.

Before dinner I popped out back to check on the bikes. I felt Patti's tyre hopefully. It was still inflated.

Lili

Day Fifty-Eight, Solothurn to Lattrigen

Shoving chunks of white bread laden with sweet apricot jam into my mouth, I tried to avoid getting the sticky jam onto the iPod. Abi and I were looking for someone to stay with in Lausanne.

'What about them?' Abi asked.

Julie was a student, with a room in the top floor of a house on the city's outskirts. Their profile offered both a couch to sleep on, or room in their garden to camp.

'Sure, I'll send them a message.'

Abi went upstairs to sort the last of the packing, while I headed out the back of the hostel to the small courtyard where we were storing our bikes. I squeezed Abi's rear tyre.

'For. Fuck's. Sake.'

It was completely flat. Again. I stood and stared at it, my anger and frustration peaking. I wanted to trash the bike. I didn't. I turned my energy to problem-solving.

'Excuse me,' I asked at reception. 'Can you recommend a bike shop?'

I refused to have another ride like the one to Solothurn. We brought our panniers down, and I parked Abi at a table in reception. I pumped up Patti's back tyre and rode it to the recommended shop. I was greeted by a young bike mechanic.

'Hallo.'

'Hallo.'

I sighed. I didn't even know where to start.

'Ich habe . . . ein problem,' I ventured. 'Mit ein Fahrrad.'

He nodded. 'The back tyre is flat,' he observed kindly, in English.

'Yeah, we keep repairing it, but it keeps going flat. The rims on the wheel are very deep and the tyre is very stiff.'

He bent down to look at the tyre, ran his hands around, stood up, lifted the back wheel and spun it round to a stop.

'This is your problem; the tyre is rubbed down here,' he explained, pointing to an area on the side wall of the tyre which was roughly textured compared to the smooth rubber of the rest of it. 'It doesn't matter how many times you change the inner tube; it will keep puncturing it.'

'How much is a new one?'

He turned to the wall behind him.

'This is about 45 francs.' He held out a Schwalbe Marathon tyre, which I had on Paula. 'It is the best; you will not get a puncture.'

I wished Switzerland was a bit cheaper.

'Sure. Let's do it.'

'Cool, pay when you pick up – an hour or so?'

'Thanks.'

I walked back to the hostel.

Sometimes I could forget how far away from home we were, or how far we'd come. I was deep in thought as I arrived back at the bike shop. Abi and I had spent the hour at the hostel discussing what we would do after we arrived in Spain; we had intentionally left the tour open-ended. This had felt ok when we were planning in Cambridge, but now, nearly two months in and over a thousand kilometres away, thinking about it left me with a heavy feeling in my gut. Something was there, in the back of my mind: thoughts or feelings I couldn't articulate. I didn't know how I felt, couldn't figure out the name for it. I let it be, hoping it would emerge eventually.

I rode Abi's bike back to the hostel. We loaded up and cycled off. We were heading for the first, and smallest, of the lakes in the Three Lake region – Bielersee. We hugged the river tightly on quiet roads out of Solothurn, past moored boats, and through several small villages. At the village of Ipsach we joined the road that circled the lake, catching only brief glimpses of the wide body of water until we climbed away towards the campsite perched in an orchard. Beneath us Bielersee reflected the last burst of early evening light like mercury.

The campsite was empty but for us. A pitch was painfully expensive – costing the same as a night in a hostel. Just-TofuOfUs were sleeping in barns and wild camping in ditches. What were we doing?

I left Abi cooking while I walked down to the village shop, easing off my legs and the knots in my head that were tightening. I was tired.

I was just tired.

Abi

Day Fifty-Nine, Lattrigen to Cudrefin

The descent from the campsite was bitingly cold and I was shivering by the time I arrived at the bottom of the hill. The first 10km followed the side of the lake and for once seemed to stay flat, rather than 'Swiss flat' – which meant not flat at all.

At the end of the lake we entered the small town of Erlach. We passed a row of gabled wooden buildings on the main road. Switzerland was full of stupidly pretty places.

My legs burned as we left the water and began to head upwards. I was trying my best to do what our Swiss mentors in Basel had told us, but even in my lowest gear I was struggling to make it. As we crested the hill, I collapsed on the handlebars of my bike. My breathing was coming in ragged gasps.

'I hate hills,' I shouted to Lili, who was also prostrate on their bike.

'At least we get the downhill now,' they replied as they got their breath back.

Ah, yes, the downhill. I still hadn't fixed my brakes after my near-death experience on the Rheinfall. I'd developed a devil-may-care attitude to my bike and had been relying heavily on traffic-free paths and long flat sections to slow my speed after each swift descent. I prepared myself and my hands and began the fall down the path.

Picking up speed and confidence I took the corners with ease. My bike travelled quicker than Lili's thanks to my weight advantage. I had given them a head start while my breathing calmed. My eyes watered from the wind and I slowed my bike, pumping on and off with both of my brakes. Another corner passed and with my view clear I realised I was once again heading straight towards a busy road. Only this time, the road was not empty and there was nowhere to throw myself.

I braked as hard as I could. I looked around for places to stop. I realised what I had to do. I moved my feet from my pedals and slowly lowered them to the ground. Lili had repeatedly told me to do this (apparently, they had grown up on bikes with relatively low levels of safety), but this was the first time I'd tried. I could feel some friction from the road as my feet made contact, but the thick rubber sole on my hiking boots made it painless. I was suddenly very thankful I hadn't worn my flimsy sandals again today. Applying slightly more pressure with my feet I leaned back onto my sit bones so I wouldn't be thrown over the handlebars. A bit more and I was significantly slowing down. As I approached Lili, boots and brakes in combination ground me to a complete stop.

'Fuck, Abs, I was so worried when I saw the hill. I was trying to figure out how I'd stop the traffic.'

'It's ok, I did what you said and put my feet down.'

'We really need to get your brakes sorted.'

I was filled with adrenaline and silently elated by my cool-headed thinking. Pumped up, I prepared to head out onto the road which wound its way to the side of Lac de Neuchâtel.

Day Fifty-Nine

So far, the route through Switzerland had been on cycle paths and quiet lanes. Now we were spat out onto a hilly, busy road. I felt like I was being tested. The route between the two lakes was busy with traffic. I looked behind to the angry tail of cars which edged closer and closer to my back wheel and fought a rising panic. Suddenly, the car directly behind me lost patience. The driver pulled past me, fast and close, honking his horn and leaving me wobbling in his tail wind. I continued to struggle breathlessly up the endless steep switchback. I wanted to stop desperately. I felt terrified but also furious; I had just as much right to take up space as these motorists.

We arrived at a campsite in Cudrefin mid-afternoon. The reception didn't open for another hour. Lili had a sour face.

'I don't think we should stay here,' they started. 'Let's go look at the campsite around the lake.'

They gestured vaguely up the road.

'I think it looks fine,' I ventured, 'and I don't fancy carrying on cycling today. Let's just wait and see.'

They were silent, but I could tell from their face they weren't happy.

'I don't understand what your problem with it is.' Something was putting them in an odd mood, but I couldn't figure out what.

We waited on the steps outside the reception in silence. Once we'd paid up, we pitched up next to the lake, much to the amusement of the owner who couldn't understand why anyone would want to camp in a tent in this weather.

Lili seemed to brighten up, despite the rain which started in the late afternoon.

'Sorry, just tired,' they explained. We pulled our sleeping bags around us and settled down for a cold night's sleep.

Abi

Day Sixty, Cudrefin

I woke up shivering violently. It was 2am and the tent was a freezer. My face was numb with cold. I couldn't feel my feet. I threw my sleeping bag off and grabbed my jogging bottoms and hoodie, pulling them on as quickly as I could in the confined space. I started rooting about for the hat I knew I had somewhere in the dry bag I was using as a pillow. Finding it, I knew the only thing left to do was the one thing I've been avoiding all tour: zipping my sleeping bag up all the way.

I hate sleeping bags. I hate having my body confined in fabric, especially as it would always wind itself around me tightly until I felt trapped. Being fat in a sleeping bag only adds to that feeling of claustrophobia. Before the tour began, I had searched hard for a three-season sleeping bag that wasn't mummy style. These, the sort which taper in at the end, locking your legs and feet together are my worst nightmare. If I did fit into one (they rarely catered for larger thighs or hips) then I would feel unbearably restricted. Unfortunately, they are also the warmest sleeping bags.

Day Sixty

I had finally found a pretty good square sleeping bag but looking over at Lili snoring gently in their mummy bag, I couldn't help but feel jealous. Wiggling closer to Lili and zipping my bag up to my neck, I tried to ignore the creeping feeling that I was slowly being suffocated and attempted to get back to sleep.

'God, it's cold.' Lili turned to me in the morning, face peeking out from the hood of their sleeping bag, breath crystallising in the air.

'I know, I've been desperate for a wee for the past hour, but I really can't bear to go outside.'

We lay for another ten minutes and then I couldn't stand it any more. I shouldn't have articulated the need if I hadn't wanted to get up.

'God dammit, I'm going!' I pulled my sleeping bag off with my feet while simultaneously pulling more layers onto my top. I looked like I was doing some sort of deranged dance.

'Make me coffee when you get back, will ya?' Lili called hopefully as I ran off towards the toilet block.

We spent the day wrapped in the tent, bargaining over the one hot water bottle we had pulled from the deepest depths of our pannier bags. Luckily the campsite had Wi-Fi, so we watched TV and checked in with Warmshowers. The cold weather was almost making us forget our time with Tommy. Almost. Certainly, the idea of a warm house was very appealing, regardless of the amount of social effort we might have to go to.

Julie had gotten back to us about their house share in Lausanne. They were away in the mountains that weekend but said we could stay anyway. It felt humbling to have this stranger's trust. Mostly I was relieved I wasn't going to have to interact with anyone.

That evening we stood in the showers, waiting for the one franc's worth of hot water to die before jumping out as quickly as possible and dressing in as many layers as we could. We waddled back to the tent and hoped for a warmer night.

Lili

Day Sixty-One, Cudrefin to Yverdon-les-Bains

I was wearing every layer I had packed and had been for the last 48 hours. It made getting ready easy since there was no dressing or undressing; I just reluctantly extracted myself from my sleeping bag. I slowly clambered up onto my feet, stiff with the cold. Packing up didn't do much to take the chill off, and it was a bitter ride through the Drei-Seen-Land or Three-Lake-Country.

A hundred and thirty years before we crossed it, the landscape had been dramatically altered – the lake level lowered, and the marshes drained for farmland. The Fens, the Netherlands, Drei-Seen-Land – all having in common the ways men and machines shaped the landscape and bent it to their will. It gave them a strange air of suspension – like at any moment, from the soil, water might rise and take back the earth. Realistically, it probably would. What cycle touring was giving us, amongst other things, was an insight into the world as shaped by humans. The fields and forests we cycled through in the Drei-Seen-Land were in some way as artificial as a shopping mall or car park. There was nothing natural about them.

This agricultural land stood in stark contrast to the lake. We'd been following its shore for over an hour, dense trees separated it from the road. Suddenly we came onto a beach – the ancient, heavy body of water crashing onto the shore in waves, turning rocks to sand, dwarfing the small towns that lay, dotted, on the opposite side. The largest lake I'd seen before was Lake Windermere, which has an area of about 15 square kilometres. Lac de Neuchâtel would swallow it. An area of 218 square kilometres of water stretched out in front of us. It felt like an ocean. We stood on the precipice, the wind whipping at us, feeling very small.

Though the Swiss route app told us the total ascent and descent for each section, it didn't describe where this was, and the map the app used lacked any gradients. As a result, we never knew if the hill we were climbing was the biggest, or last hill. This denied me a crucial way to talk myself through any period of exertion – I couldn't count the hills down or promise myself that this was the hardest part.

We began the climb into the village of Vernay. With the first few pushes of my pedals, my legs let out a series of sharp complaints at the sudden change in effort. To appease them, I clicked my gears down. The pain subsided and I counted every time my legs rose and fell. My thighs started to burn. My handlebars creaked as I pulled hard at them, desperate for some part of my body other than my legs to take on the burden of ascent. My knee twinged, I shifted my feet, pushing down with the ball of my foot like I'd seen cyclists on the telly do. I wasn't going to make it. I looked up at line where the road ended in sky – the top of the hill. It was so close. I grunted with every push. I felt my bike pitch forward slightly, the pedals turned more easily. Blood rushed back down my legs, washing away the lactic acid, as I freewheeled the short flat to a bench by the church. I waited for Abi to arrive, panting behind me. From there we made constant progress and arrived in the town of Yverdon.

Day Sixty-One

On the banks of La Thielle river tributary we found a gîte housed in a whitewash building with red wooden shutters. The reception was not open till later and the building seemed closed up, but walking around the back, I could hear voices from an open door into a conservatory. A man and a woman were inside, talking. They were teachers supervising a school trip from the German-speaking part of Switzerland. I left Abi sitting in the warm while I walked to the nearby supermarket for food.

When I returned, Abi was deep in conversation with the woman.

'Hey.' I threw over a bag of crisps.

'Hey, Sandra was just telling me that we should follow the minor road around the lake from Lausanne to Geneva. She said that the traffic has all mostly shifted to the new road, and that the cycle route winds up and down vineyards a lot.'

'Great.' I nodded, sitting down.

'She also said that it's harder to get lost that way!'

I laughed. 'Abi still hasn't forgiven me for getting us lost on our first ride,' I explained.

'She told me all about it!' Sandra replied, laughing and looking at us both. 'Are you two sisters?' she asked.

'Oh, no, no.' I looked at Abi, telepathically checking she was ok with disclosure. 'We're together, a couple.'

'Oh, sorry, sorry!'

'That's ok,' Abi reassured her. 'We've spent so much time together the last two months I think we've gotten weirdly similar.'

Sandra laughed. 'And you both wear glasses.'

When the manager showed up a few hours later, we secured two bunks in an empty six-bed dorm and revelled in stripping off our layers and laying down in the warm. The gîte was loud with the noises of 30 schoolchildren running up and down the hallways and in and out of dormitories above us, but this couldn't break through the heavy fog of tiredness.

Abi

Day Sixty-Two, Yverdon-les-Bains to Lausanne

'There's a map over in the corner with the route on it. Let me show you.'

A female cycle tourer and her husband had arrived yesterday and were keen to give us tips on the route to Lausanne.

'Look.' She pointed to the gradient map on the back of the route. 'There are only three hills, so you know when you can relax.'

I smiled and looked over at Lili. They pored over the maps, memorising every up and down.

The route was predominantly on roads. We found ourselves battling angry motorists who weren't used to slow, panting cyclists labouring up hills. My legs burned. My chest burned. It hurt. A lot. The worst thing was not being able to stop. I was desperate to give up, to collapse onto the side of the road and wave my white flag, but without a pavement and with the road on a constant bend, there was nowhere safe. The only option was to keep going, to keep pushing. I hated this cycle tour.

At the top of the hill was a chance to rest. I pulled onto the verge and waited for my heavy breathing to calm while the traffic passed. Over the past few days my mood had been shifting between joy and despair. Sometimes I would triumph-antly conquer a hill, proud that I had pushed through the pain and was now a real cyclist. Sometimes I would push on and on only to find my legs had turned to jelly and I had to get off and push my bike, embarrassed that even after almost two months of cycling I still wasn't as fit as the average Swiss child.

'That's two of the big hills done now, love,' Lili shouted back to me. It might have been two of the big hills done, but the route had still surprised us with lots of little ones.

At least the view was distracting. It was bright and cold with clear views of the Jura mountains. Alpine foothills were appearing to the east of us as we made our way towards the largest lake in Switzerland.

'I think this is the last one,' Lili called.

I looked ahead and saw a set of switchbacks snaking up a sheer mountain face. As far as I was concerned, we would need climbing harnesses to summit it.

'I think this is the one JustTofuOfUs took a pic of.' Lili had turned and doubled back to me, a manic smile on their face. 'I'm gonna try and do it in one.'

'Fine with me, at least I can stop if I need to. There's not much traffic, thank God.'

As soon as I began to struggle the cars appeared. Switzer-land was trying to shred my nerves to pieces. I pushed on. I wasn't fuelled by my irrational hatred of JustTofuOfUs like Lili and found the only way I could maintain a rhythm was to count. One, my right foot pushed on the pedal . . . two, my left foot . . . three, my right foot. On and on. I struggled to control my steering as I slowed to a snail's pace. Finally, I saw Lili waiting for me at the top.

'Keep going. You're almost there!' Lili was shouting words of encouragement.

Day Sixty-Two

'Blheaugh,' I replied.

'Try standing for the last bit, it uses slightly different muscles.'

I tried standing and immediately fell back into my saddle.

'Ok, maybe not. Just keep going!'

I pushed up the last few metres and collapsed hyperventilating onto my bike.

'Well done, babe! That was amazing.'

'Thanks,' I panted.

'All downhill from here.'

We waited until my breathing had stabilised and then cycled the short flat along the top of the hill.

'It's gorgeous up here.' Lili smiled. 'I took some pics of you coming up. I'm so proud of you.'

I looked around. Hills of yellow, purple and green rolled off into the distance, until they were lost in the long shadows of mountains. After endless rides through valleys and around hills, it was strange to see the whole sky, the Alps a faint shadow in the distance. The wind whipped across the high plain uninterrupted. I took my helmet off and let the cool air blow-dry my sweat-drenched scalp. I felt like I was standing on the painted set of an old film, everything precise and intentional.

I still hadn't fixed my brakes. We'd tightened the cable as much as possible using the small plastic cog at the brake lever, but we were just too cold to keep trying to fix it properly. I had accepted that occasionally I was going to find myself hurtling downhill, my feet scraping the pavement.

I set off, rolling, the road switchbacked back and forth on a gentle gradient. The steepest parts were at the corners. I felt comfortable; seeing the entire route was reassuring. I knew what I was going to have to deal with and when.

It was then I noticed, racing up the road below me, a large articulated lorry.

My preferred course of action would have been to get off the road and onto a bank or pavement, but there was nowhere to pull in.

The lorry got closer and closer. My main concern was passing it on the straight to give myself as much room as possible. I saw Lili slow and edge past it. Its bulk took up most of the path. At least Lili hadn't died.

The lorry speeded towards me, head on. My knuckles were white from squeezing my brakes. I pulled as far as I could to the side of the road. Just stay on course and keep slow, I thought to myself.

'OH, DON'T WORRY ABOUT SLOWING DOWN OR ANYTHING,' I screamed.

My voice got lost in the roar as it passed, a metre between us. I had created a tail of cars behind me.

I was fed up of being bullied by cars and vans and lorries in Switzerland. I pulled into the centre of the lane. I was realising that taking up space on the road was an important way of making myself safe. At some point I had absorbed the message that I was a less legitimate road user; I didn't pay road tax like car owners. I was struck by a sense of indignation. I was tired of the ways capitalism conspired to make life harder for people living outside of the proscribed system. Cyclists, like me, weren't willing or couldn't afford to enter into the monetary obligation and environmental catastrophe of car travel. We still deserved space on the road.

The road gave way to a path running through a deep valley. We sat and ate our sandwiches under a walnut tree.

'JustTofuofUs definitely took a picture of this, they were foraging here, I swear.' Lili kicked around the empty walnut shells. Once again, we weren't living up to the free-spirited cycle tourer lifestyle.

Day Sixty-Two

We filled our bottles at another of the stone basins, which we'd discovered, thanks to social media, were public water fountains, pumping perfectly clear Swiss mineral water around the country. While social media was a stick we routinely beat ourselves with, it was also an invaluable source of information.

The route rose away from the valley floor and into tiny villages nestled amongst vineyards. We laboured up and up and then stopped. My legs had simply had enough.

'We'll just have to walk it.' Lili sighed, they stepped off their bike and took a second to stabilise themselves. I wasn't the only one feeling it.

The muscles in my forearms and shoulders ached as they took the weight of my pannier-laden bike. An old man in dungarees shouted encouragement to us from his garden, at least, I assumed it was encouragement; it might have been gentle mocking.

A grey stone church marked the top of our ascent. From there, I could see the beginning of a steep decline through woodland to Lausanne. I got on my bike, let go of my brakes and leaned back on my seat. Brown leaves papered the forest floor. I flew down, riding straight through puddles which splashed mud up my legs and over my luggage. The trees thinned. Stretching out endlessly before me was the crisp cobalt waters of Lac Léman.

The path flattened and we rolled onto a busy cycleway heading into the city.

Like most old student houses, the two-storey building looked like a strong wind might knock it over. Hand-painted murals of owls covered the shutters of a single central window. A moss green front door, and matching garage, stood out against the grey pebble-dashed front. Following instructions from Julie we found the spare key and let ourselves in. We stood in a long dark corridor, the walls painted with strange animals and psychedelic patterns.

'Do you think we should say something?' Lili whispered.

We knew that Julie had flatmates, and we weren't sure of the etiquette of entering a stranger's house. Loud music blared from the room to our right.

'We should probably introduce ourselves, right? There's obviously somebody here.'

We stood in the hallway whispering to one another, neither of us wanting to break the peace and engage in awkward conversation.

'At the same time?'

'Ok . . .'

'Hallo?' our voices squeaked through the corridor. Nothing.

'Oh, shit, should we be saying bonjour? Or should we just go hello?' Lili whispered furtively.

'Uh . . . bonjour?' I ventured more loudly this time.

The house stayed still.

'Hello!' shouted Lili.

We heard a shuffle from the room next to us. The door creaked open.

A young blonde girl appeared in the doorway, a cloud of pungent smoke followed and then dissolved into the air. She was wearing a powder blue flannel dressing gown.

'Uh, bonjour, nous sommes . . . ugh . . . les amis de Julie?'

'Oh, you are the cycle tourers, yes? I am Irma. Julie's room is upstairs.' She began to lead us up the pitch-black staircase. 'This is Luc's room, he is in class.' She pointed to a room to her right. 'And this is Julie's room.' She opened the right-hand door to a brightly lit attic. A stud wall divided the main area from a bed made from pallets.

'Thanks so much!' We turned to Irma, but she had already disappeared.

*

Day Sixty-Two

That evening, a thick grey mist descended on the house. We had a guest. Lili beamed and dropped their task, falling onto the floor to play with the cat.

'What are you gonna call him?' I asked Lili, who was currently cat-whispering; turning him into putty in their hands.

Lili pulled up a wet jumper sleeve. 'I guess we'll call him Dribbles.'

I sighed. 'I'm so glad you're wearing my fleece.'

We lit the wood burning stove which had a hand-drawn sign above it: a cartoon of a lit cigarette and the words *La cheminée fume beaucoup.* We settled down into the cosy double bed, deciding to keep the window open a notch so the smoke wouldn't suffocate us.

Abi

Day Sixty-Three, Lausanne

'I don't want to go downstairs,' I moaned.

'We need to meet them eventually, plus we really should cook some lunch.'

It was midday and I still didn't want to get out of bed. The room was warm when the stove was on, but otherwise it was like many student houses – badly insulated, no double glazing, no central heating – the transient nature of its occupants allowing landlords to get away with minimal work. Plus, I really wasn't sure I could cope with meeting and chatting with strangers. I was tired and people were effort. I wanted to conserve my valuable energy.

'Let's just go say hi so they know we exist.'

I sighed. So far I'd only ventured downstairs to use the toilet in the hallway. 'Ok, just give me a second to get dressed.'

Heading into the kitchen we found two students who were drinking tea and sharing a joint.

'Hello?'

They looked up at us. 'You are Julie's guests, yes?'

'Uh, yes.' I replied.

'I am Luc, this is my friend, he does not live here.'

We all gave nodded hellos.

Day Sixty-Three

'Is there anything you need?' he asked.

'Not really. We're very tired. Where is your shower though?'

'Ah.' He indicated to the other side of the kitchen. 'There.'

In the corner of the kitchen was a sink and shower. A heavy curtain on a rail marked out the space for the 'bathroom'.

'When the curtain is shut nobody will open it, you do not need to worry.'

'Thanks.' Lili and I looked at each other. 'I think we'll be fine for now.'

Luc turned back to his friend and they chatted in French while we quietly cooked some pasta. I appreciated that there was no pressure to chat and after a while they left the room, smiling as they passed.

For the rest of the day we bedded down in the attic. Lili played with Dribbles and we kept the stove going for heat. Empty crisp packets built up in piles around the room like miniature cairns marking our movements. We fell asleep warm and happy.

Lili

Day Sixty-Four, Lausanne to Geneva

We extracted ourselves from Julie's room, where we had spent the last 48 hours nesting. We left behind a note of thanks in a DIY guest book, and the lingering smell of the BBQ sauce we'd been eating with everything. As we decanted the panniers to the outside of the house, the rain started in a fine mist. We both changed into wet-weather gear, which essentially involved stripping down to as few layers as possible.

We didn't want to spend money or waste space in our bags on waterproof trousers; we were camping pretty much every night and figured after a day of rain they'd be impossible to dry out. We were cycling in midsummer and early autumn, so they had seemed more hassle than they were worth. Plus, it's hard to find good-quality and affordable waterproof gear in Abi's size. Instead we had waterproof jackets, that also doubled up as windbreakers in the cold, and we wore our cycling shorts. We'd avoided cycling in significant rain so far, but Switzerland was clearly going to keep challenging us.

We followed the advice of the teacher Abi had spoken to in Yverdon and stayed on the N1 out of Lausanne. It was a single carriageway, with a cycle path marked on either side of the road with white dashed lines. It was heavier with traffic than I would have liked, but the occasional glimpses of the steep roads up to the cycle route reassured me we'd made the right decision.

Crossing a roundabout, I spotted a solitary figure on a loaded bike, clad in all black waterproofs that were already shimmering, saturated with rain. After another 500m they were still behind us, and so as soon as we reached a pavement I stopped. The figure pulled up and removed his balaclava to reveal a bearded face.

'Hallo.'

'Hallo,' the man replied. 'Are you cycling to Geneva?'

'Yeah, someone recommended we take the road as the vineyard route is too hilly.'

'They were right!' He laughed. 'I started out on it but couldn't face it any more.'

'Are you going to Geneva too?'

He nodded. 'Shall we all ride together?'

'That'd be great,' I replied.

I appreciated the anxiety of riding alone, and he cut a sorry figure dripping with rain. From a selfish perspective, I was happy to have met another cycle tourer at such a fortuitous point. Though there was a continuous cycle path, sharing the road with cars in a rainstorm wasn't very appealing. The more of us there were, the more visible we were, and the more of a legitimate presence on the road we became. I'd become so aware of the attitude of many Swiss drivers, who passed very close, often accelerating as they went. It felt safer to be cycling as a three rather than as a two.

He smiled. 'I'm Michael.'

'Lili.'

'Abi.' We each replied with a small wave.

Heads down, the three of us powered through the rain for several hours. I kept my eyes on the white lines which blinked by, disappearing under my front tyre. We took turns at the front. I sang old folk songs to keep myself entertained. The road was flat, and occasionally through the grey I caught a glimpse of the broad expanse of Lac Léman. Mostly it was a monotonous ride.

We paused around midday on the outskirts of a town, which stretched up a steep hill from the shore of the lake.

'Maybe we should stop to eat lunch?' Michael suggested.

We skirted the town looking for shelter, but none of us felt like climbing much. Occasionally we pedalled part way up the hill into the centre of town, before giving up and free-wheeling back down.

We continued on the road until it passed through the centre of the small town of Coppet. Here we stopped at the tourist information which, although closed, had a sheltered courtyard attached.

'Better than nothing.' I shrugged.

Michael agreed. 'You ride very fast, and I normally stop much more.'

I looked at Abi sheepishly. We'd been pushing the pace in the rain without noticing. Abi and I rested our bikes against the wall. Our companion did the same, pulling off his balaclava to talk.

'I really needed a break. I am not used to cycling yet.'

'How long have you been travelling?' I asked

'Only about three days.'

'Oh, yeah, you'll definitely get used to it, we've been cycling for nearly two months now,' I said, trying not to sound too much like a know-it-all.

I opened the tin of chickpeas, added the last of our BBQ sauce, salt and chilli, mushed it with a spoon and spread it between thick slices of white sandwich bread. With a final flourish I added a sprinkling of ready salted crisps and smushed the two slices of bread together triumphantly. I looked up to see our Michael observing me thoughtfully.

Day Sixty-Four

'Is this an English thing?' he asked

'Well, crisp sandwiches maybe, but this,' I gestured at the empty chickpea tin, 'is just us.'

He stood up and turned to his bike, pulling off a large bag from the back-pannier rack. From this he pulled a huge sheepskin rug which he unfurled and laid out. He then proceeded to get out his camping stove, a Tupperware of pasta sauce and some dried spaghetti. He settled in to cook.

'Where are you headed?' I asked, through my mouthful of sandwich.

'Spain. A friend of mine has a farm and wants help with the olive harvest.' He stirred his pasta. 'I've only been travelling three days though, and I am already behind schedule.'

It didn't take a genius to figure out why. Half an hour after we had sat down for lunch, Abi and I were getting cold and impatient to get moving again. Finishing off the last of his pasta, Michael pulled a tin kettle from his pack, filled it with water and lit his stove again.

'Where are you staying in Geneva?' I asked.

'I found someone through Couchsurfing, you?'

'We booked a flat for a few days, as a treat. We have not enjoyed Switzerland.'

He laughed.

'And it's very cold,' I said, pointedly.

Perhaps noticing that Abi and I were shivering in our cycle shorts at this point, he finished his tea, rolled up his rug and we headed off again.

We didn't stop again until we arrived at the central train station in Geneva. It had been a long time since we'd been in a city of this size. I was alert, trying to navigate the wide streets filled with cars, buses and trams in the heavy rain. Finally pulling up outside the station, we hurried under cover.

'It was nice to meet you.'

I meant it; riding with a third person had been a nice change.

'You too, and thanks for keeping the pace up.'

I smiled: the cold had been rather motivating, especially as Geneva was getting close. It had been easily 60km and we'd not let up. I gave Abi a questioning look and she nodded. He seemed sound.

'If your couchsurfer falls through this is my mobile.' I scrawled my number on a scrap of paper from my bumbag. 'You can crash on our floor.'

We waved goodbye and navigated the streets to Anton's apartment. Figuring out how to enter the code on the outside of the building, we pushed our bikes through the glass doors, barred with metalwork. In the cool, tiled hallway we unloaded our bikes and began the slow process of carrying all our stuff up the stairs. We dumped the panniers, tent and sleeping bags in the hallway and went to find a supermarket, where we loaded up on food for the next three days.

Walking back into the flat, a strong smell of damp mould hit me.

'Eurgh!' Abi started. 'What is that?'

I looked at the pile of panniers on the floor. 'Abi, I think that smell is us.'

Lili

Day Sixty-Five, Geneva

I slowly stirred out of bed and started to locate the necessary elements to make coffee in Anton's flat. There was a large wooden bureau on one side of the kitchen, its shelves heaving with crockery, pans, trays of cutlery and there, at the back, a stove-top espresso maker. The night before we'd delighted in cooking on a hob, making a huge ratatouille with one of every vegetable. I clattered the dirty pan and plates into the sink, unwilling to face the washing-up.

The rain from yesterday continued, falling heavily onto Geneva's wide streets. We walked in the gloom, feeling small beneath the tall buildings and towards the city centre. We located a large bookstore, palming maps and guidebooks between us, lingering in the small English language section and recoiling at the prices. We bought two, unable to resist the allure of lying in a bath with a book. We also bought a large green map of all the French cycle routes, the same version that Karen had recommended in the campsite in Basel.

The rain drove us inside. At the apartment we ate ratatouille and bread for lunch. I lay in the bath with the newly purchased collection of essays by Roxane Gay driving me to

265

finish my current book (we only ever wanted to carry one book each at a time, so I had an encroaching deadline). The rest of the afternoon passed in a blur. Abi again cooked a huge dinner on the stove top. She was clearly enjoying making use of the hob, and not having to cut corners to save money or camping gas. We ate till we were past full and fell into fitful sleep.

I woke sweating, the geometry of the room shifting, caught mid-flux between place to place, bedroom to bedroom. Where was I?

I threw off the heavy cover, heaved myself out of bed, and blindly ran towards the door.

'Lili? Lili? You're asleep.'

My heart was still pounding, but I could feel the floor beneath my feet. I turned to Abi. She sat up in bed and turned the light on.

'Come back to bed.'

'What time is it?'

'It's 3am.'

I lay in Abi's arms, anxious and tearful, until about 6am. I missed our tent. I missed the routine of cycling, camping, living outside. In the time and space and quiet afforded by Anton's apartment I couldn't avoid the flurry of thoughts in my head.

Despite how much I was enjoying the tour, I was feeling worn out. I could only hope some rest would recharge me, but the nightmare was a clue to something deeper, something that had been growing since I first noticed it in Solothurn. With the first hints of dawn turning the night sky from black to deep blue outside the bedroom window, I fell back asleep.

Lili

Day Sixty-Six, Geneva

I woke again at 10am. Keen to do some sightseeing while we were here, Abi and I headed out to the Red Cross Humanitarian Museum. Situated in large grounds opposite the United Nations building, the museum front was panes of mirrored glass which reflected the paving stones and sky in fragments. In a far corner of the entrance courtyard stood ten grey stone figures, hooded and bound. Inside, the museum explored family, survival, resilience, humanity, and hope through the work and archives of the Red Cross. I wandered through room after room, absorbing the testimonies of persons and communities, evidenced by bureaucracy and paperwork, brought to life by the 12 interactive witnesses who guided you through the rooms. We walked past thousands of yellow cards, documenting civilians and prisoners of war in the First World War, past art from patients in psychiatric institutions. We stood side by side facing a wall adorned with the photographs of children, used in an attempt to unite families. We tried to decipher the French cursive of the original Geneva Convention, signed in 1864.

As I walked through I was struck by this idea of bearing witness – how often we consider it a passive role, how it can be powerful, how it can heal, and bring its own kind of justice. How it isn't enough, how sometimes it's all that's possible.

We left the main body of the museum in silence, and entered a temporary exhibition called 'Ados à corps perdu'. Lost bodies. It was a glimpse of another life, my other life. There was no room for restricting my food intake on the tour – I ate and I cycled, and if I didn't eat, I couldn't cycle. There were still things I found difficult to swallow. Cycling nearly every day, my body was changing in ways out of my control and not by my intention. Wading through these personal accounts of young women deep in their eating disorders, still using food to express such deep distress, I felt a distance and perspective I never thought I would. This used to be the only thing I had, the only thing that made me feel comfortable, safe, the only way I knew to interact with my body, with its needs, with the world. Now I felt like I was in a different place, bridging old and new. Maybe I would never leave it completely behind. Maybe I would always be somewhere along this bridge. But things had already changed in ways beyond my imagination, so who knew what was possible.

I was quiet as we walked down from the museum. The glassy surface of the lake reflected the wide expanse above it, stretching out in a crescent shape from Switzerland, where we stood, to France. We could see in the distance, piercing the bright blue sky, the snowy peaks of Mont Blanc. We followed the shore round, through the Parc de La Perle du Lac. Across the water the Jet d'Eau erupted from the harbour and surged 140m into the air like a strange, wet plinth. We navigated back to the flat through streets lined with expensive shops. The oversized back-lit storefronts, and mannequins dressed in strange clothes, felt totally absurd.

'What do you think then?'

We were sitting at the round wooden dining table in Anton's kitchen, looking over the OS map that included our route from Geneva into France and comparing it to the various descriptions, blog posts and route maps on the netbook.

'I think I don't want to have to cycle over the Alps, when it is already getting cold, when it's all on these yellow roads, when Matteo said it wasn't that good to ride, when we don't have a map and campsites are starting to close.'

Abi nodded her head.

'But I also don't feel great about taking the train. Is it cheating? It feels like cheating.'

'Cheating by whose rules?'

'I don't know, ours? The rules of cycle touring?'

'What's the point if we don't enjoy it?' Abi intentionally echoed my mantra from the start of the tour. She was right, and I was glad that one of us was managing to reason with the invisible rules I'd laid out for the tour.

'Ok.' I pulled up *The Man in Seat 61* – a travel website created to make it easier to navigate trains in Europe. 'So, we could take the train to Vienne, which is just south of Lyon. The Rhône route is all green from there?'

The ViaRhôna is a long-distance cycle route (now a Euro-Velo route), which stretches the length of the Rhône river, from Geneva to the Mediterranean Sea. It is in various stages of completion, with long stretches of signposted, off-road cycling. Abi looked at the map of French cycle routes we'd bought at the bookshop.

'Yeah, it's green from there until way down south in Provence.'

Gears for Queers

I continued to read around – you had to book a bike onto the train and make sure you had proof of that booking as, apparently, they could sometimes try and fob you off. We bought our tickets and downloaded them to the iPod. We didn't have a printer, so that would have to do.

Lili

Day Sixty-Seven, Geneva

'ABBBIIII.'

I flipped back and forth in bed, flailing my arms and legs out and squirming against the sheet.

'Everything feeeellllss wrong.'

Everything felt wrong. The novelty of the flat had worn off; I was getting sick of the walls, the ceiling, the lack of natural light, the warmth. All our clothes were washed, the contents of our panniers scattered around the flat. The washing-up was piled up in the sink from the last few days of enthusiastic cooking, the discipline of living with three pots (one of which doubled up as one of our two bowls) hadn't lasted once we had a seemingly endless amount of crockery.

'What are we going to do today?' I demanded, striding through to the living room.

'Rest?' Abi ventured, knowing this wouldn't do.

We put something on Netflix but I couldn't shake the feeling, couldn't silence the thoughts.

'Maybe we should get high?' I suggested. The joint from our ill-fated trip in Amsterdam was still in an old tobacco tin I also used for spare bike bits. I'd kept the joint more out of a reluctance to throw it away than a desire to keep it.

'I guess. Maybe it will relax us?'

I lit it and we sat out on Anton's balcony, overlooking the modern glass building of a public library across the street. I took just the one toke, handed it to Abi and then extinguished it. My head started spinning. Maybe it was the high anxiety of being away, maybe it was the type or brand of weed, or maybe it was the lingering feeling that I wasn't ready to face or examine. Whatever it was, I was not having a good time.

'I'm throwing it away.' I grabbed the joint and marched to the kitchen bin.

I couldn't wait to get back on the road again, to numb this feeling out with tiredness and movement.

Abi

Day Sixty-Eight, Geneva to Vienne

'We still need to take out the rubbish and download the train tickets,' I called to Lili across the flat. I was fighting to get the tent neatly back into its bag.

I heard a scuffle at the door, as though somebody was trying to get in, and then a knock.

'Who on earth could that be?' Lili rushed in, alarmed. 'We have the flat till midday!'

We opened the door to Anton, recognisable from his online profile. We all stood there in surprised silence for a few seconds.

'The app, it said you had checked out . . .' he began.

'We thought we had until midday,' I replied.

'You do, but it said you had checked out.'

'Oh! We don't know how that happened.'

We stood for a bit longer, not sure how to proceed. I glanced through to the kitchen we still hadn't cleaned and the large bin bags full of our rubbish.

'I will go?' Anton asked.

'Oh, no, no, it's fine, we have to leave at 10 for a train anyway.' I didn't want to stop him from entering his own flat.

Anton hesitated then came through to the living room.

'I'm really sorry, we haven't finished cleaning yet, we thought we had a bit longer.' Lili emerged from the kitchen, rubber washing-up gloves coated in suds.

Anton was very kind and sat at his computer desk as we frantically tidied, cleaned and packed around him.

Lili began trying to charge the iPod so we could use the tickets we'd booked from Geneva to Lyon. 'Abi, it's not turning on, what are we going to do?'

Neither of us are relaxed when confronted with the fixed departure of a train, bus or plane. It's guaranteed we'll be there a few hours before departure time, just in case. Without access to our tickets, I could tell that Lili was immediately close to panic-point.

'It's probably the charger. I'll go get a new one from the shop. You try and get the tickets on the phone.'

It was easy enough to find a charger but arriving back it became obvious that the iPod was not going to wake up. We were coming up to the time we'd planned to leave, and we were both getting frantic.

'Look, let's just do it on the phone and wait and see.'

Anton looked at us in amusement. He had been trying to help but didn't have access to a printer. Downloading them onto the phone took half an hour. Finally, we had our tickets.

We carried our bikes downstairs, grabbed our panniers, thanked Anton for letting us use his flat and apologised for leaving him with a bin bag of rubbish. We set off down the street as bundles of nervous energy. Racing through Geneva's streets we pulled into the huge station and navigated to the correct platform. The waiting room was empty. We checked the time. We still had an hour.

I sat on a bench, rehearsing how we would get our stuff on board. I remembered the pain of pulling our bikes onto the train in the Netherlands. I couldn't stop picturing the train leaving while one of us was left stranded on the platform.

I patted my pocket to make sure I had my bank card, just in case.

As the train pulled into the station, we wheeled over to the conductor to ask him where the bike carriage was.

'There is no bike carriage.'

His curt reply sent me spiralling into a panic.

'Um, what? But we booked our bikes here, it is on our tickets,' my voice squeaked.

He looked down at our tickets. 'Hmm, maybe there is, it will be at that end of the train.' He pointed to the far front carriage.

'Ok, merci, merci.' We hurried along. We had 15 minutes before it departed.

At the front end of the train we couldn't see any evidence of a bike carriage. Usually there would be a bike symbol of some description. Flustered, we asked another member of train staff.

'Where is the bike carriage, please?' we asked. 'Uh . . . où est la carriage du vélo?'

She looked at our tickets and then with a sweep of the hand directed us to the rear of the train. 'C'est à l'arrière!'

We rushed down the length of the train. Ten minutes left. Finding the carriage with the bike symbol on it, we waited anxiously as a portable lift transported a person using a wheelchair on to the train. The doors were narrow, and the wheelchair only just fit, but they made it on, with just enough room for us to squeeze through. All we had to do was get our bikes up eight narrow steps.

'Let's do this thing.'

We had already formulated a plan. Stage one: remove all the panniers and throw our bikes onto the train, one of us pushing from the platform, the other heaving from the carriage. Stage two: after the bikes were in place, chuck the pannier bags in one by one. Stage three: the person on the platform jumps onto the train, just as the doors close.

Lili stood at the top of the steps while I thrust the bike upwards. Then they navigated three more steps onto the bike carriage.

'It's not really a bike carriage!' Lili called back. 'And there's already a bike here.'

'Well, we'll just have to squeeze on, won't we!' I called back, furious at the terrible train system. We'd paid to get our bikes on, and I wasn't going to give up.

Throwing the rest on, I climbed in with seconds to spare. We dragged our panniers through and packed them into the luggage rack. Exhausted and adrenaline filled we collapsed into our seats just as the train pulled out of the station. I looked at the 'bike carriage', an alcove with three bikes spilling out into the aisle. It was typical that cyclists and wheelchair users were forced to share already limited space on the train. It was ridiculously inaccessible.

We arrived at Lyon and Lili took the lead, having travelled through the station once before. We boarded a step-free train and sped across the French countryside to the small town.

It was slightly warmer in Vienne and we changed into our shorts in the filthy station toilet. I was glad that we had skipped the Alps, I think another few weeks in the cold weather would have marked the end of our trip. Our destination for today was a campsite only 25km south of Vienne. It was a relief to be back under our own steam. Train travel was great, but it was never going to be enjoyable with bikes.

Day Sixty-Eight

We cycled down the main street in Vienne. I noticed for the first time the stark change in scenery that came from travelling quickly by train, rather than the gradual changes I observed on bikes. Everything felt suddenly very different: the architecture, colour of stone, layout of streets, location of signs. We turned onto a smooth path which wound its way close to the Rhône. It was our third water route, and I wondered if it was possible to get bored of this type of scenery.

I pedalled alongside the flowing water. Bright green vineyards covered the landscape. We cycled up past orchards and forests, stretching out our legs in the warm sun. After four days cooped in a flat, I felt free again.

The campsite was a large complex with caravans which screamed holiday park. We rode up to the office. It was closed.

'Are we too late?' I looked at my watch. It was 4.30pm.

'They said they were open till 6pm online. I don't get it.'

I wandered vaguely through the park and found the toilet block open. 'It must be open, the loos are!'

I walked back to Lili who had their phone out.

'Look.' Lili pointed to a sign. *Le parc de campement est fermé pour la saison.*

'It means it's closed.' I sighed.

'I'm just phoning to double-check.'

Lili phoned to no answer. It didn't look like we could stay there tonight.

We had a choice to make: keep going or wild camp.

'I really don't want to wild camp,' I moaned. 'I will if I have too, I just don't feel like I have the resources right now.'

'I know. I don't think I do either, but we can't keep going indefinitely.'

'Let's cycle through the village. If we spot anything cheap, we'll stay, if not we give up and wild camp.'

We crossed a wide park and conducted several laps of the commune of Saint-Pierre-de-Bœuf, nestled beside the river. Everything was closed, and there was nowhere we felt comfortable camping.

'Let's cycle back to the path, there were a few spots there which might work.'

We made a beeline through the park back to the cycle route. Beside the road was a small chalet. A sign on it read *Gîte Maison D'Lône*.

'Lili, wait, I think this might be a hostel?'

We cycled around it, the top half sat level with the road and the bottom half seemed to house two holiday apartments built into the hill. There was what looked like an office, but it was currently closed.

'There were definitely a group of people upstairs, shall we try in there?' I asked Lili.

'Sounds good.'

On the road we stood and peered into the room. It looked like a hostel kitchen, busy with people sitting around the kitchen table and preparing food.

'I mean, we may as well check, right? They can always tell us if they're full.'

Lili opened the door and nervously walked in. I was straightening my bike to follow when they ran out, red-faced.

'What happened?'

Lili didn't have time to answer before a confused-looking French woman came out. She turned to Lili quizzically.

'Je suis très désolée, très désolée,' Lili stammered. 'Nous sommes bicyclists, et nous sommes besoins de accommodation. Camping?'

'No, not here. This is a private group. Maybe down the

road.' The woman gestured. 'Maybe camping.' And she shut the door on us.

I looked at Lili, who was bright red and looked mortified.

'I walked in and everyone just turned to stare at me. It was a group of disabled people and their carers. I didn't know what to do. I just thought "well, disabled people stay in hostels too" . . . so I just started chatting in bad French to one of the people, but they didn't understand and then everyone was silent and staring at me then she ran me out. I'd just crashed into their private kitchen like a fool.'

I burst out laughing at Lili's faux pas. 'I doubt they included lost cycle tourers in their risk assessment.'

'Oh, don't! Let's just get going, please.'

We cycled down the sandy path. At the end of it was a modern activity centre. It was nestled on an inlet where the river split. Large posters of kayakers and white-water rafters hung on the building. I wasn't hopeful.

We walked into an empty reception. There was a bell on the desk, so I rang it. On the wall were rates for hostel rooms, but so far, I could see nothing about camping.

A surprised-looking man appeared from a little office to the right. 'Bonjour.'

'Bonjour. Avez-vous des accommodation pour une nuit?'

'Ugh . . . English?'s

'Yes, please.' Apparently, my French was as incomprehensible as all my other languages.

'I am sorry, we do not have any rooms tonight.'

'That's ok.' Lili and I sighed. 'Merci.'

We turned to walk out.

'But you are cycling, yes?'

'Yes.'

'Then you could camp maybe?'

The campsite was completely empty. It had officially closed for the season. The man explained that we could not use the campsite facilities and would have to use the hostel facilities instead. Fine with us!

We arranged to stay for two nights. I hadn't anticipated that campsites would be closed, and this new knowledge left me feeling anxious and vulnerable. Who knew when we'd next find a campsite?

LILI'S STAPLE OILY-COURGETTY PASTA

Essential Ingredients
Courgette (diced), Dried Pasta (spaghetti takes up the least space for its weight), Tomato Puree, Paprika, Oil, Salt and Pepper

Additional Ingredients
Garlic (2 cloves, minced), Onion (Diced)

Method:

Pan 1
1. Put water onto boil. Add the spaghetti and cook until al dente.

Pan 2
2. Sweat the courgette, with the onion and garlic if you have them, in a good glug of oil until soft. Adding a pinch of salt helps them soften faster.
3. Add a load of paprika and black pepper and stir.
4. Add a good squeeze of tomato puree, and a glug of water to make a dry-ish sauce. Keep stirring as it cooks for a few minutes.
5. Add a final glug of oil, and combine your cooked pasta and sauce.
6. Finish with salt and pepper to taste.

France

Abi

Day Sixty-Nine, Vienne

I woke up in a bad mood. I felt terrible. The tent had gotten mouldy after it had spent several days half-heartedly unfurled in Geneva. It smelt like wet dog. My back, hip and knee hurt. I wanted to be back home, where it was warm and easy, and I could lie down on the sofa. We had planned a year away on this tour, but right now I just wanted my mum.

I sat amongst the tall grass outside the tent. It prickled my legs. I was hungry. It seemed I could never eat enough. I reached and started pulling the cooking stuff from the porch – stove top, gas canister. I shook it and listened for how much was left: enough.

'What did you get at the supermarket?' I asked Lili, who was lying inside the tent.

'Food,' they grunted back.

I emptied the shopping bag; out tumbled an onion, canned spinach, baby potatoes and chickpeas for to-morrow's lunch. I pulled a tube of tomato puree and the zip-lock bag of stock and spices from the pannier. I was going to cook us a feast.

I diced the onion and fried it with spices. I cut potatoes one by one into the pot, squeezed in the tomato puree, covered them with water and waited. Everything took longer on the tour. Single bubbles rose in the water. It wasn't like I had anywhere else to be. Back home, everything seemed focused on reducing the time spent performing the tasks of living. We invented electric kettles, ready meals, dishwashers, cars, computers, to free up time for what? I didn't spend my free time at home like this, sitting in nature, nourishing myself. I listened to the rush of water from the rapids, the crackling of autumn leaves in the trees above us. I looked up from the simmering pot. A large pheasant was observing me.

'He's very close,' Lili whispered, having crept out of the tent without me noticing. They sat beside me as I stirred the curry.

The pheasant waddled back into the undergrowth.

Lili

Day Seventy, Vienne to Glun

I sped along the path, stretching my legs on the traffic-free greenway and settling into another day's ride. Sixty kilometres away in the small village of Glun, a little north of the city of Valence, there appeared to be a municipal campsite which was still open. It was getting late in the season and while it was warmer than Switzerland our options were narrowing. We set this as our goal.

The trees were just turning, the yellow-edged leaves cutting crisp outlines in the sky, rivalling the sun for brightness. I was thankful for the paved path and smooth tarmac that took us alongside the river. We passed under bridges: blue metal suspension bridges; bridges with old stone supports that must have predated their current structure. Abi was grateful that we didn't have to cross them. After wearing tracksuit bottoms throughout Switzerland, I was glad to strip back down to my cycle shorts and enjoyed the feeling of the wind on my legs.

We ate lunch on a wooden deck that extended over the bank of the Rhône; standing at its edge I felt suspended over the deep, fast-flowing water. Inlaid into the cycle path beside it was a sign; an arrow pointed one way – 'LA SOURCE – 577KM';

a second arrow pointed the other way. 'LA MER – 235KM'. Only 235km until we reached the Mediterranean. This seemed such a small distance compared to what we had already travelled.

Cloud was rolling in as we crossed a bridge into La Roche-de-Glun 30km later. The town was on an island, the river flowing down either side. The sun was obscured, and the town felt grey and dark. The sharp contrast with the bright and idyllic path was unsettling. We circled the area where the campsite allegedly was, struggling to make out the buildings, closed up for the winter. We stopped.

'What should we do?' Abi asked.

'I thought the woods on the edge of town looked ok, there was a bike track there, and it's already starting to get dark so . . .'

'You think we should wild camp?'

'Yeah, why not?'

We both feigned bravado, not wanting to spook the other, aware our other options were dwindling. We pedalled back towards the trees. We'd drunk most of our water, and didn't know where the nearest shop was, or if it would be open. We would need more, to drink and cook that evening. Just before the entrance to the woods, I spotted an elderly woman gardening. The allotments she was working sprawled out from the blank wall that was the start of a small enclosed village. Abi went over to speak to her.

'She says there's a water pump in the centre of the village, by the church.'

Our French comprehension was significantly better than our speaking. It was a welcome change from Germany and the Netherlands where we had been useless at both.

We found an entrance to the village, squeezed between two houses of an identical light sandstone. We rode up through winding narrow streets. Young children, shouting to each other, scattered as we cycled through; a group converged the other side of us, kicking a football about and sending it flying down a side street. The sound of it echoed through the passageways. At the top of the hill, just down from the church spire that cast a long shadow down the street, was a water pump. Its wooden handle was secured with thick rope, making it impossible to use.

'Guess it's out of action.'

'Shall we just knock next door and ask if they'd fill up our bottles?'

I turned to the house beside the water pump, resting my bike on the traditional brick wall, and stood in front of a modern frosted glass door. With a nervous glance at Abi, I knocked. A small girl answered.

'Bonjour, je peux parler avec votre mère, s'il vous plaît?'

She looked at me quizzically, then turned to face inwards. She was joined at the door by a tall, dark-haired woman.

'Bonjour?' she said.

'Bonjour, s'il vous plaît, je peux avait l'eau?'

I held up my empty water bottle, hoping this would communicate what I needed better than my terrible French.

'Nous sommes cyclists.' Abi gestured to our bikes, stacked up against the wall next to the house. 'Et le pump . . .'

'Of course, of course, bien sûr.'

Her face broke into a smile, and she beckoned us inside. The front room was an open-plan kitchen and dining room, the walls filled with family photos and large pictures of the Pope. The girl regarded us with curiosity as her mum grabbed our water bottles from us and shooed her over to the sink to help her fill them up.

'Je m'appelle Isabelle,' she said over the sound of the tap.

'Je suis Lili, et c'est ma copine Abi.'

'D'où êtes-vous?'

Abi and I looked at each other, attempting to break up the phrase. Où . . . Où . . . where? The woman came back over and, handing us our water bottles, cleared the dining table of papers to reveal a glass-plated world map that covered its surface.

'Where . . . ?'

Two more children had appeared at this point. I recognised the small boy with glasses as one who had been kicking a football outside.

'Ah,' suddenly comprehending. 'Angleterre.' I pointed on the map to Cambridge as they peered over. 'Et après . . .' I traced my finger across the water to Amsterdam, and then south through Europe.

'Et voilà, ici!' I gestured.

'Camping?'

'Oui, oui. Nous avons un tent, mais il n ya pas un campsite ici, donc nous restons dans le . . . ?' I gestured. I was struggling to both retrieve and properly conjugate any French word.

'Quoi? In the woods?'

We laughed and nodded, as if this was something we did all the time.

Isabelle looked thoughtful for a moment.

'You could stay here.' She paused. 'My husband is back late. I have to take the children to piano practice. After that you could come and eat and sleep here.'

'Really?'

'Yes, yes, of course.'

'Merci, merci beaucoup!'

'Come back at 6pm, then I will be back and we can cook.'

'Don't worry about cooking for us er . . . nous sommes vegans, mais nous avons pasta et beaucoup food, ce n'est pas une problem.'

'No lait, fromage, oeuf, et vegetarian?' Isabelle asked.

Day Seventy

We nodded.

'C'est bon, it is . . . not a problem.'

We left and sat on a bench by the cycle path as the sun set. I read in the dwindling light, putting on layers as it got cooler. At 6pm we cycled back into the village, and nervously knocked on Isabelle's door. It opened to a kitchen of heat, light and noise. The little boy ran out.

'Jean-Claude will show you where to put your bikes, around the side.'

We left our bikes in the crowded garage and stepped through. The table had been cleared of papers, and the kitchen was a hub of activity.

'Bonsoir, girls. This is Louise-Clare.'

Isabelle gestured to the child beside her at the stove who was standing on a wooden stool to stir a large pot, steam erupting.

'That is Marie-Anne,' Isabelle gestured to the girl setting the table, who smiled and waved. 'And that,' she nodded to the blur of small boy that ran past us, 'is Jean-Claude.'

He turned and smiled, his eyes magnified by his thick glasses.

'You must want to get changed and washed.'

Suddenly I realised how we must have looked in Isabelle's eyes: weathered, tired and with a perpetual layer of dirt from being outside all the time.

'You are in Louise-Clare's room, there is a bed and we have also a mat. Upstairs, on the left.'

We grabbed our two sleep panniers from the back of the bikes and went upstairs to the room. Louise-Clare's room was simple, with white walls and dark wooden floorboards. It was divided by a curtain. On entering we came into an enclave. This area was clearly used for prayer; it was dominated by a large fireplace, lined with grey stones, with a low wooden bookcase, stool and two small benches. On the bottom shelf were books, a simple large wooden crucifix and candles. In the centre of the top shelf sat an image of Joseph, Mary and the baby Jesus, all gilt in gold. To its left there stood a framed photo of a pope. To its right, the most recent Sunday school teachings sat open on a book stand. Scattered everywhere across the surface of the shelves, the items and trinkets of ritual. The main part of the room was the room of a nine-year-old; a single bed, a small bookcase with collections of *Harry Potter* and *Lemony Snicket*, a desk for her homework decorated in metallic stickers.

I laid out my sleeping bag on the mat by the fireplace.

'I'm thinking,' I cocked my head towards the large photo of the Pope staring over at me, 'that we're just friends here.'

'Yeah, I agree,' said Abi. 'I don't think it's a big deal.'

'No, me neither. I think it's probably obvious, but it's not relevant and I don't want to make them uncomfortable. Isabelle is making us feel so at home, why make a point of it?'

'Agreed. We are friends. We share a flat. Simple.'

I went through to wash my hands. I tucked my hair – scruffily grown out from a buzzcut – behind my ears and smoothed it with water. It was far from simple. Visibility is powerful. As someone with privilege many in my community do not have, I felt a keen sense of responsibility. I did not want to perpetuate the shame that it is so easy to internalise, I wanted to help hold the space open for others and I wanted to hold my partner's hand in the street.

Submerging my queerness was a reflex, I reflected. In the years I'd spent under mental health services I'd hidden it; I didn't want this private part of me pathologised or problem-atised. I wasn't prepared for my gender or sexuality to be examined under that lens. Even before then, I'd been so concerned with hiding any difference from my peers that I'd refused to look at it. It took years of feeling safe to allow me to be seen, and it didn't take much to send my hands scrunched anxiously back into my pockets. Visibility was a choice that didn't come easily to me.

I wanted to hold Abi's hand in the street, and being visibly queer felt like a price I paid for that. I wanted to stay at Isabelle's house, and not being visibly queer felt like a price I paid for that.

None of these internal and external discussions and calculations diminished how welcome I felt in that house, in part I suppose because it was no different than navigating every other house, every other space on the tour, in our relationship, in our lives, where Abi and I had stayed 'friends' until we read the signifiers that it was safe to be more. During this conversation I slipped on my long-sleeved layer. The house was warm, but I didn't want them to see my self-harm scars which, thick and ranging from bright white to bright pink, criss-cross the length of both my arms. We could count ourselves lucky that we could choose to make these things, these parts of ourselves, invisible for a night.

We came back downstairs.

'Can we help?' Abi offered.

'No, no. Sit, sit!'

We sat at the table, and it filled with crusty batons of bread on a long wooden bread board and bowls of thick, black olive tapenade. We were joined by the three children and Isabelle.

'Je ne sais pas en anglais,' started Isabelle, 'c'est tapenade.'

'C'est le meme en anglais, tapenade,' Abi ventured.

We demolished the salty black paste, spooning it onto thick chunks of fresh baguette. The children tucked in enthusiastically. The plates were cleared, and the tapenade replaced with mounds of pasta and vegetables.

'Jean-Claude est allergique au lait.' Isabelle gently stroked his head. 'On ne mange pas beaucoup de lait.'

I did French up to GCSE, while Abi had studied an extra two years, up to A-Level, and was overall the better linguist. However, what I lacked in vocabulary or grammar, I made up with enthusiasm and a desire to tell a story. This worked particularly in my favour with the kids who all seemed to greatly enjoy my part-mime, picture book storytelling as I described our journey so far.

We were full of bread, olives and pasta, relaxed and warm and happy. The table was cleared a second time. Poached pears, sprinkled with flaked almonds and drizzled with dark chocolate, were placed in front of us. I couldn't believe our luck.

With dessert demolished and the table cleared, the kids got on with their English homework while we sat and chatted and attempted to help. They were doing a vocab exercise centred around a traditional English Christmas.

'Bunting?'

'Would you call that bunting?'

'Is there another word for it?'

'Garland? Would you call that a garland?'

The kids looked at us bemused.

Abi

Day Seventy-One, Glun to Saint-Georges-les-Bains

'Merci beaucoup!' I called to Isabelle, her husband, David, and the kids as we pedalled off down the cobbled path. We were both glowing with happiness. They had surprised us that morning with a breakfast of fresh bread straight from the local bakery and a selection of jams, including a home-made chestnut spread. Then, in another act of kindness, they had sent us off with two large baguettes.

'I can't believe how lucky we are!' Lili gushed.

'That was so lovely. They were so lovely.'

'It just makes you feel better about the world, right? Like, you go through life being told you should fear strangers and then you realise that actually the majority of people don't want to hurt you.'

We'd asked Isabelle for water, and been met with a whirl-wind of kindness, food, warmth, shelter. The people we'd contacted on Warmshowers had been unflinchingly gener-ous. Even Tommy, if unsettling, had let us camp in his garden and fed us huge bowls of porridge.

Still, my assessment of risk was haunted by the people I'd been taught to be afraid of: strangers who wanted to hurt me, farmers who guarded their land with shotguns. Some people *would* want to hurt me. Us.

My anxiety, and the limits it placed on both of us, stopped me from doing the tour how I felt it should be done. The stories I read about cycle touring all suggested that if you asked, the world would provide. Ride hard, pitch camp wherever, don't be afraid. Cycle touring culture encouraged looking for the best in people. To suggest I felt scared and that maybe not everyone could be trusted felt at odds with everything I'd come to believe cycle touring was.

Last night, our vulnerability had left us open to a lovely experience but I was still afraid.

Lili and I crossed a short bridge and cycled down onto the riverside path. From overhead, a man on a moped kept honking his horn. I tried to ignore it, hoping he wasn't heckling us. Lili stopped and turned.

'Is that . . . ?'

We waited, the man on the moped drove down to us. It was David.

'Bonjour, c'est bon?'

'Ah, oui. Tu as oublié ça!' He pulled out my fleece and handed it to me.

'Oh my God, merci, merci! C'est mon seulement.' I tried to express my relief as the fleece was my warmest layer and I definitely needed it for the rest of the tour.

'Pas problem, pas problem.' David got back onto the moped and rode off, waving as he went.

'THEY ARE SO LOVELY,' we practically screamed at each other.

The ViaRhôna ran straight along the river again. My tyres glided across the smooth tarmac. Rolling white and green hills rose to the east of us, whilst the sky stretched on forever to the west. The earth was pale and parched, and tiny lizards took full advantage of the autumn sun, bathing on the path and causing us to swerve around them.

In Valence we needed to cross the wide river. I gripped my handlebars tightly as I rode onto the pavement beside the busy road, the water rushing beneath me. The wind whipped around my head as I rose to the middle of the bridge.

'Just keep heading straight.' I whispered my mantra. I was cycling too slowly, my handlebars swayed under my grip. One wrong turn and I'd flip over the metal barrier and straight into the river below.

I stopped and stepped off my bike. My eyes were struggling to focus. I tried not to look down or around. I didn't want to orientate myself, didn't want to remind my brain that I was suspended 50 foot above water. A strong gust of wind swiped at my glasses. The bridge was trying to blind me. It wanted me to stumble around unseeing till I tripped and threw myself to a watery grave.

I tried to get back onto my bike but knew that my unbalanced leg would tip me instantly into the water, or the traffic. I began plodding, pushing my bike towards the other bank. I could feel its full weight. If I dropped it, it would somehow bounce over the railing.

Lili waited for me on the other side.

'You forgot this.' They handed me a piece of string which attached my glasses round my neck. I grabbed it and put it in my basket. I'd be better prepared for the next bridge.

I had a renewed confidence that we would find somewhere to sleep after staying with Isabelle, and I let myself simply enjoy the route. We hadn't been riding long when we spotted a small municipal campsite.

'It looks open!' Lili exclaimed.

'Shall we go for it?'

'We've only cycled 20km.'

'I know. I wouldn't mind a rest though.'

Lili looked at me kindly. 'I'm not gonna lie, I would too.'

It was decided. We pedalled up to the entrance, paid the cheap fare to the person behind the bar and found a nice grassy pitch. As soon as we had pitched our tent, we both fell straight asleep in the afternoon sun.

Lili

Day Seventy-Two, Saint-Georges-les-Bains to Mondragon

Waking sluggishly in the sunshine, I kept my eyes closed as I flexed first my right foot, then my left, working my way up from my toes: heels, ankles, knees. Arching my butt off the floor in my sleeping bag, I pulled back my shoulders. This process conducted an orchestra of joints and tendons, which clicked and grated and popped.

I willed myself out of my sleeping bag and towards the stove in the porch. I lit it, poured the remainder of a water bottle into our saucepan, and settled it on top of the flame. Once it boiled, I poured it straight into my cup, added a glug of instant coffee granules and stirred it with the first piece of cutlery I could lay my hands on: the handle of last night's fork. I felt the furthest possible from the athletic Tour de France riders that illustrated the enamel mug I was drinking from.

Abi was starting to move about in the tent, so I kept the stove on and started the process of making porridge, despite her never-ending complaints. We plodded through our morning routine and left at 10am. It was going to be a long ride to Mondragon. Today was the end of the signed ViaRhôna route. We were heading into uncharted waters, and for the last 20km we would be riding on roads without a formal cycle route (or any signs) to cling onto.

The greenway sped out from under us, its slick, frictionless surface a sharp contrast to its German equivalent. The route was taking us straight through the south of France, the Rhône river we followed dividing the Drôme region from the Ardèche. We were heading towards Provence.

The sun was bright, and though the air had a chill it was dry and comfortable. The path was sand-coloured, and soft hills were speckled with greens and purples and browns. The leaves on the trees were now starting to fall and the skyline was shaped by the hills we passed. We stopped at a park to eat, with public toilets (including an accessible toilet for wheelchair users) and a view of the river. I enjoyed our usual chickpeas with a fresh baguette, serving them to Abi with a flourish. The upgrade in bread from the thick and cheap sandwich bread of Lidl in Germany (and Denner in Switzerland) had elevated my chickpea and crisp mush to 'smashed chickpeas' served with artisan bread. It had the same basic ingredients; the key was in the presentation.

We followed the river further into the shadow of a huge cooling tower. Staring up at its looming bulk, I was struck by the stark contrast with the image painted on it: a small child playing in a swimsuit on the shore of a beach.

Zone Nucléaire. À Accès Réglementé. Accès Interdit Sans Autorisation was written in thick white letters on a red sign secured to the chain-link fence.

We skirted the edge of the large complex. France's main energy source is nuclear power, but other than an ominous warning at the campsite near Vienne this was the first sight of it. We continued down long straight paths, bordered by tall grass and white cliffs carpeted in shrubs of a deep green. We crossed the wide river on a concrete bridge, Abi muttering silent prayers, and continued on the opposite bank past

Day Seventy-Two

freshly ploughed fields, picking out the shadows of castles on top of hills as we passed. French villages snaked up roads away from us; the houses small lightly coloured boxes suspended on the hillsides.

'Fuck off. Fuck off. Fuck off.'

Abi's profanity-laden spell didn't work. The bridge was still there. Stretching out from an old stone gateway was a long metal suspension bridge, wide enough for two people, or one person plus bike. The path across it was suspended by vertical bars and half encased with mesh. It was so long there was a second tower in its middle, dividing it into two seemingly infinite halves.

Ne pas utiliser en cas d'orage was written on a red warning sign, accompanied by an image of a figure being struck by three bolts of lightning from a low cloud.

'Nope. It's not happening. Nope. Nope. Nope.'

Abi had tolerated every bridge so far on our journey. Even on the longer ones across the Rhône, she had gripped tightly to her bike, attached her glasses to string around her neck and powered on, step by step. This one would be testing. We made our way under the gatehouse and looked out across the expanse of the bridge, crossing the wide valley of the Rhône from region to region.

'I can't. I just can't.'

'Ok, I'm going to wheel both of our bikes across. Then I'm going to come back for you, and we will walk it together and I will keep you safe.'

I started off with my bike.

'Please be careful.'

I turned around to see Abi's face looking as if she was waving me off to my death. Second only to her fear that she would clumsily plummet over the edge of a bridge was the fear that I would do the same.

I tried to give her a reassuring smile, but my mouth could only form a half-hearted grimace. Steadily walking across, I got into a rhythm, the bridge swaying and wobbling slightly as I crossed it. Suddenly I felt it jar and jolt, as if it was tensing to throw me off. I braced. I shot a panicked glance behind me, trying to figure out what was going on. A small child was bounding towards me on the bridge, sending waves reverberating along it. He seemed to be enjoying himself. I hurried to the midway point; the swaying increased the further from the bank I got. In the middle stone gatehouse, I rested my bike, waited for the child to run past me, and returned the way I had come for Abi's bike. I wheeled it across. I then returned a final time to collect Abi. I put my hand around her waist, took her hand in front of me. We were dancing a Gay Gordon.

'Ok, we are just going to take it one step at a time.'

'Does it wobble?'

'Yes, but not a lot,' I lied. 'It's perfectly safe. Just fix your eyes on the gatehouse, and don't look down.'

'Ok.'

We made slow progress across the first half of the bridge. Arm in arm.

'It's ok. Everything's fine, we're just going for a nice stroll. Just one foot in front of the other.'

Abi was having none of it. 'We're going to die, we're going to die, we're going to die.'

'Just one foot in front of the other,' I repeated in a singsong voice.

Once we'd reached the stone support in the middle, I set off again with Paula, then Patti, and finally retrieved Abi. Stepping off the bridge, she let out a long breath.

We continued along the other side of the river on a wooden path made of planks through a nature reserve, tall cliffs on either side. Back on the road, we passed a sign for *La Ferme aux Crocodiles.*

'This is like the start of a *Godzilla* film.' I pointed to the sign.

'Yeah, let's just put a crocodile farm down river from the nuclear power plant,' said Abi. 'No foreseeable problems there!'

'This is it.'

We came out onto the road from the cycle path and stopped. That was it, the end of the completed ViaRhôna. We'd graduated from greenway to road. We didn't have time to linger on this; the campsite reception closed in a little under an hour, and we were still 17km away. All the anxiety about cycling on roads again was replaced by an urgency. I pedalled hard and fast, nose to the white lines, assertively taking on turns and roundabouts. We crossed the river, swung off a final large roundabout and through an underpass taking us beneath the N7 (the large French motorway heading south) and up, up, up through the village of Mondragon. We staggered through a forest of tall, rusty pine trees that climbed the steep hillside. Abi fell behind. Bum off the saddle, I powered up the last 100m, even though the few minutes between myself and Abi wouldn't make a difference, and pulled up breathless and triumphant at reception.

Camping la Pinéde en Provence was a holiday park with static caravans, space for tents and, in the summer season, a swimming pool. Our pitch was at the very back of the campsite, which sprawled upwards, on one of the ledges cut into the hill and surrounded by trees. It was a steep walk down to the toilet block and back up again. The air was damp and the forest floor carpeted with pine needles. Abi pitched the tent while I cooked our current favourite: chickpea curry.

As I crouched over the stove, Abi started flailing her arms and legs in an erratic happy dance, releasing some of the adrenaline from the ride. Her happiness was catching and I stood up to join her, moving in some kind of forest ecstasy.

Lili

Day Seventy-Three, Mondragon

Rain was gently pattering onto the tent. It wasn't as cold as Switzerland, but the dampness was heavy in the air. It made everything suddenly, unavoidably, autumnal. I unzipped the tent door. I scanned the porch for any animal or insect that may have taken up residence during the night. I spotted a small brown object the colour of a dead leaf, furled in on itself, in the far corner. A dead spider. I reached out to pull one of the smaller red pannier bags towards me to start making coffee. As I grabbed it, the dead spider sprung to life, jumped over and scurried out under the tent.

'Ah!' I recoiled back into the inner tent, zipping the door behind me.

Abi startled awake. 'What? What?'

'Spider,' I whimpered.

Abi nodded. Everything made sense. She lay back down as I composed myself. Slowly and cautiously I unzipped the tent and, keeping my eyes peeled, proceeded to rearrange the panniers and make coffee.

As I was boiling the water, I could hear Abi hacking in the tent. This was not a good sign. The day before had been nearly a 100km ride, and I'd known from our mad and exhausted dusk-time dancing the night before that we were heading for a fall. I watched the flames tickle the bottom of our cheap pans.

I was finally acknowledging the heavy feeling in my gut, the reality that I hadn't wanted to face. I wasn't feeling right. I wasn't sure why, or what quality of 'not right' and I didn't want to put it into words for myself. I certainly didn't want to talk to Abi about it. I poured the boiling water into my enamel mug and stirred in the instant coffee granules.

'*What's the point of doing this if we don't enjoy it?*' What was the point? I had already well surpassed the limits I set for myself, the limits set for me by mental health services, probation services, limits set by years of diagnoses, blue flashing lights and chaos. Now I felt myself edging close to my actual limit. Every time I tried to think about what came next, about our plan to stay away indefinitely, I came up against a block. It all felt so completely overwhelming. I was used to feeling like I couldn't do something and pushing myself to do it anyway. It was a new feeling to know, somewhere deep down, that this was too much. When we'd left, everything had seemed impossible. Now two months later, I was getting a clearer picture of what was possible. I'd been out of hospital two years, out of mental health services six months, out of probation services three months, and on the road for two. Maybe I was running before I could walk.

I did what I do best, what I'd practised for years and years and years. I boxed it. I took it and pushed it far back. I called it tiredness. I silenced it. I looked away.

Abi

Day Seventy-Four, Mondragon

The night was hellish. I had wrapped up as warmly as I could and still I couldn't stop shivering. The cough which kept me awake was deep and chesty. Every time I lay back I would be jolted up, spluttering up green phlegm. Our last ride was still in my mind. It had been the best ride ever and I was desperate to hold onto the feeling of speed, and competence, and sheer joy. I had planned to keep going today, to ride hard and fast with my new-found confidence. I couldn't help but feel I was being punished.

As dawn rose, I finally fell into a fitful sleep.

When Lili woke me it had only been half an hour. 'How you feeling?'

I could tell this was a formality, that they only wanted one answer and that any other might send them spiralling into misery.

Lili had been finding the tour harder and harder. It was mentally and physically challenging in ways neither of us had expected, and I could tell they needed to keep going.

As much as I didn't want to let them down, I had to be honest. 'Terrible,' I wheezed. 'I think I have a chest infection.'

Lili looked at me. I could see the struggle occurring in their head: the strong desire to care for me versus the desperate need to keep going, to not stop, to block out whatever thoughts they were finding unbearable.

'It's ok. Try and get some more sleep, yeah?' Lili closed the tent door. I was worried about them, but I knew there was little I could do. Propping my head up with Lili's dry bag, I fell back to sleep.

Later that afternoon Lili came crawling in with some food. 'Eat this?'

I looked at the pasta. 'I really don't think I can. I think I'm really ill.'

'I'm sure it's just a cold, baby. You'll feel better tomorrow.'

I wasn't convinced. The cold and damp weren't helping the pain in my chest. What I wanted now, more than anything, was to be inside. 'Can we look at hotels, please? I really don't think I can keep going.'

Lili looked at me again. I could tell that whatever was eating them up wasn't allowing them to care for me in the usual way. 'Honestly, I don't think there's anything near here.'

'What about one of the caravans in the park then? Would you go and talk to the man? I don't care if it's expensive.'

Lili frowned. 'Sure, just let me work myself up to it, yeah?'

Agitated, they ate their pasta. I felt myself falling back to sleep.

At length, the tent unzipped and Lili crawled back in. 'I went to check and they don't have anything here. You're just gonna have to keep going in the tent.'

I was snuggled under both sleeping bags, in all my clothes, surrounded by phlegm-covered tissues. I hadn't peed all day – the toilets were just too far.

I knew Lili wasn't trying to be unkind, they were doing their best to look after me, but I couldn't keep going like this. I burst into tears.

'Oh, baby.' Lili snuggled up to me, face softening. 'It's ok, you'll feel better soon.'

'I just need to have a look for somewhere else.'

'That's fine, we'll do it in a bit. I just, I . . .' Lili's features started to curl inwards. They burst into tears.

The two of us held each other in the tent, both sobbing violently.

I stroked Lili's hair and pulled them closer. 'Baby, what are you thinking?'

'I just don't think I can do this any more,' they began reluctantly. 'I definitely don't think I can stay away for a year. I just feel at my limit. I feel done.'

'What do you mean? Do you want to stop?'

'No. Yes. I don't know. I just know I never thought I could do this and now I have, I am, but there's a part of me that is reaching its limit. I'm fed up of having limits.'

'It's ok.' I manoeuvred myself so I could cough some more.

Lili held me tightly. 'I don't want to stop now, but maybe we could stop after Christmas. Maybe we don't cycle into Spain. I don't know. I feel like I'm letting you down.'

'Don't be so stupid,' I replied. 'You never let me down. We had no idea how we'd find this, and we always said we'd stop if it got too much.'

Lili sniffed. 'Are you sad?'

'Of course I'm sad about the idea of stopping, I'm not going to lie, but let's find a way to do this that works for both of us.'

Lili nodded and fell into my arms.

As Lili cried next to me, I let my emotions wash over me. I felt a strong sense of loss for the tour we'd planned, but there was also a sense of relief. We'd talked about spending winter in Spain then heading through Italy and Croatia, but now Lili was saying that not even Spain was looking possible. Lili had vocalised a painful fact: I was reaching my limit too.

I knew, though, that finishing now wasn't the end of the world. There would be another time to cycle other routes. What mattered now was working out what we could still manage.

That and finding somewhere warm for me to bed down.

Lili

Day Seventy-Five, Mondragon to Bollène

Abi lay hacking up phlegm while I assessed the situation. We had two bikes, all the bags, a motel room booked 6km away and Abi wasn't in a state to ride. Keeping my eyes peeled for spiders, I pulled the panniers out of the tent porch and began packing up everything but the tent and Abi's sleep stuff which she was currently cocooned in.

'Ok, darling, I'm going to need to pack up the tent.'

Abi shuffled out, clasping her unzipped sleeping bag around her shoulders. She had dark rings under her eyes, and underneath her tan she was pale. I walked her down to one of the picnic benches and continued to take down the tent.

Leaving Abi sitting with the tent and four pannier bags, I started off on my bike. The D26, a small wiggly white road on the map, took me straight from the campsite to the town of Bollène. The road was quiet. A lot of traffic was using the larger motorway that ran parallel, and there was a marked cycle lane. I was used to cycling on my own, on my exploits to find food or water after we'd pitched camp somewhere. I settled my anxiety with the rhythm of the pedals, setting a relaxed pace. The road was bordered by fields and lined with trees, the only building the occasional farmhouse – rough casted in an off-white. I arrived in Bollène, the buildings lining the streets a mix of new build and traditional Provençal buildings, different shades of yellow, ochre and brick with bright blue or teal wooden shutters and terracotta roof tiles. Traffic merged with the small road. I slowed and navigated across town to a final, huge roundabout. There the hotel sat, at a junction with the motorway that curved past.

I dismounted as I approached. There wasn't a cycling infrastructure built in, and given the size of the roundabout and speed of the cars I wasn't keen on navigating it on my bike. Walking round, I could see the tollbooth to the motorway, and to its right the McDonald's which backed onto the cheap motel we had booked the evening before. I followed the small road. Leaving my bike outside I went in.

'Bonjour,' the receptionist greeted me.

'Bonjour. J'ai un réservation. Mais, je voudrais un taxi, parce que ma copine est malade et en Mondragon. Nous avons vélos. Si vous plaît.'

'Un taxi?' She spoke slowly, kindly. 'Pour ici?' She pointed down.

'Oui, de ici à Mondragon, et après, de Mondragon à ici.' I made a series of circles with my finger, trying to indicate a return journey.

'Bon.'

She picked up the phone and spoke for a while in French.

'Votre nom?' she asked

'Cooper,' I replied, hoping I'd understood.

'Dix minutes,' she said, holding up ten fingers.

'Merci. Il y a un place pour mon vélo?'

She showed me through to a cleaning cupboard, where I was able to leave my bike.

'Votre chambre est prête.'

Day Seventy-Five

I dumped the panniers in the simple hotel room and sat outside waiting for the taxi.

A silver car pulled up, and a friendly-looking woman beckoned me over from the driver's seat.

'Un taxi pour Cooper?'

I climbed in.

'Mondragon?'

'Oui, merci.'

How I pronounced these two words was enough for her to figure I was not a native, or even competent French speaker. I wanted to communicate the round trip to her, how she would be dropping me off, but picking Abi up, because I wasn't sure how much had been conveyed on the phone.

'Ma copine est très malade. Nous restons—' my intonation went up, as I guessed the conjugation of the verb '—en un campsite en Mondragon. Nous voyageons,' I committed at this point to sticking -ons onto every verb I was trying to say in the plural, 'en vélo, en Hollande, Deutschland . . . no . . . Allemande, Suisse et, en présente, ici en France. Ma copine est en campsite. J'ai fait du vélo ici, et après, elle est en un taxi, et je faire son vélo.'

We were heading quickly out of Bollène and back along the road I'd just travelled. I hadn't been in a car for a while, and the speed was disconcerting. At the campsite, what I'd been trying to explain became obvious with the sight of Abi, looking like death, surrounded by pannier bags. I loaded her into the taxi, they set off and I followed on Abi's bike. As the taxi disappeared down the road, I realised the flaw to our plan. I had all our cash in my bumbag, which was currently around my waist, which meant Abi had nothing to pay with. I could have called, but that would have wasted time, especially if the taxi driver decided to wait for me to arrive to be paid. Instead, I started sprinting.

It was strange riding Abi's bike, markedly smaller than my own and significantly lighter too. The thin racing tyres, lack of a load and the fact that I'd ridden this route before meant I was able to push the speed. It was a 6km dash. We'd ridden fast for the joy of it before, pulling back when our legs started hurting or our lungs burning, and I always kept something in reserve – because I didn't know what would come up. On the road to Bollène I didn't have to hold back, because I was heading to a hotel room, and I couldn't afford to ease off when I was tired because I needed to get there as quickly as possible. Chasing an invisible taxi was an effective motivation. After the emotional turmoil of yesterday, riding in an uncomplicated way, with a single purpose and to my physical limits, broke through some of the lingering cloud of fear and anxiety and reminded me that I did, at least, enjoy cycling.

I crashed into the hotel car park to see Abi sitting at the bench out front.

'I'm so sorry, babe.'

'I didn't have any money to pay her with!'

'I knew, I realised literally as you headed off. I pegged it here.'

'It's ok, she didn't understand at first, but I think she trusts us. I said I'd text her when you got here.' Abi was composing a message on her phone.

'Let's go inside and get warm. I'll sort it.'

The taxi driver arrived a few minutes later, and I paid the full fare plus a big tip to apologise. I came back to the room to find Abi, a grey dot inside a bundle of bright white duvet. She fell asleep almost immediately, curled up in the single bed. I lay on the other bed and read. At lunchtime, I walked across to the McDonald's next door and bought several large portions of chips and a huge Diet Coke. I ate them in bed, Abi picking at bits. I refilled the Diet Coke cup with tap

Day Seventy-Five

water. We spent the evening watching telly. Our only link to the outside was the small square window of blue sky and flat roof beside my bed.

I felt better for having been able to look after Abi. I felt better for having vocalised my greatest fear – that I wasn't able to do this. I felt better for having ridden in a way that made me feel physically confident.

I felt as if I could do some of this after all.

Abi

Days Seventy-Six, Seventy-Seven and Seventy-Eight, Bollène

The next three days blurred into one. The room was tiny but clean and warm and I felt safe snuggled into the duvet. After the first night my breathing felt easier. I slept a lot, relying on Lili, the hunter-gatherer, to bring regular meals of Subway salad sandwiches, McDonald's chips and peach iced tea.

On the second day, I spent more time awake, already feeling stronger after a good long sleep. We watched *Friends* and I dozed on Lili's chest. In the afternoon I decided to join them on a walk to the supermarket around the corner. We stocked up on throat lozenges and paracetamol and attempted to choose cheap healthy food to make in the room. We ate warm baguettes filled with beetroot, pickles and salad, and I collapsed back into bed.

Lili was beginning to get cabin fever and was happy to see me feeling better by the third day. I felt guilty about making them spend so much time locked in this cell-like room, but I was relieved I wasn't going to need to see a doctor. The single window of the room looked directly onto a flat roof, so Lili decided to cook some real food and sat on the windowsill making spaghetti bolognese with the stove, which we ravenously ate, enjoying the break from sandwiches.

Days Seventy-Six

Lili had spent the day unpacking and repacking our pannier bags. We had decided we would follow the Rhône to the sea and reach Montpellier. From there, we would send our bikes home and travel into Spain on foot, giving us the flexibility to hop on and off trains and allowing us to make the journey back to the UK whenever we needed to. I hoped this change of pace and the ability to 'tap out' would help Lili. With the decision made they had gone into a flurry of activity; since we were going to send home a large amount of our kit in Montpellier, it made sense to use the sheltered space of the hotel to organise our stuff. There were a few items left to sort.

'What about this?' Lili asked.

I laughed.

'Yeah, I'm not sure when we thought we'd use that in a tent.'

Out of all the ridiculous things we'd bought on the tour, there was one which stood out as the most ridiculous, yet each time we'd sent stuff home it had somehow survived the cull.

Lili held up our purple strap-on.

'Well, better make use of it before we send it home.'

I smiled. I was definitely feeling better.

Abi

Day Seventy-Nine, Bollène to Avignon

I may have given the impression that I was on the mend the night before, but I still feeling rough the next morning. Lili was beginning to cough, and I was secretly hoping that their illness would keep us grounded in the hotel for a bit longer. I didn't want to overdo it and end up sick again in another campsite.

'Are you *sure* you're ok?' I asked Lili, for the fortieth time.

'I'm fine, stop asking,' Lili replied, clearly agitated. 'I really can't stay here any more, and you said you were feeling ok.'

'I know. But I need to go slow, ok? I'm still not 100 per cent, y'know.'

I packed up my panniers and got ready to go. I was uneasy about the ride and I found myself feeling frustrated with Lili. Maybe I needed to stay longer. Why did they always push me so much when I wasn't ready?

We paid up and headed to the McDonald's next door. Sitting in the sunshine on the outdoor seating, I pushed my frustration down and sipped on a peach tea. If we were heading off today, I may as well make the most of it. I did

Day Seventy-Nine

enjoy cycling, after all. I had missed the feeling of the sun on my face.

We were both nervous about our first day off a signed cycle path and we had scoured online for the best road to take. Google Maps had suggested a path which ran alongside the Canal de Donzère-Mondragon.

The towpath was gravelled and bumpy. Potholes and large rocks littered the surface, designed specifically to throw the unprepared cycle tourer off their bikes. It was a punishing ride. I hit a particularly deep pothole, which sent my front pannier flying up and crashing down.

'Google Maps is a sadist,' I muttered.

'We're going to have to walk,' said Lili.

We both dismounted and started pushing our bikes along. There was a road which linked to this path not far ahead. Stopping at the junction, we checked the Michelin map to make sure it would take us in the right direction. I just hoped the surface would be slightly better than this.

'At least it's pretty,' Lili remarked, looking off at the hills and water.

I didn't reply. I was feeling too ill and upset to even try and make the most of it.

We followed the new road and finally found ourselves pedalling along at speed. I was finding the cycling hard, my chest tight and my breathing more laboured than usual. Lili just seemed happy to be back outside.

The route turned into an outdoor leisure park, mid-completion. It was surrounded by fishing lakes.

'Can we stop here, please?' I begged. 'I'm feeling pretty rough.'

'Sure, we'll have lunch.'

I sat back and gulped down a sandwich and a few crisps. Mostly I suckled on the chocolate milk carton. I really wanted to feel better.

319

'Ready to get going?' Lili asked, after about ten minutes.

'Um.' I could have sat there all day.

Lili didn't seem to notice how ill I still was. They jumped up and started packing the food back into the panniers. 'Now, how do we get out of here?'

We looked at our maps, but these lakes didn't seem to be marked on them. Confused, we cycled roughly in the direction we needed to go. The path led to a dead end. We cycled back and found a map of the lakes on a board, which showed a path which should lead to the next road. We cycled onto it and around it, to find ourselves back at the picnic area.

'What the actual fuck?' Lili asked.

We stopped and got off our bikes. I identified a road on the map which we should have been able to reach, but so far, we had had no luck. We considered cycling back the way we had come, but it was a long way to another crossing in the road.

'What about this way?' I pointed to a point on the map.

'No, I'm pretty sure it's this way.' Lili pointed elsewhere. I didn't have the energy to argue.

Back on our bikes we cycled in circles some more. Lili was adamant they'd find the way. After 40 minutes stuck in the park, we were close to giving up.

'Let's just try my route, please,' I said.

We cycled along a path designed for walkers and found ourselves at a locked barrier gate. We squeezed through a gap between the gate and a hedge. Coming onto a road, we looked up and down.

'I think it's this way.' I pointed downwards.

'It's definitely this way.' Lili pointed upwards.

I gave up and followed Lili up the road. I had needed this day to be short, so I could rest, but it was turning into a nightmare.

*

Day Seventy-Nine

We had escaped the lakes, only for a detour to take us hurtling off on minor roads, under train tracks and through fields. The constant twists and turns were totally disorientating. Half an hour in, neither of us had much idea of where we were. Heading straight, we passed a small family farm.

'If this road turns left, we should be on the right track,' I called to Lili.

The road turned left and we followed it around. Then it turned left again and then once more. We were back where we started.

Lili and I looked at one another, both of us were feeling the strain. We had never gotten so lost before. Were we really this incompetent without route signage?

We scouted out the roads in all directions but could never find one which went the way we wanted to. Intensely frustrated, tempers fraying, we retraced our steps and found ourselves back under the railway bridge.

'Look,' I said, pointing to the map. 'We know roughly where we are by the train tracks, so we know we need to follow them this way, because we know where the river is.'

'Yes, but there's no road going that way. We've established that.'

'I know that.' I looked angrily at Lili. 'So, do you want to go back? Or do you want to try and get onto the other road?'

I had seen a road across the fields which seemed to head in the right direction, but there was no obvious way to reach it.

'I did see a pretty dodgy path back there. We'll have to walk but I think it will take us to the road.'

'Fine.'

We cycled our bikes to the path and peered down it. It wasn't really a path, more like a mud trail, and it was hard to see if it continued the whole way as it was surrounded by tall bamboo and palm-like plants. We began the push. Thick mud coated my boots which were occasionally submerged in wide puddles. We trampled down the plants around the edges and tried not to get our feet too wet. It felt a bit better to at least be trying something.

'Oh, thank fuck!'

I looked up to see the road just ahead. We traipsed the last few metres and got back on our bikes heading, we hoped, towards Roquemaure.

After half an hour of silent riding I was beginning to get nervous.

'Lili, shall we check the map?' I called ahead. I felt exhausted.

Lili continued. I could tell from the way they were cycling that they were angry. They weren't the only one of us who was stressed though. I felt my frustration rising. We needed to work together if we were going to get anywhere. I couldn't deal with Lili having a tantrum right now.

I wiped my eyes and steeled myself. We could do this; we just needed to get out of this maze of country roads.

'Talk to me!' I desperately shouted ahead.

Lili stopped. I cycled up beside them.

'I don't want to be Bette and Tina,' I pleaded, referencing a toxic on-off relationship from *The L Word*.

Lili braked to a stop. 'We. Are. Not. Bette. And. Tina,' they choked out between sobs. I reached over to give them an awkward one-armed hug, and they collapsed into the crook of my elbow, letting their tears subside. My anger instantly dispelled.

'We'll work it out. Let me have a look at the map.'

I stared at the useless bit of paper. It just wasn't detailed enough. I looked up at Lili and there, coming up the road behind them, was a cyclist.

'Let's ask him, hey?' I pointed.

Day Seventy-Nine

We flagged him down and in faltering French asked him the way to Roquemaure. He pointed us down the road we were on. I felt relieved we had gotten one thing right. Maybe we could get this day back on track?

In Roquemaure we were able to orientate ourselves. The maze of minor lanes had been more trouble than they were worth. A D-road was marked clearly on our map. It seemed the best option.

There wasn't a huge amount of traffic to contend with and either way it didn't matter, I had begun to get used to riding on roads and after a day of stopping and starting, I was ecstatic to just be moving.

We left the D-road an hour later, turning off at Sauveterre under another railway bridge. At the first right turning we stopped and got out our maps.

'I'm pretty sure we can take this road and we'll end up near the bridge.' I pointed to the right. A road ran under an arch of trees. It looked ideal; small, tarmacked and without heavy traffic. It wasn't marked on our map, but it seemed to head south. I was confident it would take us straight towards Avignon.

'Well, there's the other path by the river, and we KNOW that one takes us to the bridge.' Lili was pointing to a line on our map which followed the canal southwards. We would have to cycle a few kilometres east to reach it, extending our route further, and without seeing it there was no way of telling what quality the path was in.

'What if it's uncyclable? I really don't want to have to walk it.' I tried to voice my concern to Lili.

'We can always come back here if it's too rough,' they countered.

I hesitated. I believed my route would take us the right way but I couldn't say for certain.

'It's a long way to go to then come back. I'm pretty sure this one just cuts through,' I pleaded.

Lili was unconvinced. 'Look, it's your choice. We can take this one and maybe get lost again, or we can take mine, risking bad paving, and know we're going the right way.'

They stood firm, tapping their feet impatiently.

I hated it when Lili did this. I knew the canal path would be unrideable and we'd end up walking. It was getting late and I just wanted to get there, but what if my route was a dead end? I didn't want them to blame me for getting us lost.

'Let's take the canal path.' I gave in. 'But I'm not happy about it.'

Lili smiled, got back on their bike and headed off. I watched my desired path disappear behind thick bushes as I cycled towards the canal. I felt like I'd made the wrong decision, and I was pissed off that I had not asserted myself. We cycled in silence. The road seemed never-ending and was adding time to our route.

I could feel my anger simmering under the surface. Why couldn't we have just gone my route for a change? Why didn't Lili trust me?

The path carried on and on. I was so tired. We would have been there already if we'd taken my route. The trees surrounding us opened out onto the canal. We turned right and faced Lili's canal path. The path I'd been coerced into choosing.

'FUCK!' I screamed. It was another gravelled path, littered with rocks and potholes, just like the one at the start of the day. It was going to take double the time it should.

'I can't ride on this.' My voice was full of venom.

'Fine, we'll get off and walk.'

We both got off our bikes.

'We should've just taken the other road,' I muttered under my breath.

'Well, why didn't you just say so?' Lili replied

'Because you said you wanted to take this path!'

Day Seventy-Nine

'I said I *preferred* this path but I was happy for you to over-rule me. You just didn't have the balls to.'

'You know I find it hard to assert myself.' I felt miserable. My anger with Lili was compounded by my anger at myself.

'And that's my fault how?'

Silence.

'You never let me decide fucking anything.' I felt the words explode out of me. Lili was such a fucking control freak and I was fed up of letting them get away with it.

'Why are you so fucking angry with me?'

'I DON'T KNOW!' I screamed back. I was seeing red. I knew I needed to just get away from the situation before I said something I'd regret.

'Fine. FINE. Why do I even fucking bother?'

I glanced at Lili, my face contorted with anger and climbed back on my bike. I didn't care about the surface of the path any more. I rode as quickly as I could, flying through potholes and over large rocks. My bike was quicker than Lili's and right now I didn't give a shit if I burst my tyre, I just had to get away from them. I looked behind me. Lili was snaking around the potholes. I hit something hard and braked. I got off to check my tyre. It was ok.

'Why did you leave me?' Lili had caught back up with me.

'Why the fuck can't you let go of even a tiny bit of control? Why can't I ever decide anything?' I wasn't going to stop. This was it – I couldn't stand Lili any more. My fury felt like fire running through my veins.

'Well, you make all the decisions from now on,' Lili screamed at me.

'Then I guess we'll camp here!' I pointed to a grassy knoll next to the canal, got off my bike and proceeded to pull the tent out of a pannier bag.

Lili flung their bike down, straight into a huge puddle. I laughed at them. Aware of how ridiculous my camping idea was I pushed the tent back into my pannier and started to cycle off. I realised that Lili hadn't followed me; this wasn't the plan – as angry as I was with Lili I wasn't going to leave them in the middle of nowhere. I looked around to see them struggling to lift their bike. I watched as they heaved it out of the water, fuelled by indignation. I cycled on.

In all my anger I hadn't realised we had almost reached the end of the path. It led to the main road, a sign to Avignon large and reassuring. I stopped to wait for Lili. I wasn't going to do this without them. I looked around me, another path opened out onto the main road. My original path. I felt my anger rising again. As Lili cycled towards me, I got ready to point out their mistake, but something in their demeanour told me something was wrong.

'I can't. Please.' Lili wouldn't look me in the eye, they slowed to a halt.

I looked at Lili, my anger still simmering. I tried to read their emotions.

'I'm not real . . . I can't . . . please . . . stop . . .' Lili was taking big gulping breaths of air.

Through the veil of my anger, I focused on their face. They were wide-eyed and frantic. This had happened before: all the overwhelming emotions were causing Lili to disassociate.

'I'm not inside my body any more.' Lili was panicking.

There was only one thing to do. I pushed my anger down – I could deal with it later, but right now it wasn't useful. I loved Lili, and even in my anger I wasn't going to forget that. I readied myself, we needed to get to the campsite. I needed to be there for them. This was more important than anything else right now. Once we were in a safe place, I could look after them and finish the argument if needed.

'It's ok, darling. We're on the road now. Do you feel safe to carry on cycling?' I said, as calmly as I could.

Lili nodded. Their breathing calmed.

'I'll lead, you just follow me.'

Lili nodded again. We set off on the road. The sun was setting and it was getting darker. We stopped to put our lights on our bikes, pulling them from the small bags under our saddles.

I turned to Lili and put my hand on their shoulder. I was worried about them and felt guilty that I'd escalated things to this point. I hated seeing them like this.

'Are you ok?'

'I'm sorry,' Lili stuttered.

'Me too, Lili.'

Lili began to cry, but I needed them to stay together, just until the campsite. 'Listen. Look at me.' I tilted Lili's head to mine so our eyes met. 'It's not important, don't worry about it now. We just need to get there.'

We gathered ourselves and kept going. I led. It was always hard pushing my feelings down for Lili, but right now it was important. I spotted the sign to Camping Bagatelle and we cycled in. I organised a pitch and then collapsed onto the grass. A curious cat and her two kittens approached us.

'Everything was terrible, and now we are in a campsite surrounded by kittens,' Lili said softly.

They played with the kittens and smiled up at me.

Lili

Day Seventy-Nine, Bollène to Avignon

I agree with Abi: it was a hard day. However, we disagree on some fundamental details and I'm inclined here to depart from sharing the narrative and give my account of our ride to Avignon. I had spent three days staring at the square of blue sky in the hotel room. I had spent three days eating Subway salad sandwiches and McDonald's chips and Diet Coke. I had had enough. Now, we'd spent much of the ride lost, making slow progress towards Avignon.

It was clear from the map that if we followed the canal path, we would end up at the bridge we needed to and the road to the campsite. After a day lost on French roads, I just wanted to feel certain we were going the right way.

'We can either go on the road or the canal path.'

'What do you think?' Abi asked.

'I would rather go on the canal path, but I'd accept it if you wanted the road.'

Abi looked at me. I knew she wanted to take the road. I didn't want to make it easy for her, didn't want to censor myself so we could do what she wanted. I wanted her to know what I preferred (which was definitely the canal path) and, if she so wanted to go on the road, she'd have to assert herself.

'Fine, we'll go the canal path.'

I could tell she was furious, but I was filled with self-righteousness. I'd given her the opportunity to assert herself and she hadn't taken it. This was her problem, not mine. It wasn't my job to babysit her. I couldn't always make life easier for her. Sometimes she had to do the work.

With every stone she hit, every pothole, I could tell she was getting angrier and angrier. This stoked a rising anger in me. Why couldn't she just make the most of it? She was as much responsible for this decision as I was.

Abi pulled on her brakes. 'I can't ride on this,' she huffed.

'Fine, we'll get off and walk.'

We both dismounted our bikes and started the laborious process of pushing them along the gravel path.

'We should have just taken the road,' Abi half-muttered.

This was enough to trigger a full-blown shouting match. After a final yell, Abi climbed back on her bike and started pedalling furiously away. I tried to follow her, but in trying to avoid potholes I couldn't keep up. My thoughts fuelled a rising fury: how could she be so unkind, so unfeeling, why did she have to make it all about her? She hit a large pothole, her back-pannier rack swaying wildly and braked. I pedalled up beside her, violently throwing on the brakes and juddering to a stop.

'Why the fuck did you leave me?' I asked.

'Why the fuck can't you get go of even a tiny bit of control? Why can't I do anything?' Abi shouted back.

'Fine, YOU make all the decisions from now on,' I replied, louder.

'Fine, we'll camp here,' Abi responded in quiet rage.

I swung off my bike and let go. It crashed down into a large pothole, filled with muddy water. Abi pushed off again, not looking back. I paused a moment and reached down to pull up my bike. It was too heavy. I pulled it part way, and dropped it again, splashing mud over my legs and the pannier bags. I gripped it with two hands, braced myself against the wheels and heaved it, dripping, upright. I followed Abi. She hadn't even noticed I was stuck. As the canal ended and we reached the road my mind was racing, my body collapsing in on itself. I felt like I was drowning in this feeling.

I can't do this.

It hit me hard, had me bent doubled. This was bad. This was bad. I can only take so much, and this was way beyond. I looked at my hands, but they weren't my hands. I was retreating inside my body. My whole self felt disjointed and dislocated. I was so far away from anything I could use to ground me; I was falling. I was frightened. I caught up with Abi.

'I can't. Please.'

She turned around to look at me.

When we first started dating, I couldn't really tolerate arguments. I needed someone to be gentle with me, and Abi was. I pushed myself to be stronger, more resilient, more able to tolerate conflict, anger, because all these things are necessary for a relationship, and I wanted Abi to feel able to express herself. I pushed myself to my limit, and then a little further each time as our relationship grew and I recovered. Once I was at that limit, I would tell Abi one way or another that I couldn't go on, and she would put everything aside for me, to take care of me.

She turned around and looked at me, and she knew what I meant.

'I'm not inside my body any more.'

'It's ok, darling. We're on the road now. Can you carry on cycling?'

I nodded.

'I'll lead, you just follow me.'

I nodded again. We set off on the road. The sun was setting, and we pedalled in the half-light.

'You ok?'

I was sorry for not being able to finish the argument. I was sorry for starting the argument in the first place. I was sorry that so often I had to be in control and that I hadn't paid attention to how Abi was feeling.

I was sorry we weren't going to be able to finish the tour we'd planned.

'It's ok. We're nearly there.'

A sign pointed to the left for *Camping Bagatelle*. We pulled in and Abi organised a pitch with reception: four nights. We needed a rest. We walked around the shower block to our pitch, backed by a grey stone wall where we leant our bikes. We sat side by side on the grey stone slab that jutted from the grass at the front of our pitch and were quickly joined by a very curious ginger cat and her two tortoiseshell kittens.

'Everything was terrible, and now we are in a campsite surrounded by kittens,' I ventured, the ginger adult cat having taken up residence on my legs, while the kittens played with my boot laces.

'It all turns out ok in the end, doesn't it?' Abi smiled.

Lili

Day Eighty, Avignon

I woke stiff with cold. It had been a difficult night, and I was still recovering from yesterday, when the feelings, thoughts and stresses of the last few days had broken the skin, messily. I opened the tent door to bright sunshine and started setting up for breakfast. Abi and I moved gently around each other; we were both still healing from our fight. I cooked while Abi watched me from the inner tent.

We were quickly joined by our friends from last night: the ginger cat climbed straight into the tent beside Abi, unconcerned by etiquette, while the two kittens sat hesitantly outside the tent door.

We crossed the bridge into Avignon and walked through the thick stone of the city wall, still intact, into the centre. Sunlight streamed down, illuminating the old building and making the whole city appear to shine. We walked under the boughs of broad, twisted trees through the gardens of a church. Hungry, we sat outside a pizzeria and demolished huge doughy pizza, hot from the oven, drenched in fresh tomato sauce, basil and oil.

From the campsite we'd been able to see the papal palace; a jumble of square towers, arches, spires and crenulations crowded atop a huge rock called the Dom. I set this as the goal of our city excursion. The largest Gothic building of the Middle Ages, the papal palace was made up of two parts – an older building and the newer – and had been home to both two popes, and two antipopes. This is a person who, in opposition to whoever has been elected pope, makes a significant claim to be pope and not, as I'd hoped, an apocalyptic, evil version of the Pope in the tradition of the anti-Christ. We started climbing, legs unused to being off bikes they protested at the first step. I stood back to regard the tall arches of the older building, carved into white stone. A large crucifix poked out from within the palace, and at the top of the rectangular stacked Gothic building, part fortress part palace, a gold statue glinted in the sunlight.

We climbed up further, to the manicured gardens. In the middle of the ponds at Rocher des Doms a mallard easily twice the size of every other floated, dipping its head underwater to feed, snapping at bread thrown by the children flocking round. We decreed it the papal duck. From the highest point of the Dom, we climbed down to its foot in the river, and took the ferry back across the water Île de la Barthelasse.

I couldn't face anything proper for dinner. Instead, Abi cooked pasta while I pulled hunks of white bread off a baguette and dipped them into a pot of apricot jam. Halfway through the pot I began to feel very queasy. I curled up into my sleeping bag. I started awake in the dwindling light of dusk, scrabbled for a cooking pot, and threw up while Abi rubbed my back. Piss pot, sick pot. Things become multi-functional on a cycle tour.

Abi

Day Eighty-One, Avignon

Lili was still feeling rough after the night before, so we spent the day in the tent, reading, watching TV and eating crisps. Throughout the day the kittens would appear, announcing their presence by clawing their way up the inner tent. We repaired the holes they made with duct tape. We played with them both and they napped on our rucksacks in the porch.

I mostly lay on my mat, bundled up next to Lili, our sleeping bags serving as pillows. We were nearing the end of our cycle tour and I was beginning to wonder what everyday life would be like when we got back. There was a part of me that was looking forward to getting home and seeing my family, but a bigger part of me was scared what being home meant. Life was at its most simple on the tour. I didn't need to worry about looking after a house or working or going grocery shopping or getting haircuts or all the other myriad of day-to-day real-life tasks that caused me so much stress and took up so much of my time (often for very little reward). All I'd really thought about was cycling, food and sleep.

After years lost in depression, I was finding a way to live. Cycle touring felt fundamentally good for me in a way my day-to-day life wasn't. There was something about this way of living that was more real than the world I had left behind. It broke through the artificiality of consumerism, of living in capitalist society. Life back home felt like I was still on anti-depressants; everything was fine, but nothing was exceptional. Here, I felt everything. I felt the pain and the beauty and misery and the deep swell of happiness that burst through my chest. I was alive.

I was being forced to face and accept my limits, but I'd learnt these would change and adjust as I grew. I wanted to see what would happen if we just kept going, kept pushing ourselves. Going home felt increasingly like heading into the unknown. It felt like setting off on the cycle tour all over again. I just wasn't sure how I'd survive.

Abi

Day Eighty-Two, Avignon (Arles)

I looked at the tourist map, an orange ribbon ran through the streets of Arles, marking a walking trail from the site of one Van Gogh painting to another. It was the perfect way to explore a new city. We had arrived that morning, the white stone hills of the *Parc Naturel Régional des Alpilles* glimmering through the train window.

'I'll lead the way.' I grabbed Lili's hand and pulled them towards the centre of town. We wound through quiet lanes of sun-bleached houses. It was early morning and we had the city to ourselves. We stopped outside Les Arènes d'Arles; a two-tiered Roman Amphitheatre. A board outside showed Van Gogh's painting of its interior: a crowd of people in blue, outlined quickly and erratically, jostling to see the faint lines of a bull fight taking place on deep orange sand. In the foreground, a woman dressed in black and white looks straight out of the frame at the viewer, an outsider to the group below her.

We walked around, staring up at the Amphitheatre, and stood on a metal platform which sat at a second-floor height. We peered through the stone arches which circled both the bottom and upper tier into the central arena. Bull fights still took place here, drawing thousands of tourists into the city each year. Each audience would be like the one in the painting, themselves a spectacle, made absurd and homogenous by the barbarity they chose to enjoy.

We followed the path back through to the town square and the ancient stone obelisk in its centre. There were no paintings here, but the impressive Church of Saint-Trophime had opened its gates. The church portal was embellished with elaborate sculptures; chained souls shuffled towards their fate, while Christ and the apostles looked down stoically; the whole frieze depicting the Last Judgement. It is one of the best examples of Romanesque architecture in the world.

'Does that mean what I think it does?' Lili asked, pointing to the words *Porte de la miséricorde*, in large serious letters above one of the church doors.

'I'm not sure . . .'

We drew closer. During the Catholic Church's Year of Mercy, the Pope had opened 'Holy Doors' throughout the world. As in the film Dogma, these doors absolved the person of all sin.

'A-mazing, shall we go through?' Lili asked. 'We may as well cover all bases, right?'

'I could probably do with instant magic absolution.'

We stepped through the magic door, and freshly cleaned of sins, I pulled Lili further into the church. Along its length were reliquaries, some of which sat behind glass in small alcoves. Each relic contained a part of a Saint. In the past, relics could be bought, offering absolution of sins to the buyer. It was these relic sellers which prompted the schism of Catholicism and Protestantism. Neither Lili nor I had ever seen relics, having spent very little time in Catholic buildings. It was fascinating to look at these gory religious souvenirs. Skulls, finger bones, leg bones, foreskins, various pieces of bodies in beautiful gilt golden containers. In the glass-covered alcoves were, presumably, the most holy relics, only viewable once a one-euro piece was paid into the mechanical box, lighting the alcove for just long enough to view them.

'Catholicism is mental,' I whispered, at the sight of a temporarily illuminated piece of St Anne.

Lili nodded. We headed out of the Holy Door holding hands. We weren't sure if this cancelled out the magic effects, but after a quick kiss in the square we were definitely back to our normal life as sinners.

Van Gogh's *L'entrée du jardin public à Arles* invited us into the long park. In the painting, the trees are a verdant green, the path a brilliant yellow, the whole garden suspended in an endless summer. The path we walked along was a patchwork of deep reds and oranges, strewn with the colours of autumn, the trees above bare limbed save for a few green stragglers.

From nowhere, an urgent feeling overwhelmed me.

'Lili, can we sit down a bit, please?'

I tried to unpack the feeling, something felt very wrong. It felt like nothing would ever be ok again.

'Are you all right, love?'

The question irritated me. I was angry and sad. I hunched over, tightly wrapping my arms around myself and rocked up and down. I tried to hold in the feeling so it wouldn't explode out of me.

'Babe?'

'Yeah!' I snapped.

Lili sat next to me in stony silence.

'I just need a second, sorry.' I looked up to Lili but couldn't make out their face properly.

It was painful, I couldn't work out why my brain had shut down like this. I sat and waited for it to pass, painfully aware that I didn't want to make a scene or have people look at me.

Day Eighty-Two

The sound of the traffic running beside the path seemed to swell and roar. I could taste the car fumes. I put my hands over my ears, squeezed my eyes shut. I wanted to turn down the dial on colour, on noise, on the bright sunshine, on this feeling.

It swelled and crashed over me. Gradually I began to return to my surroundings. The park was bathed in subtle orange sunlight. It had taken on the feel of a cool summer's evening. The light twittering of birdsong entered my consciousness. I felt Lili's hand on my back. I sat up.

'I think I just felt a bit overwhelmed. It's been a hard week.'

We followed the map towards the hospital where Van Gogh had stayed. The hospital garden was less colourful than he had painted it, the shrubs less lush, lost again to the turning weather. The only thing the same was the yellow of the building's arches, they remained as vivid as the colours in the painting. That same shade of yellow threaded through Arles, through the buildings, through Van Gogh's paintings.

A small tour group was walking around the courtyard. In a gift shop, the same scene was replicated hundreds of times, on postcards, tea towels and posters.

'It's nothing like the hospital I was in,' Lili said thoughtfully, staring out across the bright courtyard. I knew sometimes they felt keenly the gap in my understanding – I hadn't been there when they were most unwell. I didn't know what it was like. I reached over to hold their hand. Sometimes there was nothing to be said.

Our final stop was by the river. We walked the windswept promenade hand in hand. Van Gogh's *L'escalier du Pont de Trinquetaille* still features dashes of the same yellow shade, but this time interwoven through pale blues and greys that threaten to drown out the hue. It is a painting of a winter's morning. We compared the painting to our own view. The bridge was now a graffitied crossing for cars, the steps empty of people. We walked on.

On the train back, a woman sat with a witch's hat on, poking up from the seat in front of us. We hadn't realised it was already Halloween.

Lili

Day Eighty-Three, Avignon to Vallabrègues

After the disaster of our ride to Avignon, I had some hesitations about leaving. But it was a bank holiday in France (All Saints' Day), and we both wanted to take advantage of the lack of traffic. Rather than cycling through Avignon we chose to follow the D2, a small road superseded by the motorways that now link the larger towns and cities in the region. Despite the fact it closely followed the Rhône we couldn't see the river – a large stone edifice towered to our right instead. The water flowed on the other side of it. We were more confident reading road signs now and followed the quiet single carriageway to Tarascon. Halfway, we had to cross a simple, concrete bridge. A metal fence, no real pavement and a narrow road stretched out across the wide expanse of river. We stopped.

'Are you going to be ok?' I asked Abi.

Abi was attaching one of the thick chords for securing her glasses. She looked at me, absurd and serious in equal measure.

'Yes.'

We proceeded across the bridge. One pedal in front of the other. In the exposed centre, the wind was whipping at

341

the bikes. Thankfully the cars kept their distance and over-took slowly.

We continued down long quiet roads. Suddenly, there was a loud banging noise.

'Shiiiitttttt.' I braked and turned.

Abi had stopped a little behind me. I wheeled my bike round and scooted towards her.

'What's up?'

'Something at the back of my bike?'

I looked around to her back-pannier rack, which was currently lolling at a very jaunty angle.

'This doesn't look good.'

I leaned my bike against a tree and came back. Abi had dismounted and was taking the panniers and bungee off the back.

'Ah.'

The weight of the panniers, the repetitive strain of the ride and (I was reluctant to admit) the punishing canal route of Avignon had completely sheared the metal on one side of Abi's pannier rack, taking out a key support strut that held it to the frame.

'Right.'

'Right.'

I dug around in one of the pannier bags for the roll of duct tape. This was becoming the most often used part of our maintenance kit. We used a tyre lever like a splint, taping it to both halves of the sheared metal. I gave it a wobble.

'That'll do. Let me just reorganise the pannier bags to take some of the weight off your back ones, especially on this side.'

I transferred the heavier stuff – liquids, tent poles and bulk foods – to my back pannier, in exchange for lighter things – clothes, a sleeping mat. We reattached Abi's back panniers.

'Looks like it's holding!'

*

Day Eighty-Three

It didn't feel like November. Something had shifted, in the trees or the dirt or the hum of crickets, that spoke of the south, of the Mediterranean. We rode along a single road, through tall rushes and past lines of poplar trees, their branches brushstrokes flowing up into their tips.

Twenty kilometres into the day's ride, we passed a camp-site at Vallabrègues. As we got closer and closer to the sea, I was getting more and more reluctant to put in the big miles. Our time on bikes was coming to an end, and I don't think either of us felt ready. We stopped at reception and were greeted by a young woman.

'Ouvert?'

'We close today, but my partner will still be here tonight, so you can stay.'

We pitched our tent in the empty campsite and watched as the last family packed up their caravan and drove off. We walked off to a small fishing lake, where we sat in the still afternoon and ate. I'd spent countless meals on benches, staring at the surface of water, over the last 90 days. Now, it felt like I was counting down.

'Are you sure we're making the right decision, stopping?'

'I think it's easy to forget how you felt before the decision, now you're feeling better after.'

I nodded. It had been so hard to say out loud. Of course, I felt better now it was out in the open. Things didn't necessarily get easier when we went back but I knew I would benefit from some rest and routine and structure. The tour had given me a real sense of what I was capable of, but it had also given me a sense of my limits. I took a bite of sandwich. It had also taught me something fundamental about living in my body. Living in my head was more comfortable for lots of reasons, but it wasn't working. A body makes us vulnerable, but it is the only way to be in the world. Maybe I was ready to take that risk.

*

I woke in the darkness to a low hum. As I sat up and strained my ears, the noise morphed into the repetitive bass of French techno music. It came closer, passed us on one side, moved away, then came closer on the other side. I could feel Abi was awake beside me.

'Can you hear that?'

'Yeah, what is it?'

'It's music, but it's, like, circling us . . . ?'

'Yeah, in a car?'

'But why?'

Abi and I were both silent, both convinced that the music was going to be used to mask the sounds of our painful deaths, both aware of the danger of verbalising this irrational fear. I mentally rehearsed where I'd put the large penknife we carried with us. Always in the side pocket of the tent. I contemplated slipping it out and holding it, just in case, but I didn't want to worry Abi.

'It's probably just kids.'

'Yeah, just bored kids in a small village driving around . . .'

Thump. Thump. Thump.

'Or a vole?'

I laughed nervously. We lay in silence, listening to the music circle us for over an hour, until it finally disappeared into the distance and we were able to fall asleep.

Abi

Day Eighty-Four, Vallabrègues to Aigues-Mortes

My bike felt like it was held together by duct tape and sheer willpower, but I felt great. I was a well-oiled cycling machine and setting out along the road I felt calm. The early morning sun was slowly rising, illuminating the flat landscape. I thought about the tour, about the things we'd seen, about how hard it had been to begin with and how natural it felt now. We cycled in silence, both deep in thought, absorbing the views. We took pictures of a sculpture of a strange hybrid turtle-man-lizard in Beaucaire. We crossed a bridge across the Rhône for the last time.

We rode into the Camargue. The silence of the landscape matched my contemplative mood. The large, dramatic skies reminded me of home in Norfolk. We cycled past Bellegarde, following the D38 south.

At Saint-Gilles we were aiming for a canal which would take us on a cycle path towards the sea.

'Which way do you think it is?'

'I dunno.' Lili smiled.

Neither of us was particularly worried about finding our way. We were so close to the end; a long detour would have been welcome as a way to prolong our journey. We both needed the loo though. We followed the signs to the tourist information hoping to find a map and a toilet.

The small roads wound up and down through Saint-Gilles. Bright posters papered all available surfaces and advertised a bull run which had taken place two days earlier. The low barriers that lined the high street suddenly made sense. I was glad we missed it. I pictured the *Daily Mail* headline: 'Lost lesbian vegan cyclist gored by bull. Probably own fault.'

We skirted the old town and I waited with the bikes while Lili asked the tourist information where the nearest public toilets were. I stood on the pavement, enjoying the feel of the sun on my face. Lili sprinted past me and straight down the road. I looked behind them for the stampeding bull.

'All all right, Lils?' I called after.

'I'm desperate,' they called back.

They reached the side of a building: part of the crumbling stone wall of the original town fortifications, where they stopped and opened a huge iron gate set into an archway. Then they disappeared down the stairs into darkness.

Emerging from the dungeon and walking back over, they handed me the key. It looked like it belonged in a museum: it was comically large and ornate.

'The loos are down the stairs through the gate, make sure you lock up after. The woman was very keen we didn't lose it – it's the only one.'

'I doubt we will.' I laughed.

After purchasing some food at a small corner shop and now with a map of the area, we navigated out of Saint-Gilles and back onto the quiet roads. After a short ride we arrived at the beginning of a canal path. It was the perfect place to eat, and we sat watching a family's drama play out as they arrived to holiday on a canal boat.

Day Eighty-Four

The canal marked the beginning of another completed section of the ViaRhôna, and I was very grateful to find the towpath tarmacked for the 25km we rode along it.

We were 5km from our destination when a curious wasp took a liking to me and started buzzing around my face. I hoped it would drop away as I got further along the path, but it was proving to be very persistent. Without traffic it was easy to be distracted by the small insect. I didn't want to swat it in case it stung me. Then, without warning, it flew straight down my bra.

'STOP!' I half garbled, half shouted at Lili.

Lili, alarmed, immediately pulled hard on their brakes.

I pulled on mine, forgetting they didn't work, and flew straight into the back of Lili's bike. In slow motion, I toppled to the side, bike and all.

I lay on the path, one leg under the weight of my bike.

'Are you ok?'

'Wasp!' I spluttered. It was still down my bra. I wafted my top to try and encourage it out while hoping it wouldn't sting.

A family cycled by. They looked bemused to see a grown woman flat on the floor, trapped under a bike and wafting their shirt up and down. They continued cycling.

'There's a wasp in my bra!' I finally verbalised. As if this had been the magic spell, the wasp nonchalantly flew out and away. I was thankful I'd avoided being stung.

I climbed up from the floor and checked in with my body. I'd grazed my right leg along the thigh and calf, and my hand felt bruised, nothing serious. Next, my bike. The handlebars were skewed, and the grip tape had been shaved off in places, but otherwise no significant problems – even my pannier rack had survived. I adjusted the handlebars and got back on.

'You nearly knocked me off again.' Lili laughed. 'Trust you to fall off because of a wasp.'

The campsite we planned to stay in could only be reached via a busy dual carriageway. There was a large hard shoulder and it was only half a kilometre to the turning, but the traffic rushed past at high speeds, shredding our nerves. We reached the campsite and cycled towards the office. It seemed to be open, there were cars parked round and the lights were on. We walked into the office together where a woman looked us up and down before explaining, 'Excusez moi, nous sommes fermé.'

Lili immediately turned to me with huge eyes. 'I can't do that road again.'

I hadn't realised how fragile Lili was feeling. I looked at them, their eyes wide with fear. I could tell they were stretched to their absolute limit, but I knew the longer we put it off the harder it would be to do. The busy road was the only route out; there was no other option.

'I know, baby, but it wasn't very far. It won't take long.'

'I just can't, I really can't.' Lili was beginning to panic. I gave them a hug.

'Let me lead. We'll cross the road on foot, and then just follow me. We can always go onto the grass if we need to.'

Terrified, they agreed. The road was full of traffic and very difficult to cross.

'Ok, now we just have to pedal. It's not far.' I looked at Lili. I understood this paralysing fear. 'Just half a kilometre and then no more big roads.'

We pedalled, one foot after the other, the heavy lorries and fast cars rushing past us. It was the first time I'd led on a busy road. It was disconcerting seeing an entire road ahead of me, without the reassuring presence of Lili to follow. I steadied my handlebars as a particularly fast lorry rushed by.

Day Eighty-Four

Staying close to the side we finally reached the small turning towards Aigues-Mortes.

I stopped and Lili cycled up beside me.

'We've cycled nearly 2000km the length of Europe, and I still shit myself on roads like that.'

They shook their head.

'I'm so proud of you.' I beamed.

Aigues-Mortes was perfectly boxed by tall, stone fortifications. As we cycled towards the walled town, we noticed signs for hotels everywhere. Lili spotted a campsite sign.

'Shall we give it a go?'

'It's that or wild camp.'

We headed along the low roads. The original sign had been a proper metal one. As we cycled onwards, they deteriorated into handwritten cardboard signs. It didn't look hopeful. We kept a lookout for areas suitable for wild camping, but as far as we could see there were only freshly ploughed fields.

'We could ask a farmer?' Lili suggested. I was unconvinced. After a long day I was beginning to get agitated, I didn't think I had the reserves to talk to other people or to stay somewhere where I didn't feel safe. I already knew what I wanted to do, but I was sure Lili wouldn't agree.

We found the campsite. It was closed. The season had well and truly finished. Deflated we cycled quickly back to the town.

'What about a hotel?' I asked tentatively.

'Or we could wild camp,' Lili enthusiastically replied.

'I'm just not sure I can.' It really was feeling like an impossible task, and a nice comfy bed was calling my name.

'I really don't want to pay for a hotel.'

'I *really* don't want to wild camp.' We were stuck at an impasse. Neither of us wanted to budge.

I looked at Lili desperately. I was so tired.

'Ok, ok. If we can find a hotel for less than 50 euros, I guess that's ok,' they conceded.

We cycled back along the canal, away from the more expensive hotels within the city wall.

'Combien?' I asked hopefully, at the reception of a run-down B&B.

The receptionist scribbled a number on a piece of paper and turned it towards us. 48 euros. I telepathically pleaded with Lili, and they pulled their purse out of their bum bag.

The room was clean and warm. We stripped off our clothes. I looked at my body. I was covered in bruises of different sizes and colours: brown, grey, blue, green. My right leg was already an impressive shade of purple after the fall, the bruise stretched from knee to thigh. My deeply tanned arms, face and legs stood in contrast to the pale flesh of my belly and chest: it was as if I'd been dip-dyed. My body had changed. My calf muscles jutted out from my shins, angular and strong. My butt and thighs were smaller.

I struck a strongman pose and laughed. This body had cycled me across four countries, and it was still fat. I was still fat. I was strong and fit and resilient and fat. It just didn't matter any more.

We walked through the walled city. It was easy to cross from one side to the other, and from the opposite gate we looked out onto a wide expanse of nothing, white dirt glimmering in the setting sun.

'We probably could have wild camped here,' Lili muttered.

I couldn't understand why Lili was so upset about the hotel and so I kept silent. I felt guilty, but also hugely relieved to have somewhere safe to stay.

We walked back through the town and popped into a few tourist shops. In a giant sweet shop, we found long vegan jelly snake sweets. We bought two and ate them on the way back to the hotel room.

Day Eighty-Four

In the room we turned the heating up high and watched French *Come Dine With Me* on the telly.

Lili had turned to me. 'I just didn't want it to end.'

'What do you mean?'

'This is our last night on the route.'

We cuddled up closer and fell asleep.

Lili

Day Eighty-Five, Aigues-Mortes to Montpellier

It was our final day. After about 2,000km, and three months, we were going to arrive at the Mediterranean Sea. We woke early in the hotel room, making use of the artificial light to prep and leave as the sun was rising. It wasn't far. We would be following a small straight road along the canal Saint-Louis to the seaside town of Le Grau-du-Roi. We rode through the wide, salt flats of the Camargue, through ponds where we were surprised by the sight of flocks of light pink flamingos feeding. A shimmering line on the horizon, we could see the Mediterranean, and we set our wheels in that direction. The tarmac fell out from under us, and it felt like we were cycling towards the edge of the earth, the road stretching straight into the sky, into blue, into nothingness. The end of the line.

At Le Grau-du-Roi we ignored the route signs pointing towards Montpellier and stayed on the road, onwards and onwards until it stopped dead. I stood on the very tip of the stone Quai and called out a series of loud whoops. I thrust my arm in the air and fist-bumped the sky. I imitated the noise of a stadium of applause.

'And Cooper and Melton cross the finish line . . .' Abi watched me, laughing. I looked out at the wide expanse of

352

water that stretched out around us, our first sight of sea since we'd crossed the North Sea three months ago. With one hand I gripped the handlebar of my bike and with the other I reached for Abi's hand, anchoring us both in the strangeness of this moment.

We started cycling along the shore. Behind my joy at reaching the sea was a creeping awareness that there was now a finite number of turns of my pedal left. We reached a sandy beach where we sat and ate breakfast (a large bag of crisps each) before padding across the sand to dip our feet in the cold water.

People were making sweeping journeys at the same time as us, journeys of great distance and importance, but they were not 'travelling'. They were migrating, fleeing, swarming. Their stories not told, drowned out by political rhetoric, silenced in detention centres. We were moving against the flow, bicycling from our comfortable home in Britain, south to the Mediterranean. We'd crossed borders without noticing. Movement and migration were a fundamental part of being human. I looked out across the water. Borders were lines we'd drawn in the sand, to claim things that were never ours.

The path continued along the shore until we became tangled up in a busy harbour, riding alongside streets between boats, tall buildings, bars and the casinos of La Grande-Motte. We came out the other side of the town and returned to the calm of the cycle path: sea, sand and grass. We could have stopped for hours, but we didn't. I didn't want to delay the inevitable: the end of the ride. We met the canal again and rode a narrow path surrounded by water, sea on our left, a huge lake to our right. At a second beach, we turned off and re-joined the road.

A cycle path appeared on the pavement and we crawled up the hill towards Montpellier. The campsite we were heading for sat between the suburbs of Pérols and Lattes on a small D-road. Google claimed it stayed open all year round, but we had learnt not to trust it. We turned along the winding road, cars speeding past at intervals.

Making our way down the gravel driveway of the campsite we were observed by a donkey and its foal, who brayed at us as we passed. The reception was open. It was a washed pink, selling postcards and souvenirs. We booked for four days; we didn't know what we were doing yet or how long it would take. As we crossed the site, past static caravans and campervans, a closed swimming pool and simple outdoor sinks, cats scattered around us. It appeared to have a similar feral cat population to Avignon, but these ones were less domesticated and regarded us warily from beneath caravans and cars. Our pitch was bordered by trees, close to the toilet block and with only a small campervan on one side.

We were both sore and tired, but keen to be set up for a few days of rest, so we decided to take the tram into Montpellier.

Montpellier was the largest city we'd visited since Geneva. We disembarked the tram at the main station. Our goal was a second-hand English language bookshop (helpfully called 'Le Bookshop'). We climbed a broad street to a large open square, the Place de la Comédie and set off towards the old town. Leaving the metropolitan main road, we navigated undulating narrow streets, on steps winding up and down past shops. It was cool; the sun not reaching past the tall buildings to the alleys below. We turned off Rue Voltaire, up steep steps and almost missed the narrow entrance to the bookshop. We ducked into the green front, through the upstairs cafe and down to the labyrinth of books in the basement. Bringing up our purchases, we sat and read with a cup of coffee. This was our last day of riding, and neither of us was quite ready to speak aloud how sad we felt about this. But this sadness was matched by a feeling of competence. We'd made it here on two wheels, despite everything, because of everything.

Abi

Day Eighty-Six, Montpellier

The beach was empty save for a group of pensioners who were taking part in an aqua aerobics session, dressed in wetsuits, in the sea. They waved their arms up and down, splashing about at intervals. It looked like a synchronised drowning.

I peeled off my shoes and socks and paddled. The water was lukewarm, and I walked in to my knees. My muscles ached after our long journey and the cold water cooled them. I felt it easing off 2,000km of cycling. I looked at my oddly tanned legs through the crystal-clear water and thought about home.

We had decided to send Patti, my bike, home via an online courier. It would cost £100, but my wheels were worth twice that. Paula had only cost £40. After going back and forth, Lili had resigned themselves to leaving her in Montpellier.

At the campsite I began to deconstruct my bike to fit in a large cardboard box. I didn't know what I was doing, but I figured if I could remove as much as possible it would prob-ably fit the required dimensions. The back pannier went into the bin, now more duct tape than metal. Lili helped me

355

remove the front pannier rack and the handlebars and I placed them to one side. I began to detach the pedals when my screwdriver broke. Overwhelmed by the emotions of the past few days I threw it on the floor. 'I'm not doing this any more.'

'Babes, it won't take long and you have to do it,' Lili said, totally misjudging my mood.

'I'm not going to do it. I need to take a fucking break. I'm so fed up with this shit.'

Lili looked at me angrily. I knew I was acting irrationally, but I desperately needed to fight someone; anything to ignore the swirl of emotions in my head.

'Fine. Go have a break. I don't fucking care.'

Lili had now become the target for my tantrum.

'You don't care? I guess I'll just leave then!' I made some vague steps away from the tent. Lili crawled into it and starting crying. I could feel tears inching down my cheeks; I knew I was saying cruel things just to provoke a reaction from Lili, and now I just felt guilty as well as angry. It wasn't like there was anywhere to go anyway.

I stomped over to the donkey enclosure to watch the baby foal in the meadow. My head felt ready to explode. I didn't know how to put a name to all the emotions I felt. Packing my bike meant it really was the end. I didn't know what to do.

I waited. As the minutes ticked by my anger began to dissipate. I remembered Lili, alone in the tent and felt a huge sense of shame. Head hung, I stepped slowly back to the tent.

'Lili? I'm sorry.'

I climbed in. I really was sorry. Neither of us wanted to face up to the fact it was over, it was almost too much to bear. We held each other until the grand swell of emotions calmed and then stepped out of the tent to try and fix the final problem of my bike.

Day Eighty-Six

'Fuck it,' Lili proclaimed.

'Fuck it,' I agreed.

Opening the box, we stuffed the bike in and hoped the courier company wouldn't notice the extra few centimetres' width.

Lili

Day Eighty-Seven, Montpellier

We were sitting in the small courtyard outside reception, either side of the misshapen box we'd stuffed Abi's bike into after yesterday's blowout. We'd been given a window: 9.30am–4.30pm, but we'd hoped they would be earlier than that so we could head into Montpellier in the afternoon. Neither of us wanted to face how we were feeling sending Patti off; we could deal with that once it was done. Instead we resolutely bedded down on the bench, wrapped in our layers, and waited. We were so fixed on ignoring the large box between us, that it was only after the damage was done that we noticed the large dog who was weeing on it. We shouted him off, his unbothered owner calling him away, and tried to dry the box off with toilet roll.

The van arrived about midday, and after helping load it (avoiding the corner which now reeked of dog piss) and sign it off we headed into Montpellier. We rode on the tram with my bike. I was chatting incessantly to avoid thinking about the importance of these moments, the ways they marked the end of our journey. We didn't have the time to sell my bike properly. We left Paula with a scheme that fixed up bikes for community use which was attached to a second-hand bike shop. The mechanic was slightly startled as I burst into tears. With sympathetic eyes, he sat me down in his workshop and made me a coffee, giving me time to say goodbye and recover before we went back out onto the street.

We took the final two panniers worth of stuff to the post office, packing them into a large box to post to my mum. Due to the box's X-rated content, this final parcel was accompanied by a phone call home instructing her not to open it under any circumstances.

On the tram back we stopped at Carrefour for cheap amaretto. It was the US election that night, and we had the same lump in our gut that we'd had pre-Brexit, pre-general election. With both bikes gone and the last of our panniers sent off, we booked a train to Portbou, a small Spanish town just across the Pyrenees from France, for the next morning. Then we lay in the tent, sharing an enamel cup of the overly sweet, almond alcohol and refreshing our computer screen as the night progressed. Earlier that day we'd walked back through Montpellier, with a growing awareness that neither of us had bikes. The sale of my bike wasn't the big moment. It was the sharp tip, the point, the proof that something much bigger and more fundamental was happening. In the United Kingdom, across Europe, and now America, right-wing politicians were breaking the surface, erupting like volcanos, signalling the seismic shifts underneath.

Lili

Day Eighty-Eight, Montpellier to Portbou

We were hungover, our mouths dried out by sugar and alcohol, and feeling as if the ways that things were changing were slowly catching up with us. We started packing and, with a train to catch, we started discarding more and more in the free shop in the laundry room. My rucksack was still ludicrously heavy, stacked high and almost impossible to even lift onto my shoulders. We left the campsite behind and took the tram to Montpellier train station. We were early, so we let our rucksacks fall off onto the seats and sat about waiting in the station. The platform came up on the board. Abi heaved her rucksack onto her back. I couldn't lift mine, so instead I squatted down to it, looped my arms through the straps and tried to stand up. I couldn't. Abi was watching me incredulously as I squatted on the floor by the bench. I started laughing at the absurdity of it, which only weakened my legs further.

'I'm stuck,' I choked out.

Abi grabbed the top strap of my rucksack and together we heaved me up. The train was quiet, and we could have our rucksacks next to us which was lucky as I didn't think I'd be able to get mine off the floor. I watched the landscape rush by. We were heading south still, chasing weather comfortable for camping, but our hostel booking in Barcelona, 200km further down the coast, wasn't for another two weeks. We hadn't decided how we would join up the two places.

Portbou used to be a busy tourist town; when trains couldn't make the journey from France to Spain in one go, everyone would overnight here. Now it was quiet, especially out of season. We walked down from the train station to the shore, without knowing where we would stay. An old-fashioned guesthouse had a vacancy sign and reasonable rates. We checked in.

We walked out along the stone pier set into the still, glassy, dark water of the bay – so different to the bright blue Mediterranean of the French coast. We continued walking round, past the stone memorial to Walter Benjamin, the German-Jewish philosopher who killed himself at Portbou in 1940 to avoid being returned to Nazi-occupied France. On the opposite side of the bay, there is a bronze memorial to him, created by artist Dani Karavan in 1990: bronze steps that lead down into the water, and the unknown in its depths.

As it got dark, we headed to the bar on the shorefront – empty but for the owner, it had a rainbow flag hanging from its front. The pride flag may have been co-opted and commercialised, but it remains reassuring to arrive at a place flying it. I reached to squeeze Abi's hand across the table.

With our drinks, the owner brought a free panini with thin slices of Iberico ham over on a paper plate. Trains move faster than bikes and I'd not clocked the cultural shift to Catalonia and tapas. Unwilling to offend, I waited until he was back in the kitchen and slipped the ham out of the panini and into a napkin which I scrunched into my pocket, and we both enthusiastically ate our empty halves. I could still sort of taste the salt from the ham, but I didn't mind.

To recover is to get back something that is lost; doctors and nurses promised I would be back to my old self one day. Instead I found myself further from my old self than ever before. I had expected the cycle tour to change me. I wasn't the person I was, but I didn't feel I had become anything, anyone, solid. It felt right that we were in a town that for years had been a part of people's journeys, rather than a final destination. Neither home, nor away, not end or beginning, but some place all of its own, in between.

In the dark, the headlights of cars taking the road along the cliffs above us looked like they were floating lights. As they turned the corner of the cliff, they vanished. The small circle of warm light created by the bar was surrounded by a deep inky darkness – even straining it was impossible to make out the borders between sky, shore, sea. If it weren't for the sound of the waves crashing against the sea wall, we could have been in nothingness.

Abi's 100km Victory Tinned Mushroom and Spinach Curry

Essential Ingredients
Tinned Spinach, Tinned Mushrooms, Spices (we packed a mix of Turmeric, Garam Masala, Cumin), Tomato Puree (1-2tbsp), Salt and Pepper

Additional Ingredients
Onion (diced), Garlic (minced), Ginger (minced), Chilli flakes/ sauce (e.g. sriracha), Oil, Tinned Chickpeas, Potatoes (pre-cut and boiled)

Method
1. If you have them, sweat the onions, garlic and ginger in oil or water until translucent.
2. Add a couple of tbsp of the spice mix and dried chilli flakes (if using), cooking for a minute until you can spell the spices.
3. Chuck in the tinned mushrooms, spinach and chickpeas/ potatoes. These are already cooked so you simply need to heat them through. Make sure they get nice and hot.
4. Add water as needed, the texture should be thick and soupy. Try not to burn it to the bottom of the pan.
5. Stir through the tomato puree, add more water if needed. Mix well with the other ingredients.
6. Season with salt, pepper and chilli sauce (if you like spice).

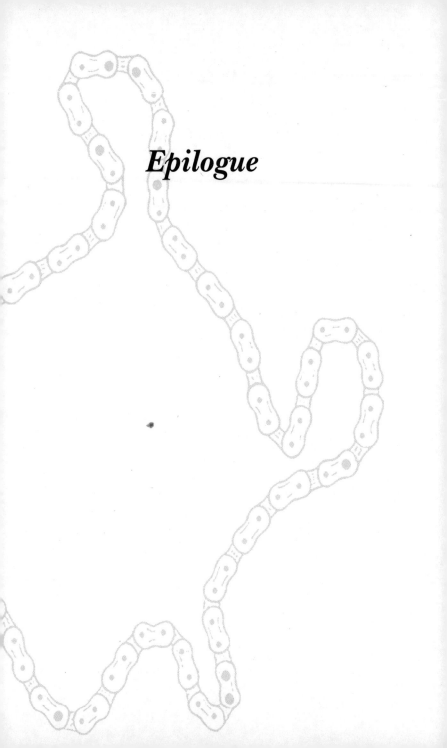

Epilogue

Abi

31st December 2018, Fife

'There's no fucking way I'm cycling up that.'

I gestured to the hill stretching off into the sky. Lili smiled at me. We were on the NCN 76, riding from our home in Kirkcaldy to a small cafe on the Falkland estate. It was 30km, and several hills, away.

We had spent two months in Spain at the end of our tour. When we arrived back in the UK, just after Christmas, we had been full of plans. We spent January and February working and saving, and in March we'd booked our train tickets back to Spain, ready to hike the Camino de Santiago. My body had had other plans. The searing pain I'd experienced after that ill-advised breakfast in Switzerland was the first of many agonising gallstone attacks. These eventually left me hospitalised with an inflamed liver; grounded in the UK for six months on an operation waiting list.

I ploughed up the hill. I'd forgotten how much it hurt, but it felt natural, and I felt more alive, more connected to myself, than I had in months. It had been a long period of illness and recovery which had tested our relationship, and the resolutions we'd made on the tour to live a different life. Sometimes life doesn't let you do what you want. Sitting in

367

my hospital bed, or bed bound at home, I'd been afraid that I'd lost everything I'd gained; that whatever intangible thing the cycle tour had given me was gone, never to be recovered.

Lili waited for me at the top of the hill.

'You're nearly there,' they called down to me.

Panting, I triumphantly summited.

Things weren't the same after the tour, and we weren't the same people. We had moved away from Cambridge to live in Edinburgh, and then moved again a year later further north, across the Firth of Forth, to the Fife coast. We'd gotten married, started a zine library and signed a publishing contract. Now, we were setting our intentions for the coming year.

We stood at the top of the hill, looking out over the Fife countryside as the sun hung low in the sky. In the distance, the Lomond hills beckoned.

Lili turned to me, breath crystallising in the cold air. The day before, the Sustrans map for Land's End to John o'Groats had landed on our doormat.

They beamed. 'Ready for another tour?'

Further Reading

This is a short list of books, zines and articles we have either referenced in the text, or which informed our writing and our cycle touring.

'White Privilege: Unpacking the Invisible Knapsack', article, Peggy McIntosh

'Everywhere All the Time', blog, Bani Amor (www.baniamor.com)

Bikequity: Money, Class and Cycling, zine, edited by Elly Blue

All About the Bike, book, Robert Penn

Mind the Cycling Gender Gap, zine, Tiffany F. Lam

Londonderry: A cyclo-feminist zine, zine, Les Derailleuses

Asking for Elephants, chapbook, Mary Ann Thomas (@postcardsfrommat) and Daniel Baylis

Bicycle/Race: Transportation, Culture and Resistance, book, Adonia E. Lugo

Chainbreaker Bike Book: A Rough Guide to Bicycle Maintenance, book, Ethan Clark and Shelley Jackson

Back in the Frame, book, Jools Walker (@ladyvelo)

Bikes vs. Cars, documentary, dir.Fredrik Gertten

Acknowledgements

We'd like to acknowledge our deep debt to our parents and family for supporting this book, this cycle tour, and us. We would be totally lost without you.

Huge thanks to our friends, our chosen family, who put up with the endless moaning, freak-outs, wild attempts at procrastination and inevitable flakiness as deadlines approached.

We'd also like to thank everyone at Kangus Coffee House, Indigo Coffee House, and Shantee House Hostel where various drafts where written. Thank you Tony and Kirsty, for the scran, support and encouragement. We'd like to thank Guy for reading through drafts and offering good advice, Irma and Jen for helping with our French and German. Mark, from Flat Planet Cycles in Cambridge, for helping fix up our bikes and telling us to just go do it. Marie and Dave, Dominic, Danni, James and Sadie, Andy, Teresa, Brian, and everyone else for buying us coffees, IRL and online. We're always and forever grateful for the zine community in Scotland, without whom our DIY ramblings wouldn't have made it into the hands of our now-publishers. Lili would specifically like to thank Chris, Richard and John, who all shouldered the pressures of working in NHS mental health service, Helen A, Chantelle, and Helen B, who helped them carve out a way to be in the world.

Special thanks go to Kay, our editor, who reached out to us, guided us through the process and helped shape our manuscript into something that people might actually enjoy reading. Thank you for not flinching when we said Lili used gender-neutral pronouns, for your commitment to diversifying the list and for working around our decision to go on another cycle tour midway through editing this book.

Finally, to the three young women we got stuck in the hallway of a train carriage with from Leeds to Sheffield, you probably didn't believe us when we said we'd write you into the acknowledgements, but here you are.

www.sandstonepress.com

 facebook.com/SandstonePress/

 @SandstonePress